MASAYA TAKA

▶ ORIGINAL STORY
FUJINO OMORI

▶ CHARACTER DESIGN
SUZUHITO YASU

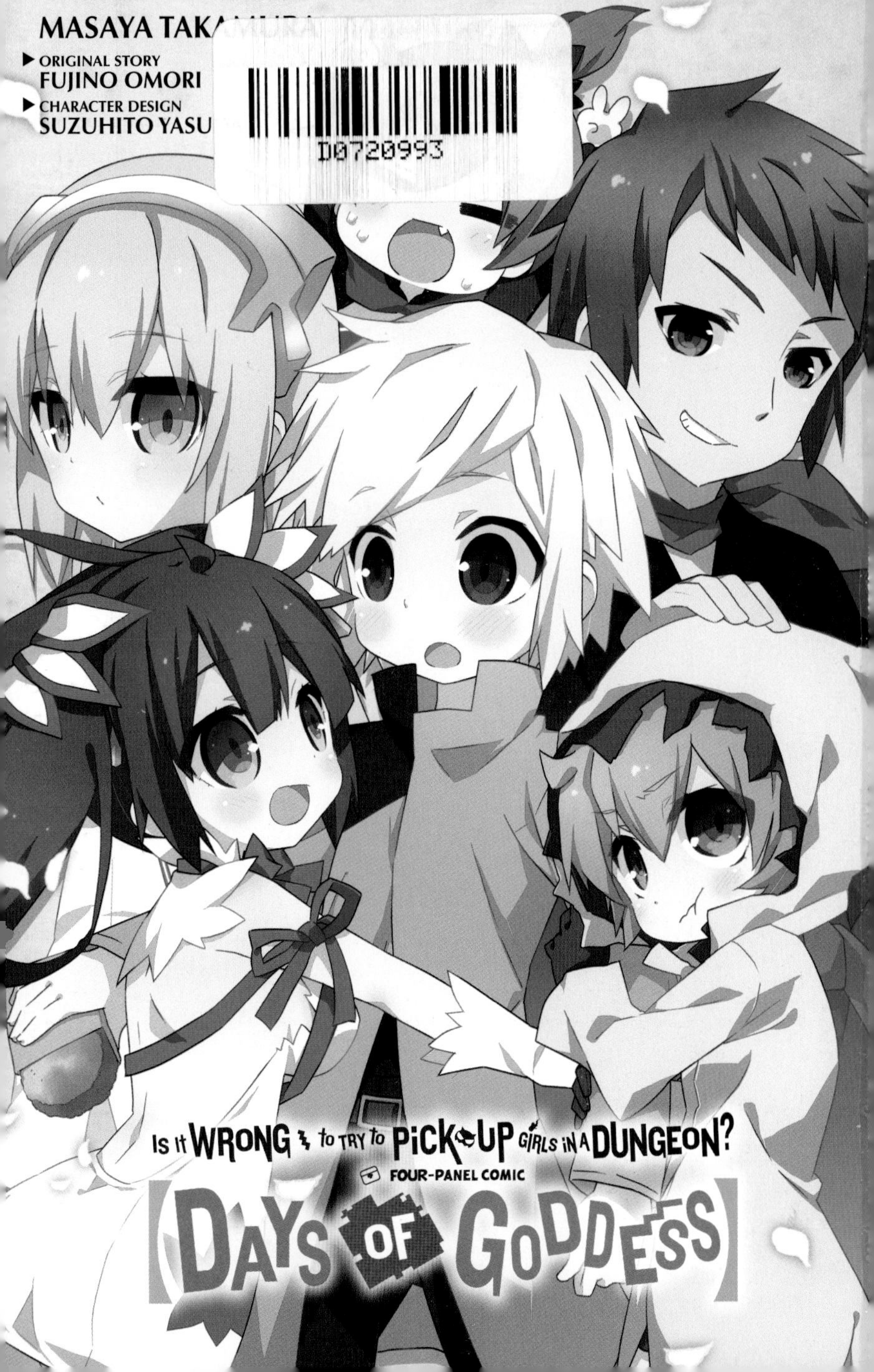

Is it WRONG to TRY to PICK UP GIRLS IN A DUNGEON?

FOUR-PANEL COMIC

DAYS OF GODDESS

【DAYS OF GODDESS】

CONTENTS

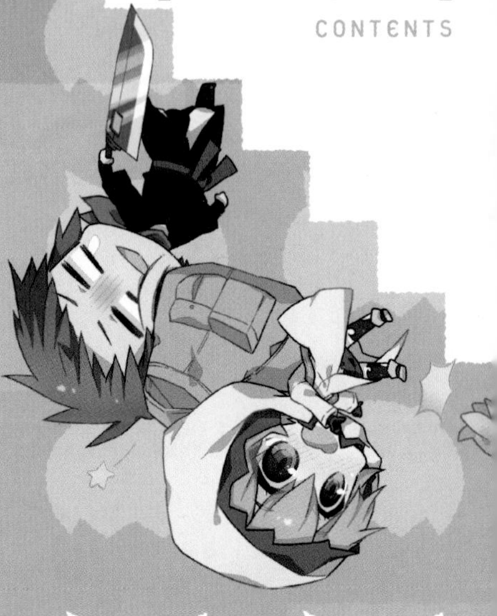

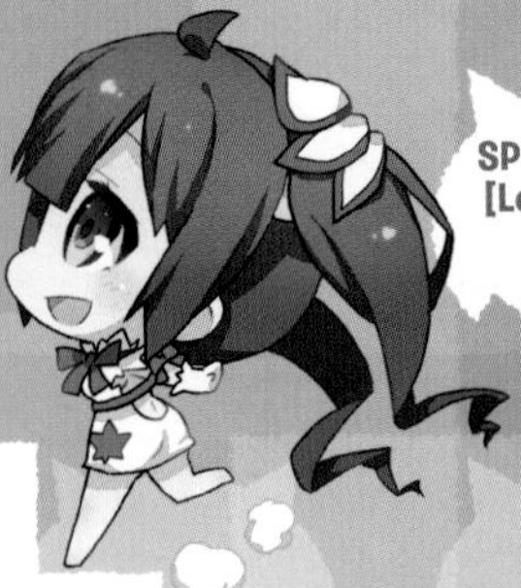

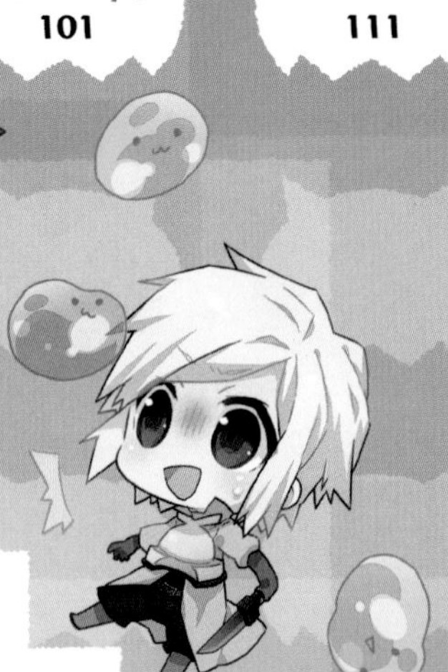

Is It WRONG to TRY to PICK UP GIRLS IN A DUNGEON?

FOUR-PANEL COMIC

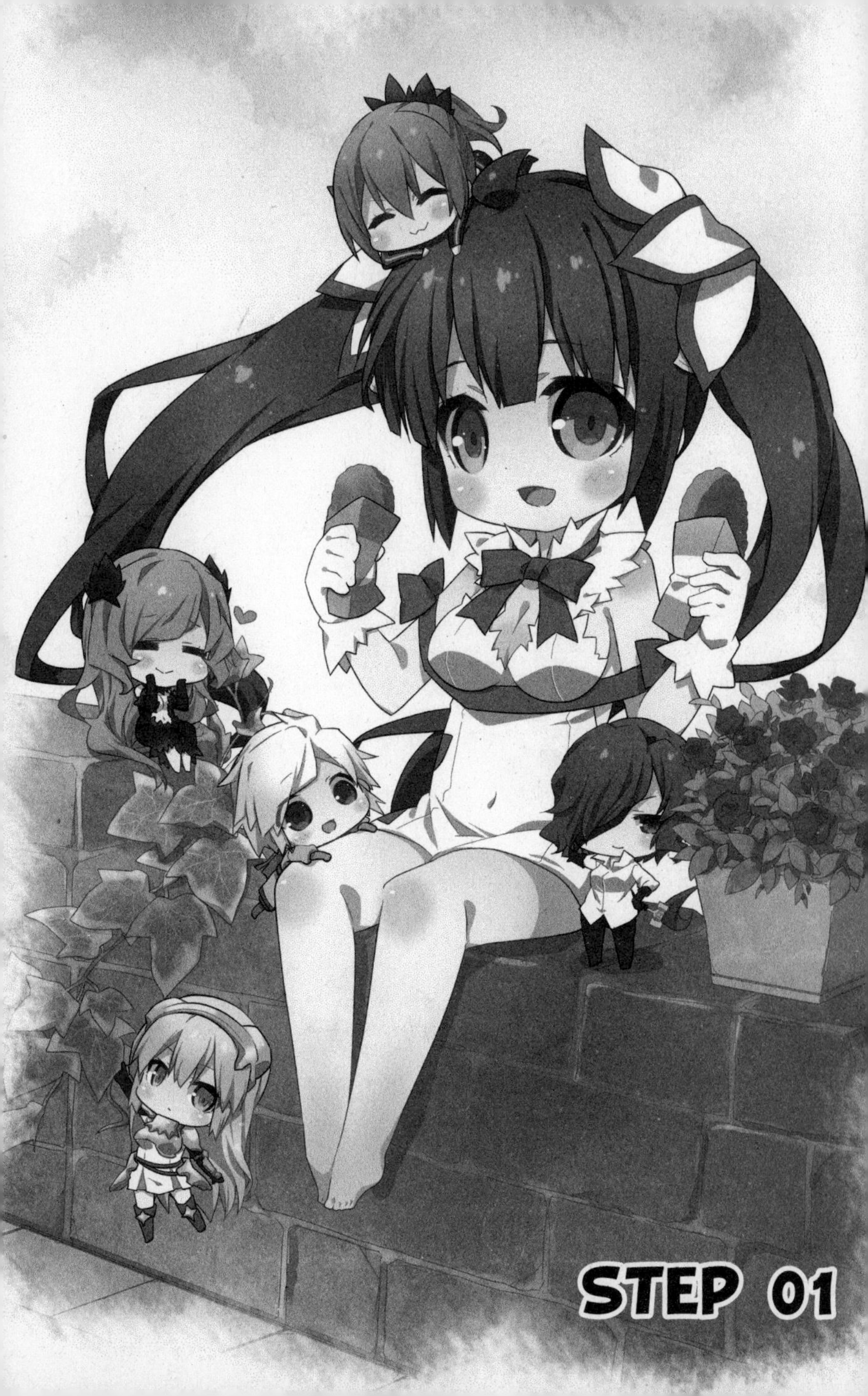
STEP 01

DEITIES AND ADVENTURERS

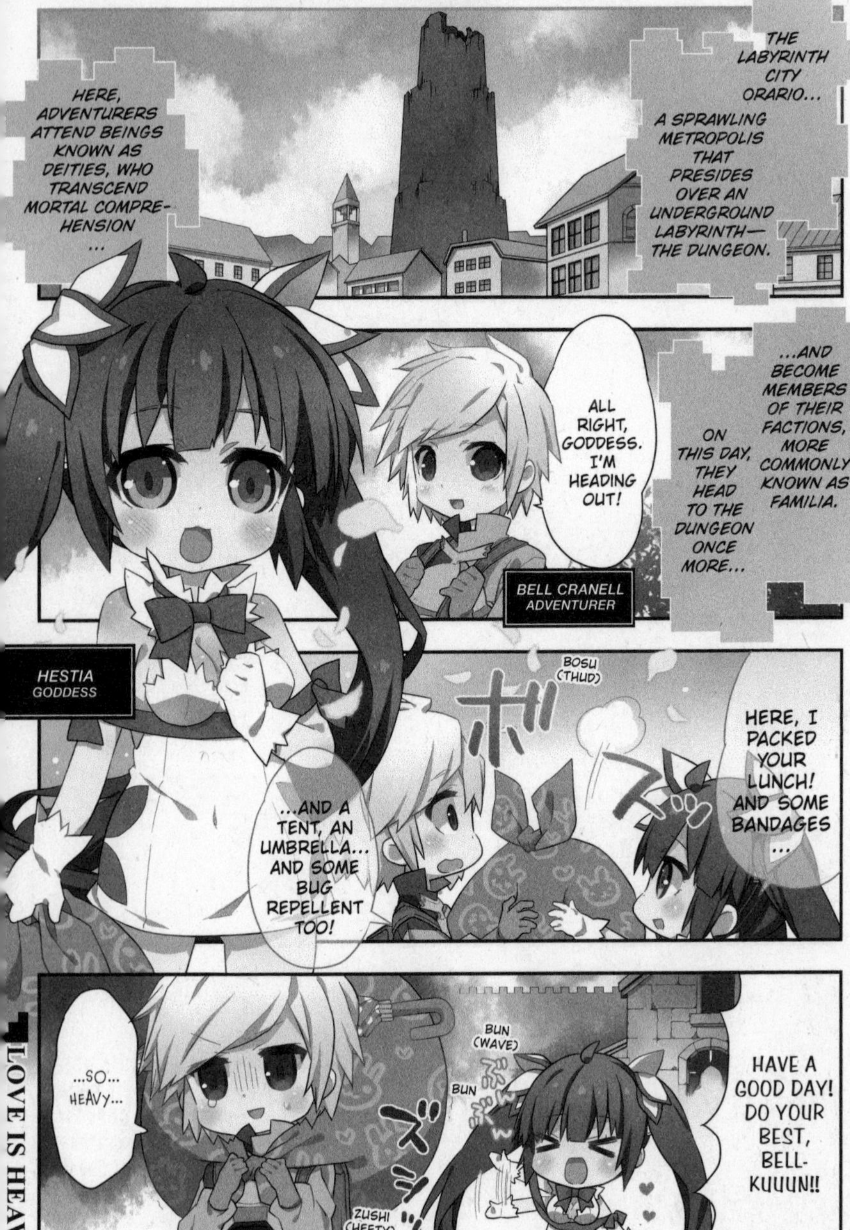
THE LABYRINTH CITY ORARIO... A SPRAWLING METROPOLIS THAT PRESIDES OVER AN UNDERGROUND LABYRINTH—THE DUNGEON.
HERE, ADVENTURERS ATTEND BEINGS KNOWN AS DEITIES, WHO TRANSCEND MORTAL COMPRE-HENSION ...
...AND BECOME MEMBERS OF THEIR FACTIONS, MORE COMMONLY KNOWN AS FAMILIA.
ON THIS DAY, THEY HEAD TO THE DUNGEON ONCE MORE...
ALL RIGHT, GODDESS. I'M HEADING OUT!
BELL CRANELL ADVENTURER
HESTIA GODDESS
HERE, I PACKED YOUR LUNCH! AND SOME BANDAGES ...
BOSU (THUD)
...AND A TENT, AN UMBRELLA... AND SOME BUG REPELLENT TOO!
HAVE A GOOD DAY! DO YOUR BEST, BELL-KUUUN!!
BUN (WAVE)
BUN
ZUSHI (HEFTY)
...SO... HEAVY...

LOVE IS HEAVY.

GODDESS AT WORK!?

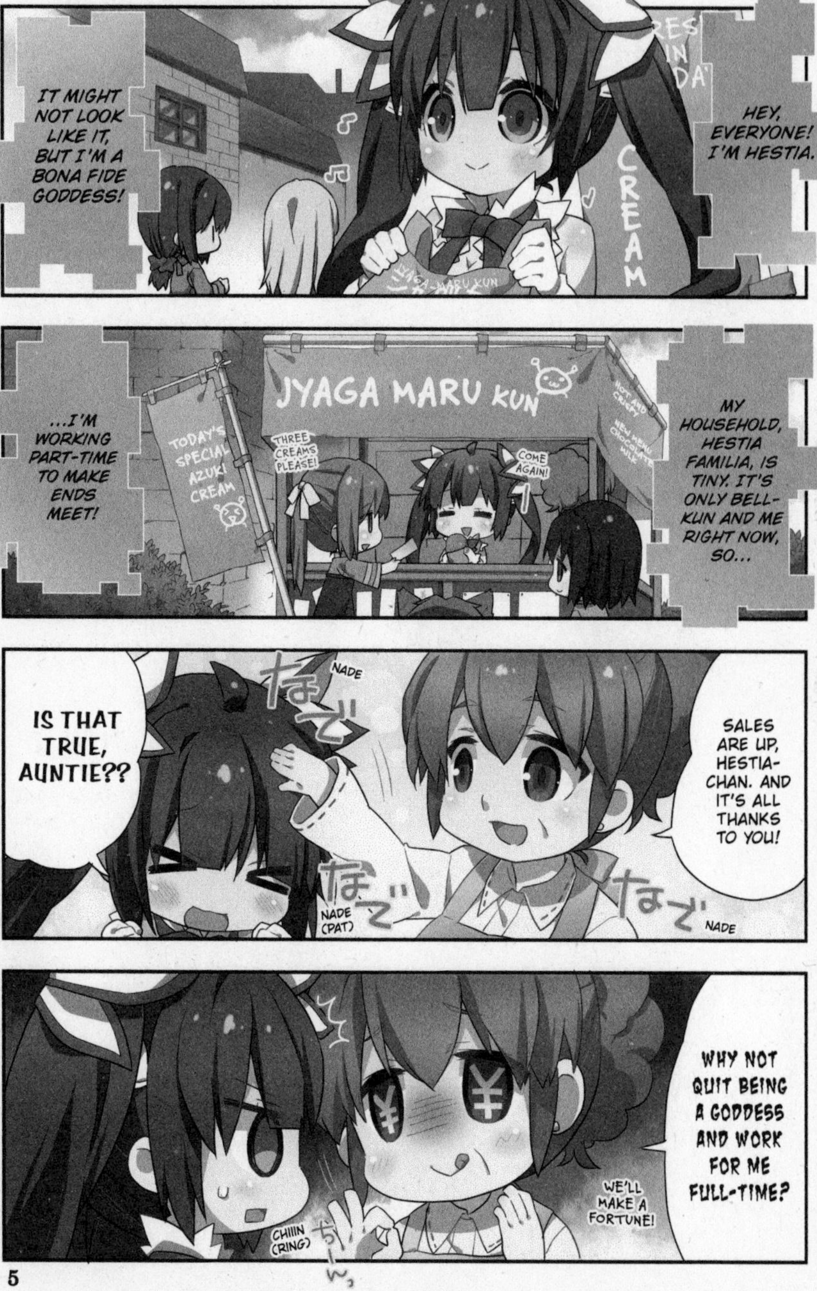
HEY, EVERYONE! I'M HESTIA.
CREAM
IT MIGHT NOT LOOK LIKE IT, BUT I'M A BONA FIDE GODDESS!
MY HOUSEHOLD, HESTIA FAMILIA, IS TINY. IT'S ONLY BELL-KUN AND ME RIGHT NOW, SO...
JYAGA MARU KUN
HOT AND CRISPY
NEW MENU CHOCOLATE MILK
COME AGAIN!
THREE CREAMS PLEASE!
TODAY'S SPECIAL AZUKI CREAM
...I'M WORKING PART-TIME TO MAKE ENDS MEET!
SALES ARE UP, HESTIA-CHAN. AND IT'S ALL THANKS TO YOU!
なで
NADE
なで
NADE
IS THAT TRUE, AUNTIE??
なで
NADE (PAT)
WHY NOT QUIT BEING A GODDESS AND WORK FOR ME FULL-TIME?
WE'LL MAKE A FORTUNE!
ちーん
CHIIIN (RING)

JOB CHANGE TO YOUR TRUE CALLING.

THE SHOPPING DISTRICT'S MASCOT DEITY

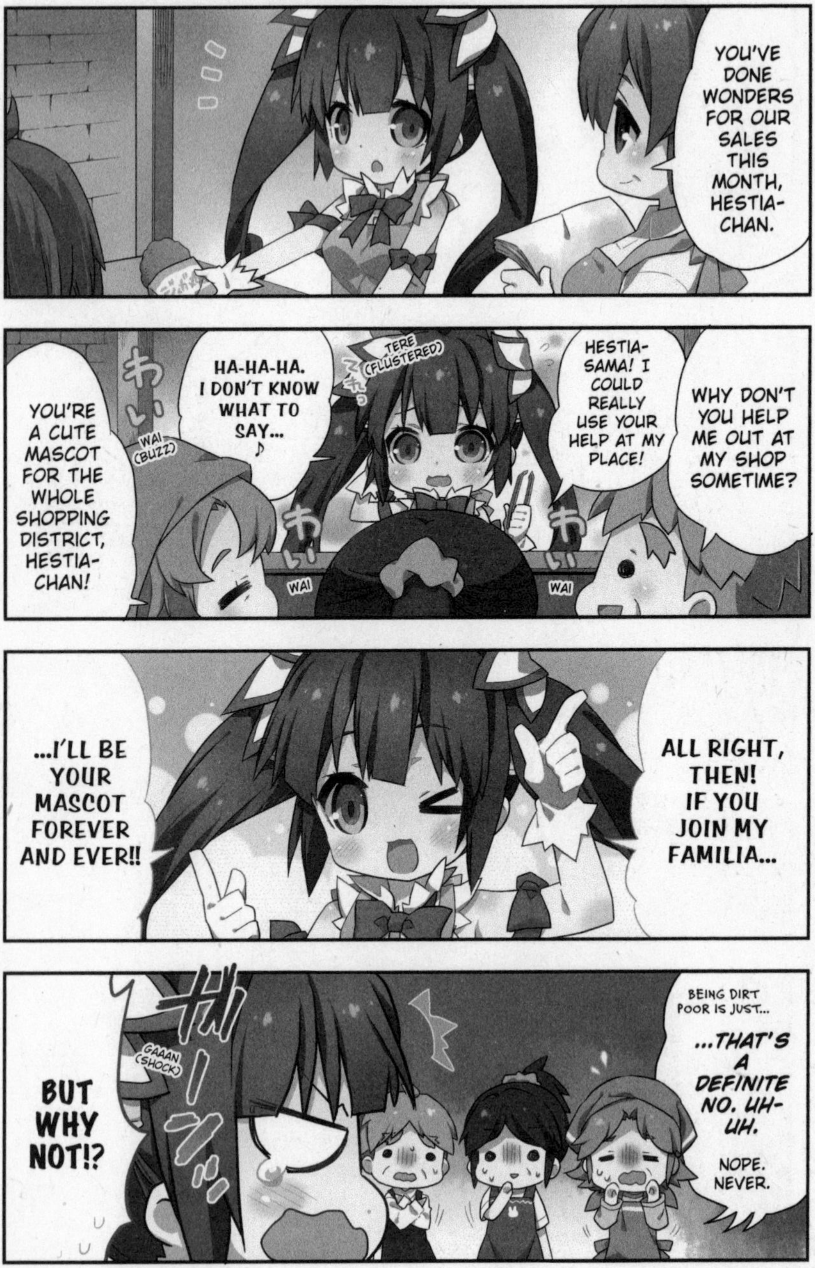
YOU'VE DONE WONDERS FOR OUR SALES THIS MONTH, HESTIA-CHAN.
WHY DON'T YOU HELP ME OUT AT MY SHOP SOMETIME?
HESTIA-SAMA! I COULD REALLY USE YOUR HELP AT MY PLACE!
TERE (FLUSTERED)
HA-HA-HA. I DON'T KNOW WHAT TO SAY... ♪
WAI (BUZZ)
YOU'RE A CUTE MASCOT FOR THE WHOLE SHOPPING DISTRICT, HESTIA-CHAN!
WAI
WAI
ALL RIGHT, THEN! IF YOU JOIN MY FAMILIA...
...I'LL BE YOUR MASCOT FOREVER AND EVER!!
BEING DIRT POOR IS JUST...
...THAT'S A DEFINITE NO. UH-UH.
NOPE. NEVER.
GAAAN (SHOCK)
BUT WHY NOT!?

HESTIA THE BABYSITTER?

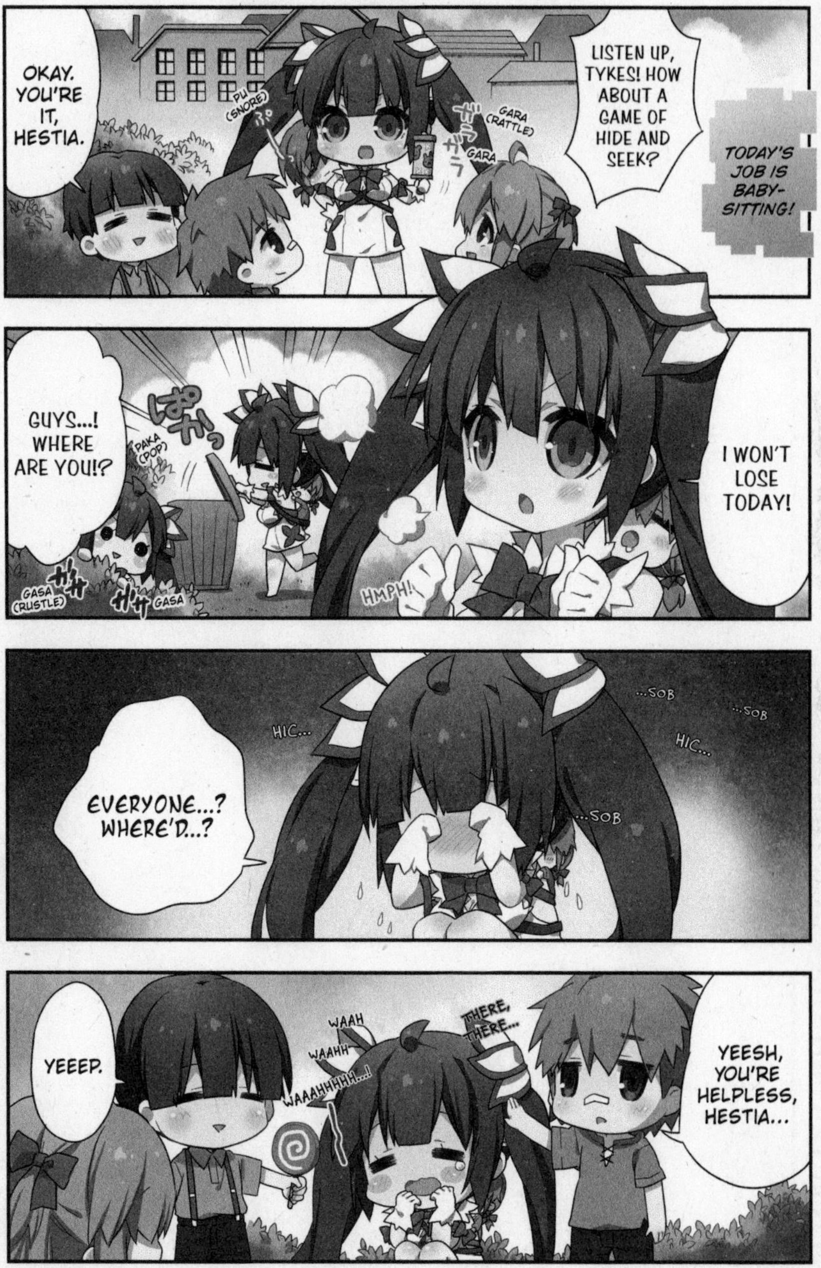
TODAY'S JOB IS BABY-SITTING!
LISTEN UP, TYKES! HOW ABOUT A GAME OF HIDE AND SEEK?
GARA (RATTLE) GARA
PU (SNORE)
OKAY. YOU'RE IT, HESTIA.
I WON'T LOSE TODAY!
HMPH!
PAKA (POP)
GUYS...! WHERE ARE YOU!?
GASA (RUSTLE) GASA
...SOB
...SOB
HIC...
HIC...
...SOB
EVERYONE...? WHERE'D...?
YEESH, YOU'RE HELPLESS, HESTIA...
THERE, THERE...
WAAH
WAAHH
WAAAHHHHH...!
YEEEP.

IT ALWAYS ENDS LIKE THIS.

WELCOME HOME, BELL-KUN ♡

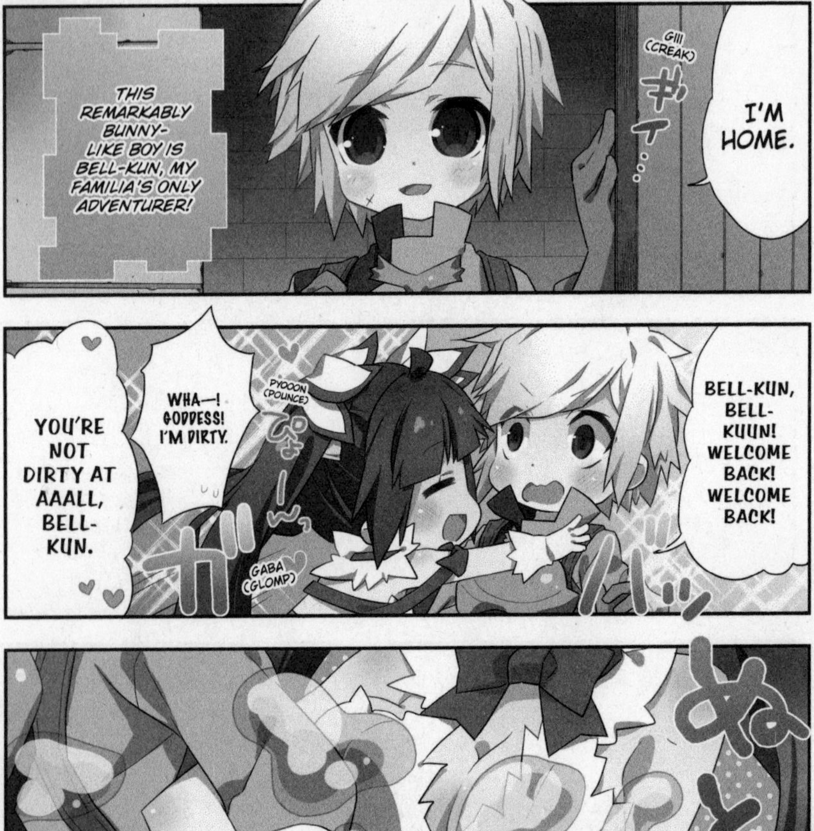
I'M HOME.
GIII (CREAK)
THIS REMARKABLY BUNNY-LIKE BOY IS BELL-KUN, MY FAMILIA'S ONLY ADVENTURER!
BELL-KUN, BELL-KUUN! WELCOME BACK! WELCOME BACK!
PYOOON (POUNCE)
WHA—! GODDESS! I'M DIRTY.
YOU'RE NOT DIRTY AT AAALL, BELL-KUN.
GABA (GLOMP)
NUTOOO (SQUELCH)
THE SLIMES WERE REALLY AGGRESSIVE TODAY...
BETTORI (STICKY)
NUTO (SLIMY)
GROSSSSSSS!!
NUTO

WELCOME HOME TO YOU TOO, SLIME.

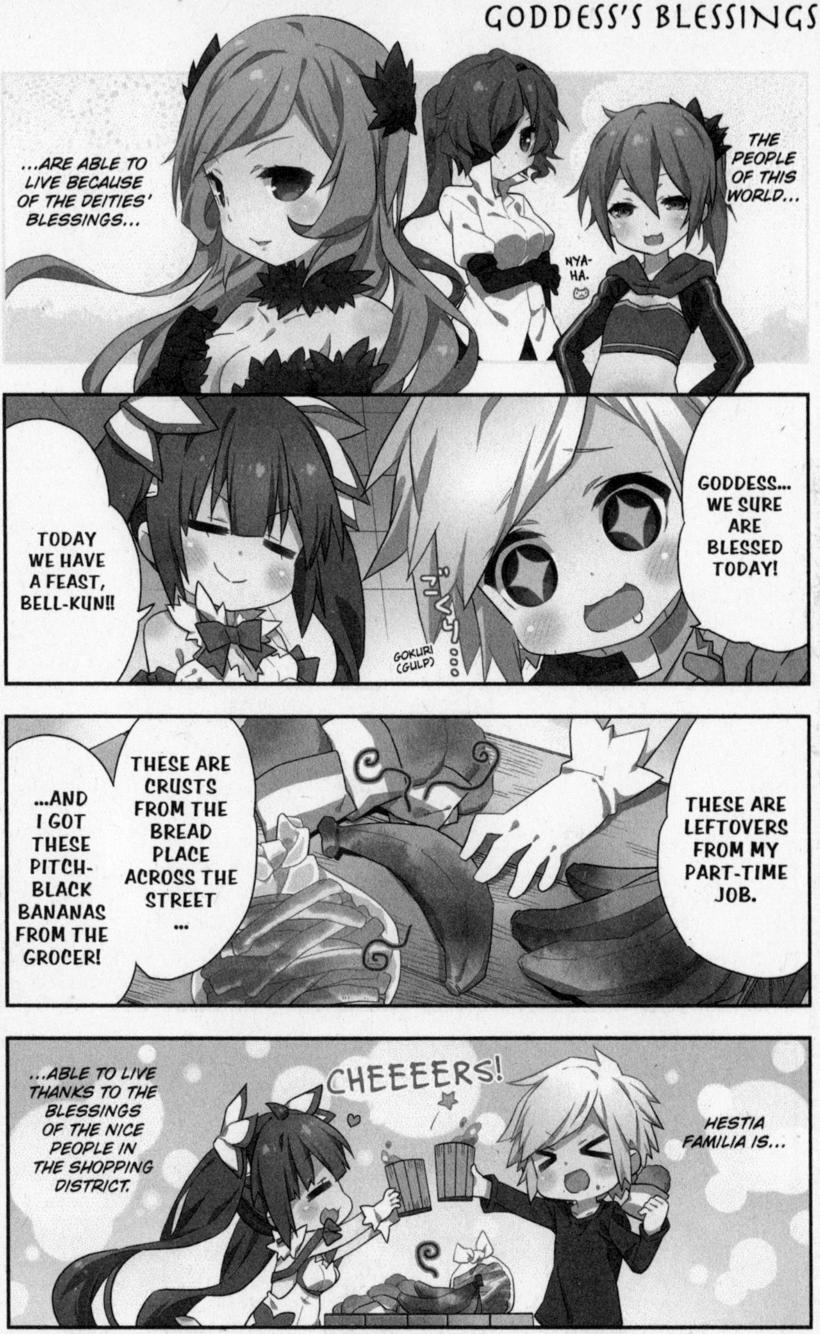
THE PEOPLE OF THIS WORLD...
NYA-HA.
...ARE ABLE TO LIVE BECAUSE OF THE DEITIES' BLESSINGS...
GODDESS... WE SURE ARE BLESSED TODAY!
GOKURI (GULP)
TODAY WE HAVE A FEAST, BELL-KUN!!
THESE ARE LEFTOVERS FROM MY PART-TIME JOB.
THESE ARE CRUSTS FROM THE BREAD PLACE ACROSS THE STREET ...
...AND I GOT THESE PITCH-BLACK BANANAS FROM THE GROCER!
HESTIA FAMILIA IS...
CHEEEERS!
...ABLE TO LIVE THANKS TO THE BLESSINGS OF THE NICE PEOPLE IN THE SHOPPING DISTRICT.

TRULY A DIRT-POOR FAMILIA.

SOMEONE STOP HER

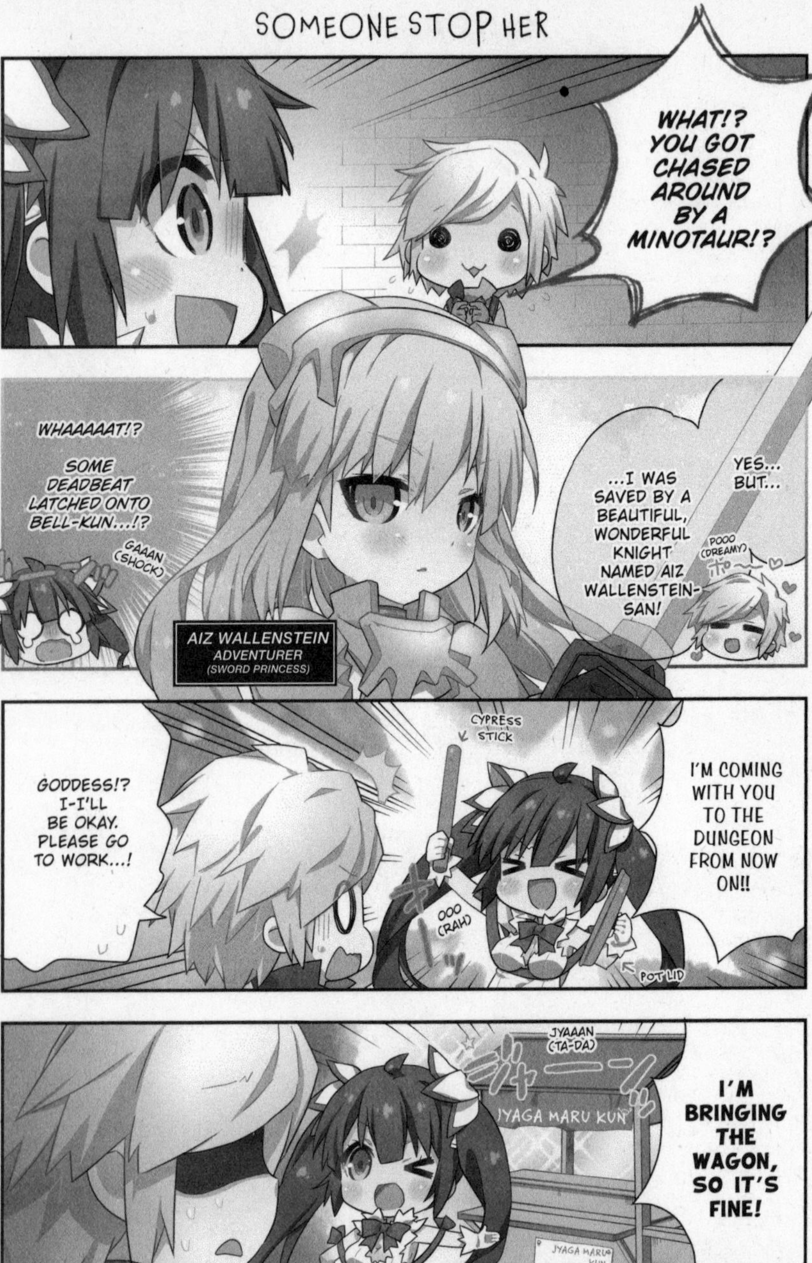
WHAT!? YOU GOT CHASED AROUND BY A MINOTAUR!?
YES... BUT...
...I WAS SAVED BY A BEAUTIFUL, WONDERFUL KNIGHT NAMED AIZ WALLENSTEIN-SAN!
POOO (DREAMY)
AIZ WALLENSTEIN
ADVENTURER
(SWORD PRINCESS)
WHAAAAAT!?
SOME DEADBEAT LATCHED ONTO BELL-KUN...!?
GAAAN (SHOCK)
I'M COMING WITH YOU TO THE DUNGEON FROM NOW ON!!
CYPRESS STICK
POT LID
OOO (RAH)
GODDESS!? I-I'LL BE OKAY. PLEASE GO TO WORK...!
I'M BRINGING THE WAGON, SO IT'S FINE!
JYAAAN (TA-DA)
JYAGA MARU KUN
JYAGA MARU KUN
HOT AND CRISPY

ENTREPRENEURIAL SPIRIT.

SAVE ME, EINA-SAN

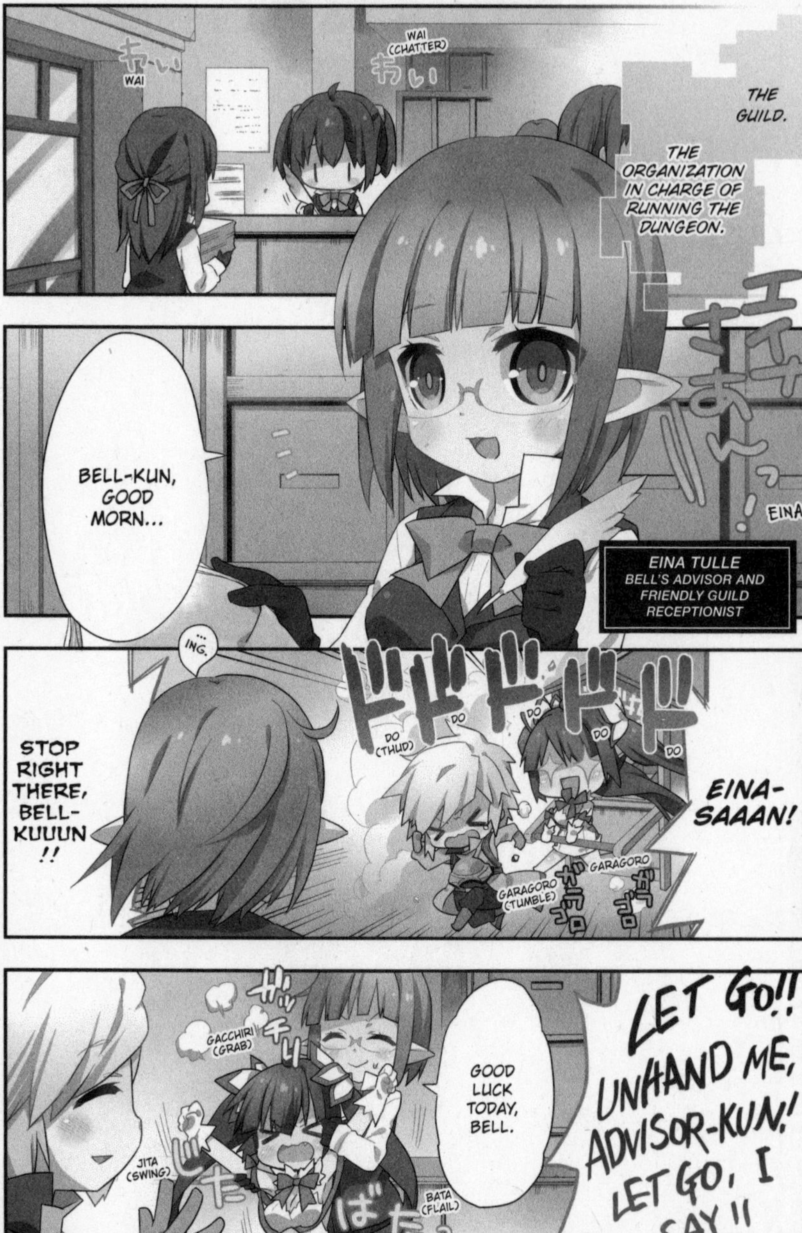

THE GUILD.
THE ORGANIZATION IN CHARGE OF RUNNING THE DUNGEON.
WAI (CHATTER)
WAI
EINA-S
EINA TULLE
BELL'S ADVISOR AND FRIENDLY GUILD RECEPTIONIST
BELL-KUN, GOOD MORN...
...ING.
EINA-SAAAN!
DO
DO
DO
DO
DO (THUD)
GARAGORO
GARAGORO (TUMBLE)
STOP RIGHT THERE, BELL-KUUUN!!
LET GO!! UNHAND ME, ADVISOR-KUN! LET GO, I SAY!!
GOOD LUCK TODAY, BELL.
GACCHIRI (GRAB)
BATA (FLAIL)
JITA (SWING)

NOT OFFICIALLY AUTHORIZED BY FUJINO OMORI-SENSEI!!

☆DEITY STATUS☆

FIRST ENTRY

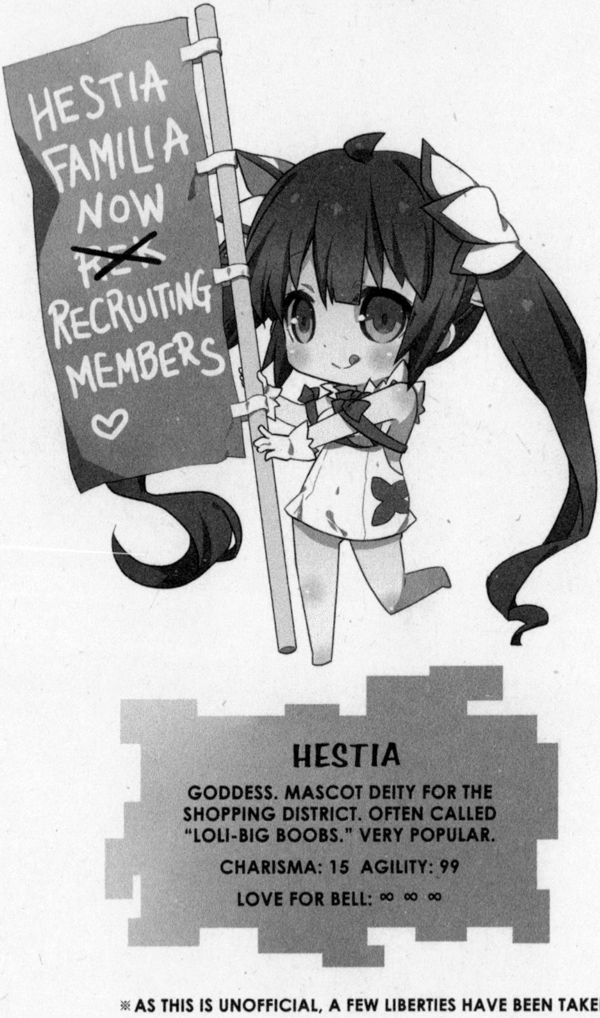
HESTIA FAMILIA NOW
RECRUITING MEMBERS
♡

HESTIA

GODDESS. MASCOT DEITY FOR THE SHOPPING DISTRICT. OFTEN CALLED "LOLI-BIG BOOBS." VERY POPULAR.

CHARISMA: 15 AGILITY: 99

LOVE FOR BELL: ∞ ∞ ∞

※ AS THIS IS UNOFFICIAL, A FEW LIBERTIES HAVE BEEN TAKEN.

STEP 02

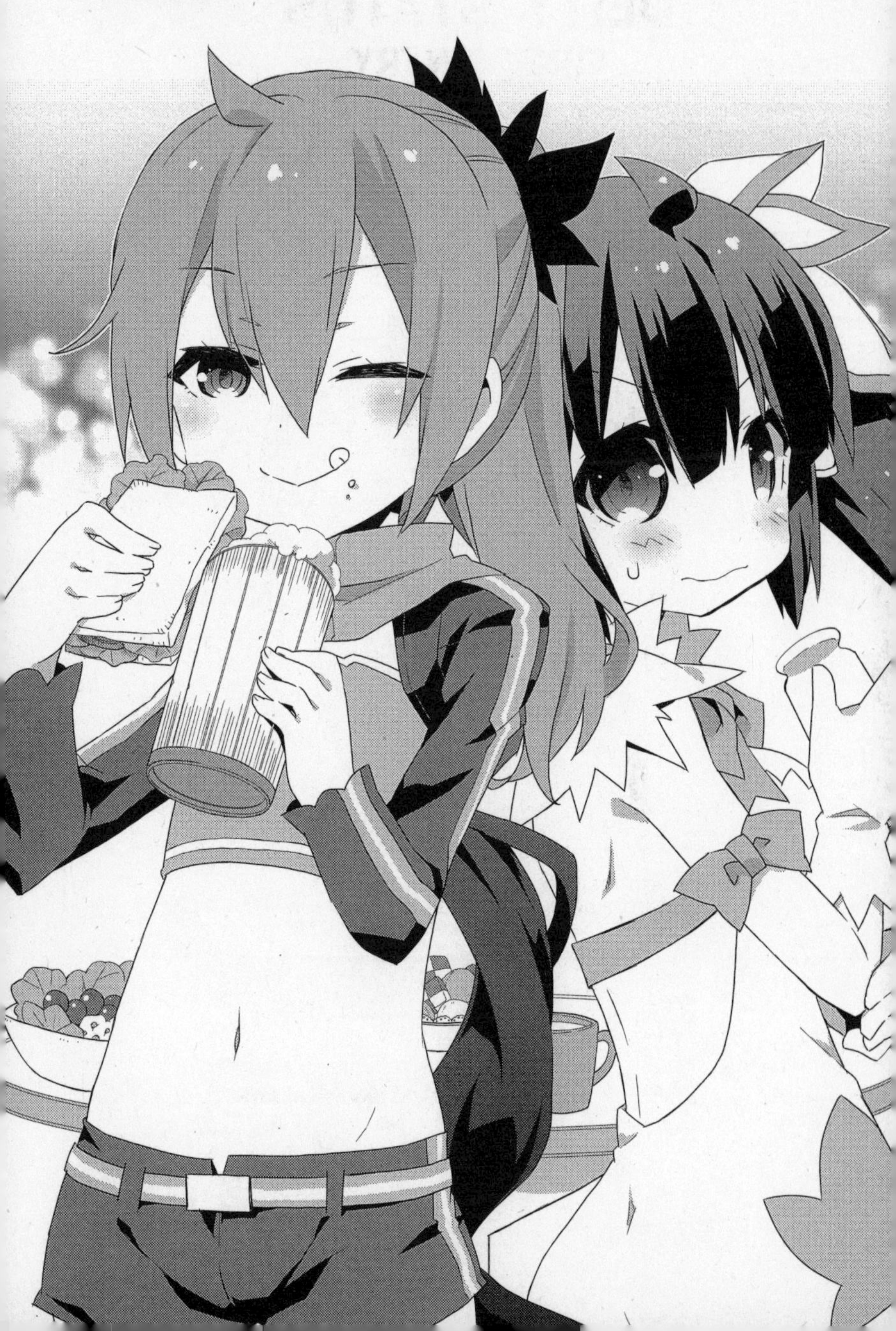

ORARIO'S LOLI-GODDESS

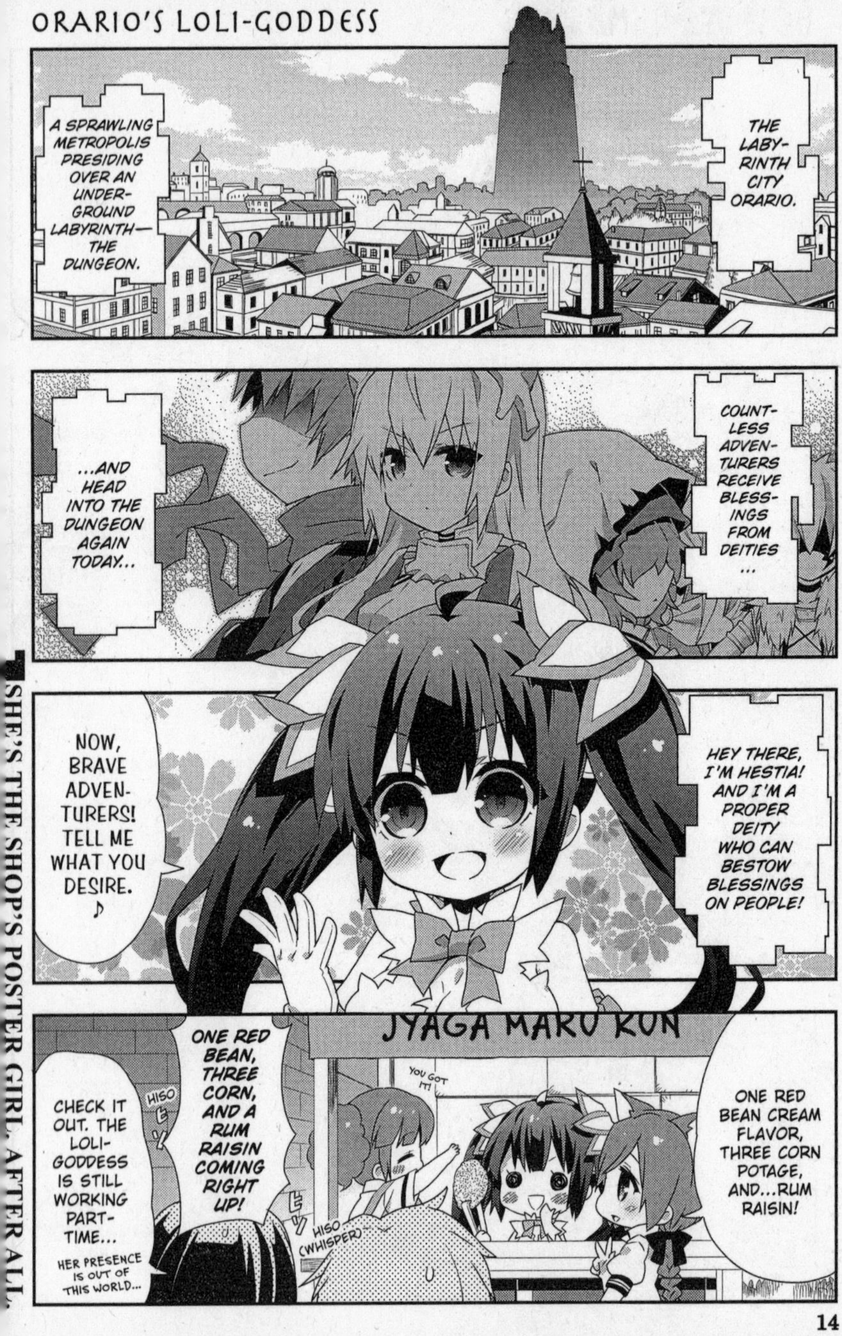
THE LABYRINTH CITY ORARIO.
A SPRAWLING METROPOLIS PRESIDING OVER AN UNDERGROUND LABYRINTH—THE DUNGEON.
COUNTLESS ADVENTURERS RECEIVE BLESSINGS FROM DEITIES...
...AND HEAD INTO THE DUNGEON AGAIN TODAY...
HEY THERE, I'M HESTIA! AND I'M A PROPER DEITY WHO CAN BESTOW BLESSINGS ON PEOPLE!
NOW, BRAVE ADVENTURERS! TELL ME WHAT YOU DESIRE. ♪
JYAGA MARU KUN
ONE RED BEAN CREAM FLAVOR, THREE CORN POTAGE, AND...RUM RAISIN!
YOU GOT IT!
ONE RED BEAN, THREE CORN, AND A RUM RAISIN COMING RIGHT UP!
HISO (WHISPER)
HISO
CHECK IT OUT. THE LOLI-GODDESS IS STILL WORKING PART-TIME...
HER PRESENCE IS OUT OF THIS WORLD...

SHE'S THE SHOP'S POSTER GIRL, AFTER ALL.

HESTIA'S NEMESIS

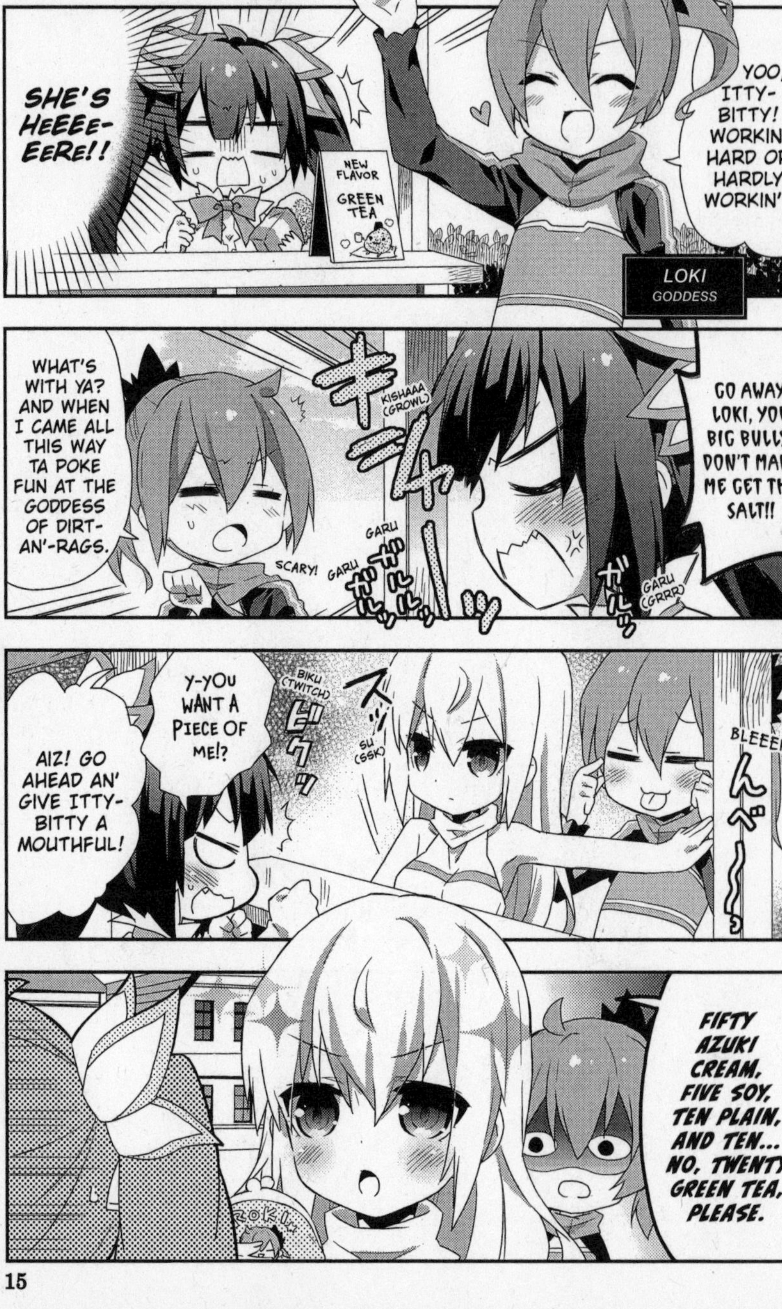

YOO, ITTY-BITTY! WORKIN' HARD OR HARDLY WORKIN'?
LOKI
GODDESS
NEW FLAVOR
GREEN TEA
SHE'S HEEEE-EERE!!
GO AWAY, LOKI, YOU BIG BULLY! DON'T MAKE ME GET THE SALT!!
GARU (GRRR)
KISHAAA (GROWL)
GARU
GARU
SCARY!
WHAT'S WITH YA? AND WHEN I CAME ALL THIS WAY TA POKE FUN AT THE GODDESS OF DIRT-AN'-RAGS.
BLEEEH!
SU (SSK)
BIKU (TWITCH)
Y-YOU WANT A PIECE OF ME!?
AIZ! GO AHEAD AN' GIVE ITTY-BITTY A MOUTHFUL!
FIFTY AZUKI CREAM, FIVE SOY, TEN PLAIN, AND TEN... NO, TWENTY GREEN TEA, PLEASE.

COMPLETELY UNEXPECTED CONCLUSION.

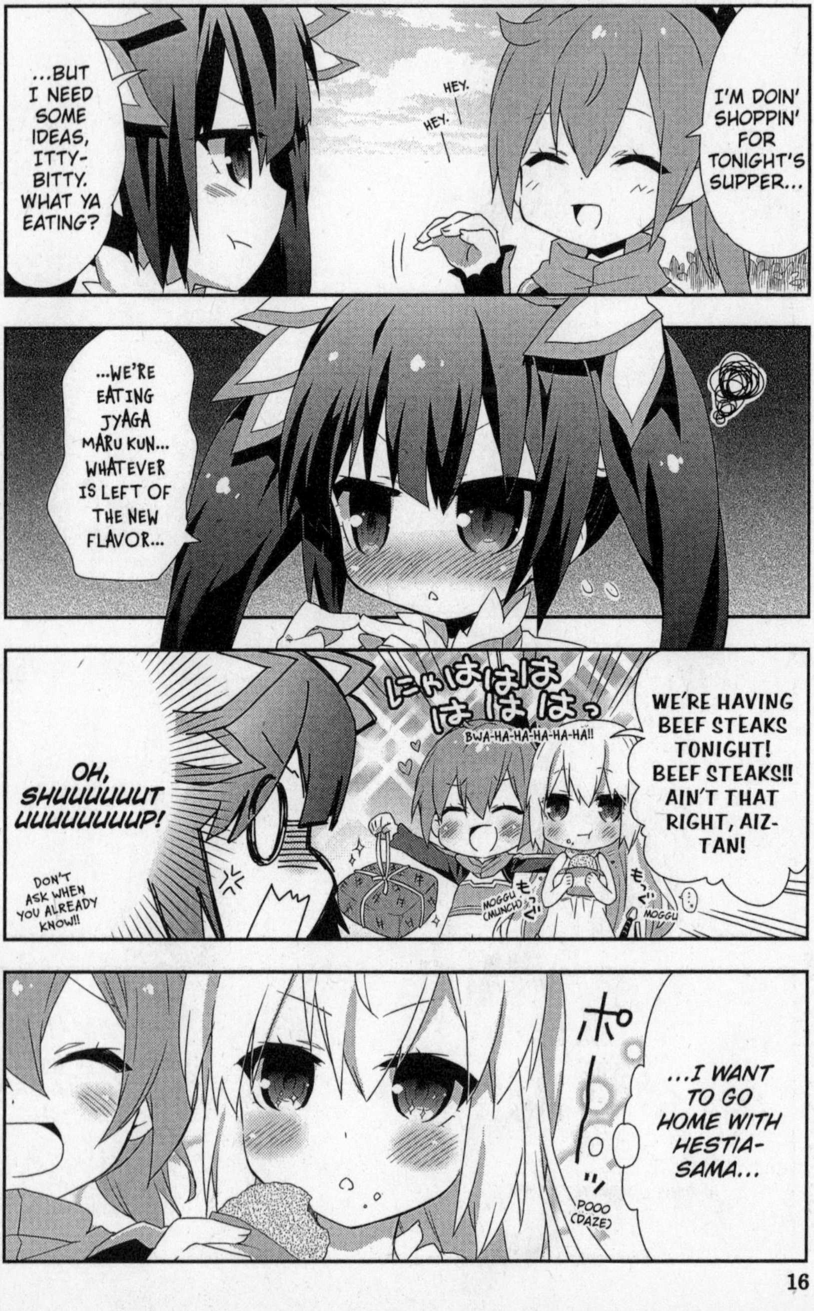
I'M DOIN' SHOPPIN' FOR TONIGHT'S SUPPER...
HEY.
HEY.
...BUT I NEED SOME IDEAS, ITTY-BITTY. WHAT YA EATING?
...WE'RE EATING JYAGA MARU KUN... WHATEVER IS LEFT OF THE NEW FLAVOR...
WE'RE HAVING BEEF STEAKS TONIGHT! BEEF STEAKS!! AIN'T THAT RIGHT, AIZ-TAN!
にゃはははははははっ
BWA-HA-HA-HA-HA-HA!!
もぐ
MOGGU (MUNCH)
もぐ
MOGGU
OH, SHUUUUUUT UUUUUUUUP!
DON'T ASK WHEN YOU ALREADY KNOW!!
ポーっ
POOO (DAZE)
...I WANT TO GO HOME WITH HESTIA-SAMA...

TOTALLY HOOKED

HEALTHY?

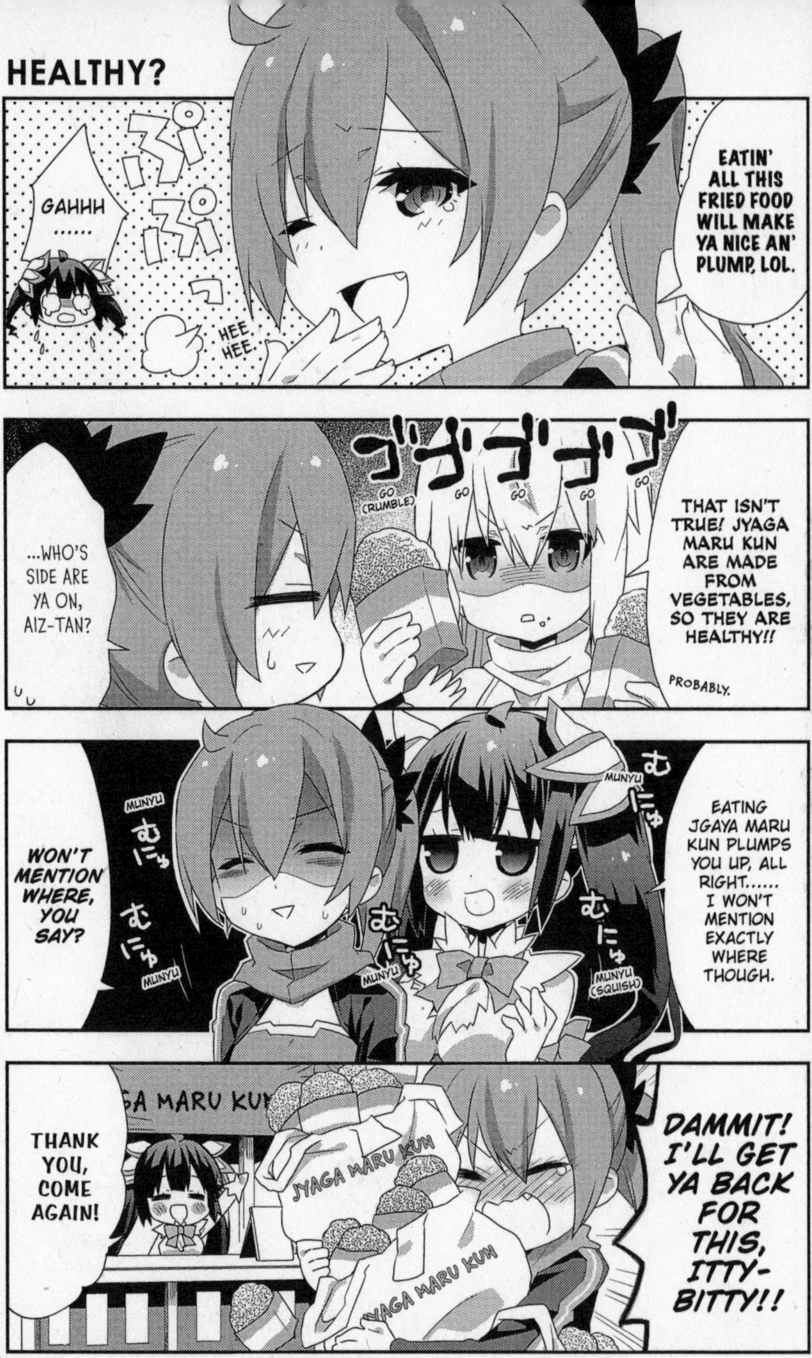
EATIN' ALL THIS FRIED FOOD WILL MAKE YA NICE AN' PLUMP, LOL.
ぷぷっ
HEE HEE.
GAHHH ......
ゴゴゴゴゴ
GO (RUMBLE) GO GO GO GO
THAT ISN'T TRUE! JYAGA MARU KUN ARE MADE FROM VEGETABLES, SO THEY ARE HEALTHY!!
PROBABLY.
...WHO'S SIDE ARE YA ON, AIZ-TAN?
むにゅ MUNYU
EATING JGAYA MARU KUN PLUMPS YOU UP, ALL RIGHT...... I WON'T MENTION EXACTLY WHERE THOUGH.
むにゅ MUNYU (SQUISH)
むにゅ MUNYU
むにゅ MUNYU
WON'T MENTION WHERE, YOU SAY?
むにゅ MUNYU
DAMMIT! I'LL GET YA BACK FOR THIS, ITTY-BITTY!!
JYAGA MARU KUN
JYAGA MARU KUN
JYAGA MARU KUN
GA MARU KUN
THANK YOU, COME AGAIN!

ABSOLUTE DEFEAT.

GOOD GIRL, HESTIA

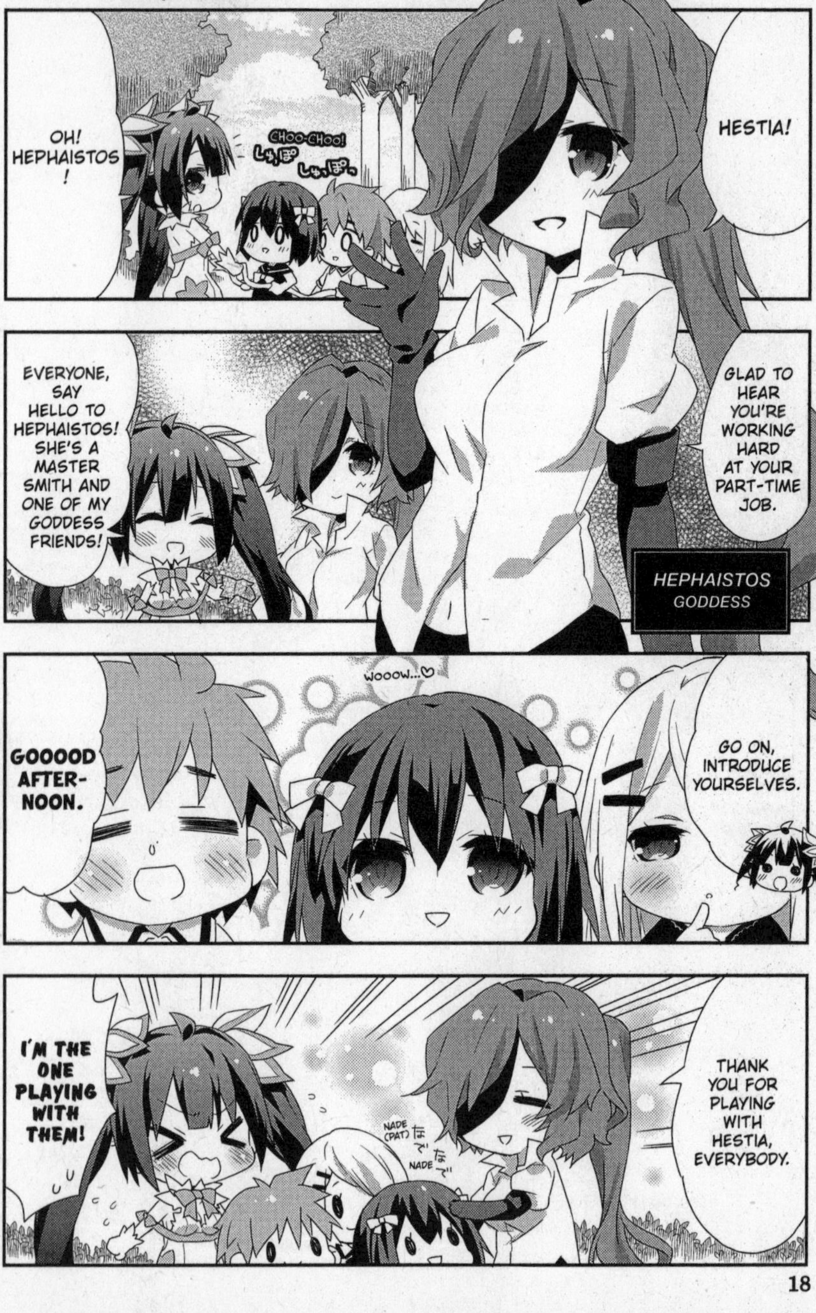
HESTIA!
CHOO-CHOO! しゅっぽ しゅっぽっ
OH! HEPHAISTOS!
GLAD TO HEAR YOU'RE WORKING HARD AT YOUR PART-TIME JOB.
HEPHAISTOS GODDESS
EVERYONE, SAY HELLO TO HEPHAISTOS! SHE'S A MASTER SMITH AND ONE OF MY GODDESS FRIENDS!
GO ON, INTRODUCE YOURSELVES.
WOOOW...♡
GOOOOD AFTER-NOON.
THANK YOU FOR PLAYING WITH HESTIA, EVERYBODY.
NADE (PAT) なで
なで NADE
I'M THE ONE PLAYING WITH THEM!

MORE OF A MOTHER THAN A FRIEND.

HEPHAISTOS THE WORRYWART

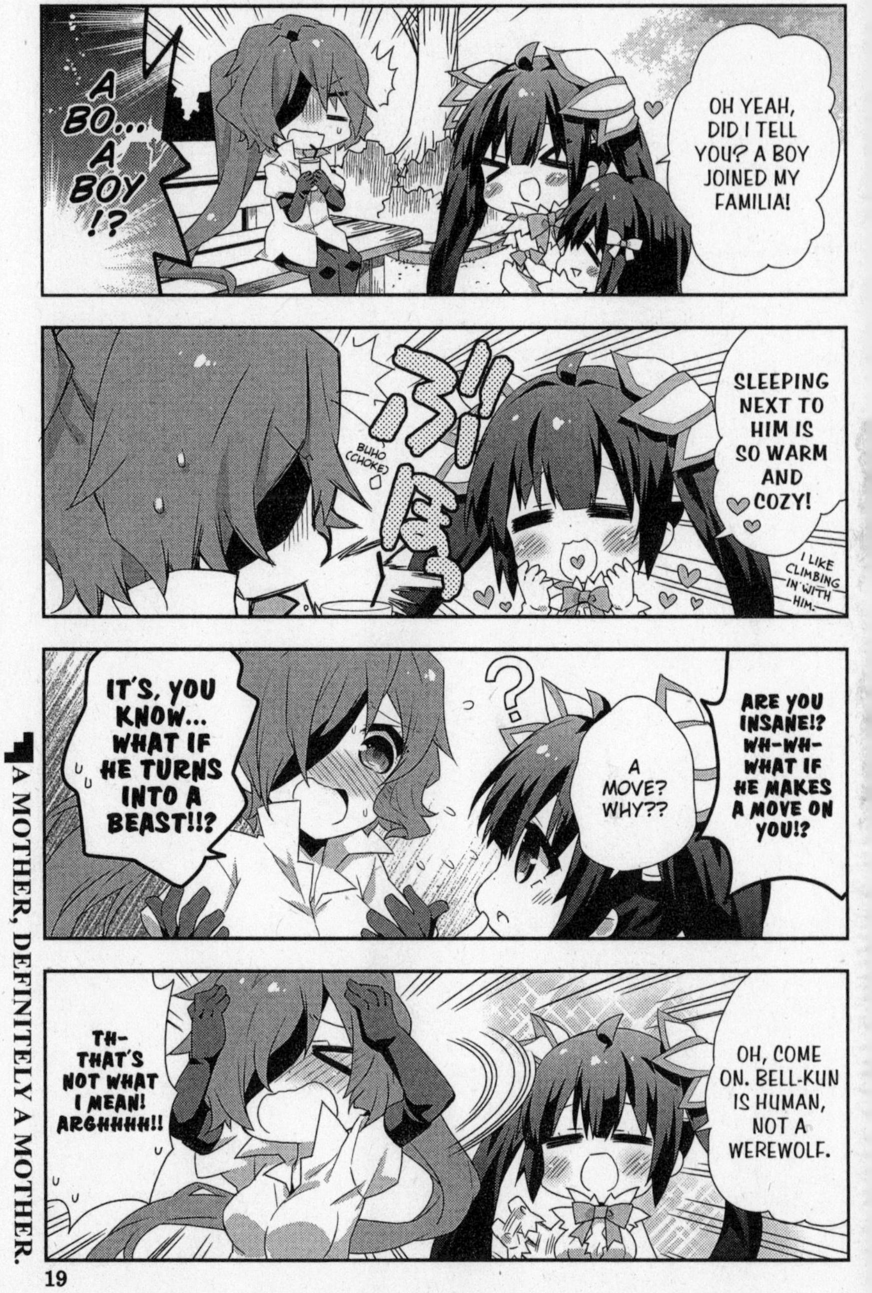
OH YEAH, DID I TELL YOU? A BOY JOINED MY FAMILIA!
A BO... A BOY!?
SLEEPING NEXT TO HIM IS SO WARM AND COZY!
I LIKE CLIMBING IN WITH HIM.
BUHO (CHOKE)
ARE YOU INSANE!? WH-WH-WHAT IF HE MAKES A MOVE ON YOU!?
A MOVE? WHY??
IT'S, YOU KNOW... WHAT IF HE TURNS INTO A BEAST!!!?
OH, COME ON. BELL-KUN IS HUMAN, NOT A WEREWOLF.
TH-THAT'S NOT WHAT I MEAN! ARGHHHH!!

A MOTHER, DEFINITELY A MOTHER.

HELP ME, HEPHAISTOS

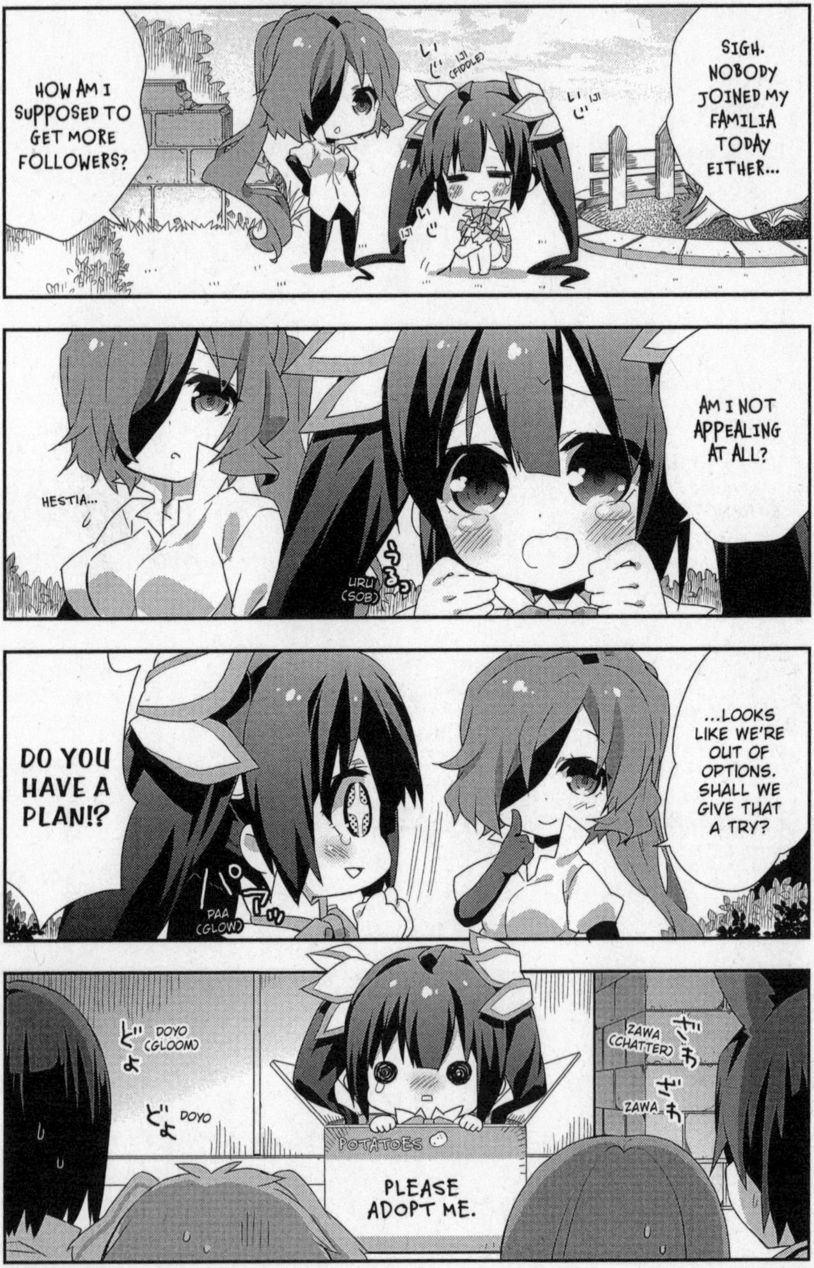

SIGH. NOBODY JOINED MY FAMILIA TODAY EITHER...
いじ IJI (FIDDLE)
いじ IJI
いじ IJI
HOW AM I SUPPOSED TO GET MORE FOLLOWERS?
AM I NOT APPEALING AT ALL?
うるっ URU (SOB)
HESTIA...
...LOOKS LIKE WE'RE OUT OF OPTIONS. SHALL WE GIVE THAT A TRY?
パァッ PAA (GLOW)
DO YOU HAVE A PLAN!?
ざわ ZAWA (CHATTER)
ざわ ZAWA
POTATOES
PLEASE ADOPT ME.
どよ DOYO (GLOOM)
どよ DOYO

NOTE: THIS IS A GODDESS.

HESTIA'S FAULTS

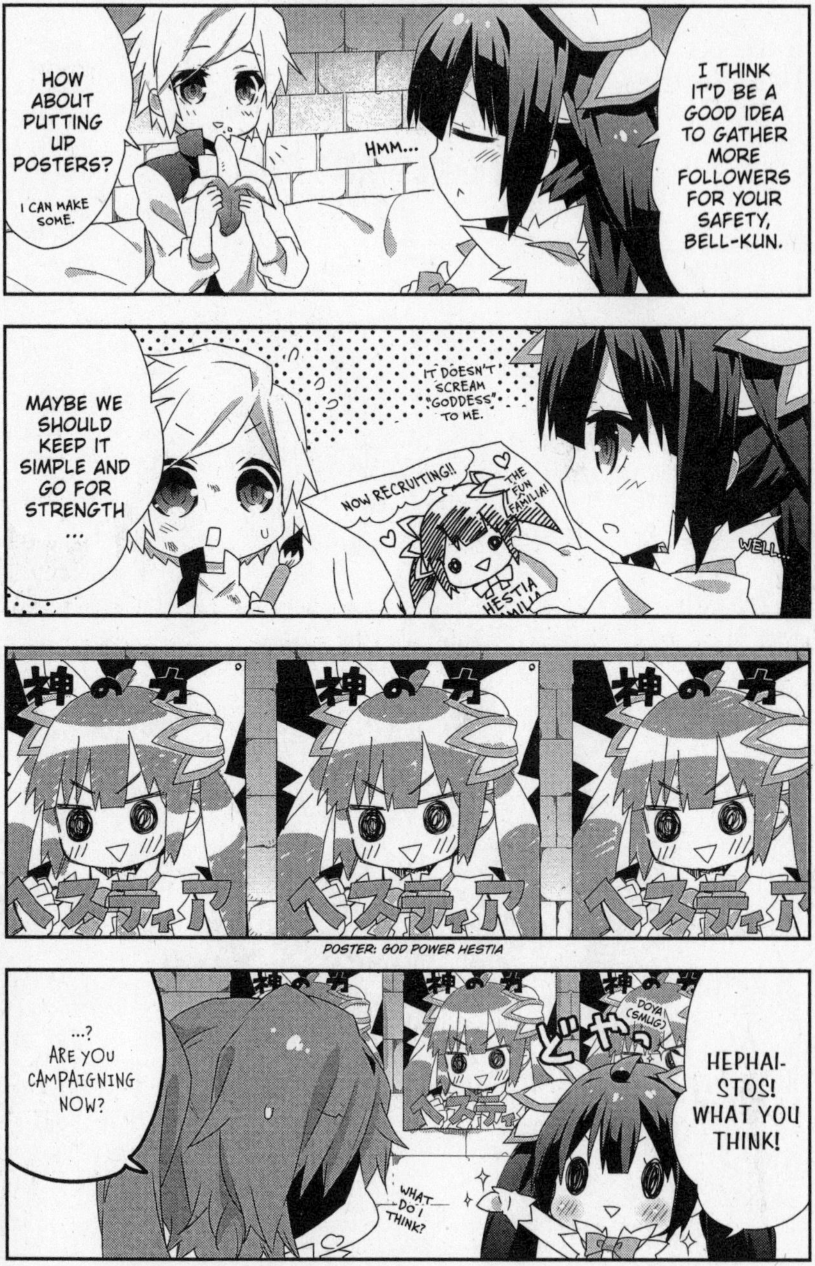
I THINK IT'D BE A GOOD IDEA TO GATHER MORE FOLLOWERS FOR YOUR SAFETY, BELL-KUN.
HMM...
HOW ABOUT PUTTING UP POSTERS?
I CAN MAKE SOME.
WELL...
IT DOESN'T SCREAM "GODDESS" TO ME.
THE FUN FAMILIA!
NOW RECRUITING!!
HESTIA
MAYBE WE SHOULD KEEP IT SIMPLE AND GO FOR STRENGTH...
神の力
ヘスティア
神の力
ヘスティア
神の力
ヘスティア
POSTER: GOD POWER HESTIA
HEPHAISTOS! WHAT YOU THINK!
DOYA (SMUG)
どやっ
WHAT DO I THINK?
...? ARE YOU CAMPAIGNING NOW?

NOT OFFICIALLY AUTHORIZED BY FUJINO OMORI-SENSEI!!

☆DEITY STATUS☆
SECOND ENTRY

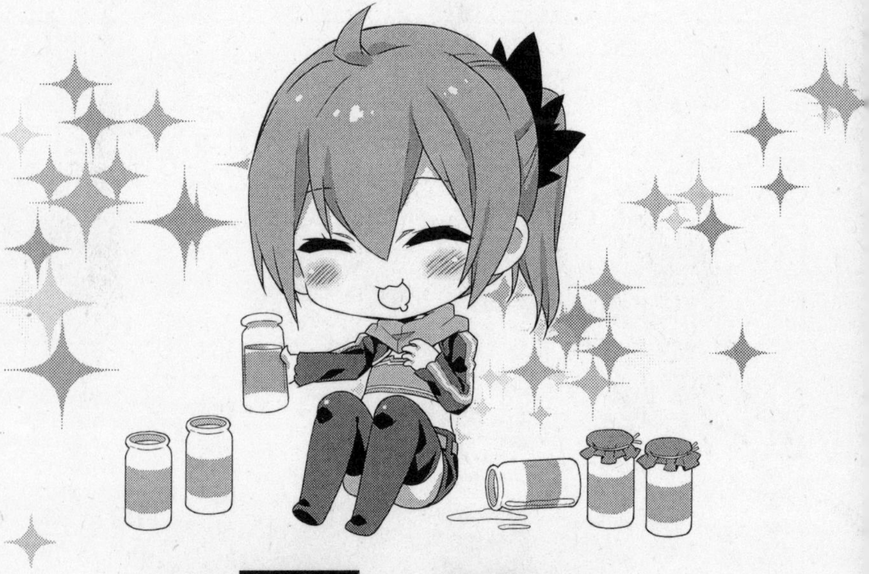

LOKI

GODDESS. HESTIA'S RIVAL. A FLAT-CHESTED DEITY HEADING UP A POWERFUL FAMILIA. ENDEARINGLY REFERRED TO AS "LOKI THE BOOBLESS."

CHARISMA: 150 INTELLECT: 35
BUST: 5 99 YA HEAR!?

※ AS THIS IS UNOFFICIAL, A FEW LIBERTIES HAVE BEEN TAKEN.

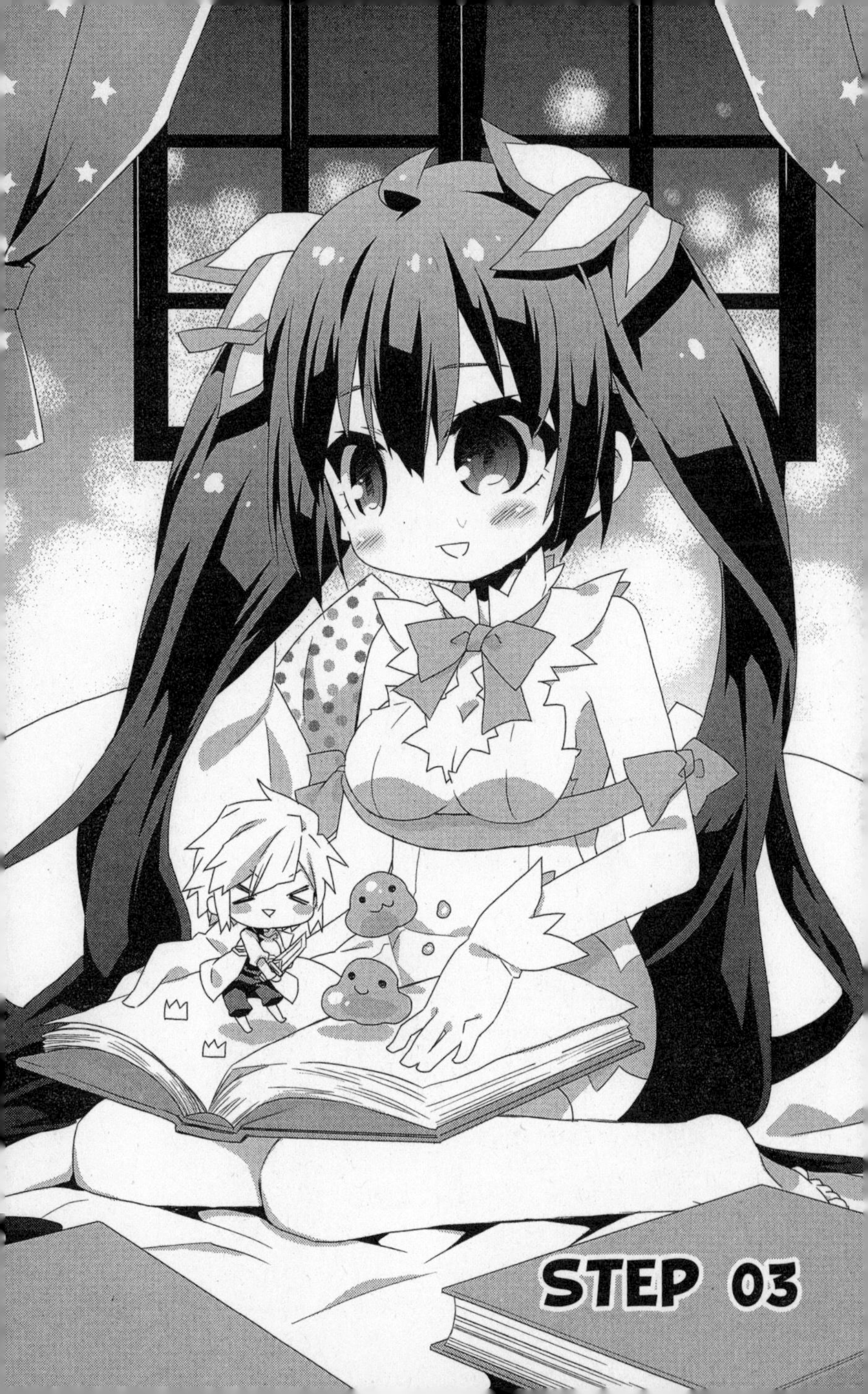
STEP 03

HESTIA-SAMA'S OPTIONS

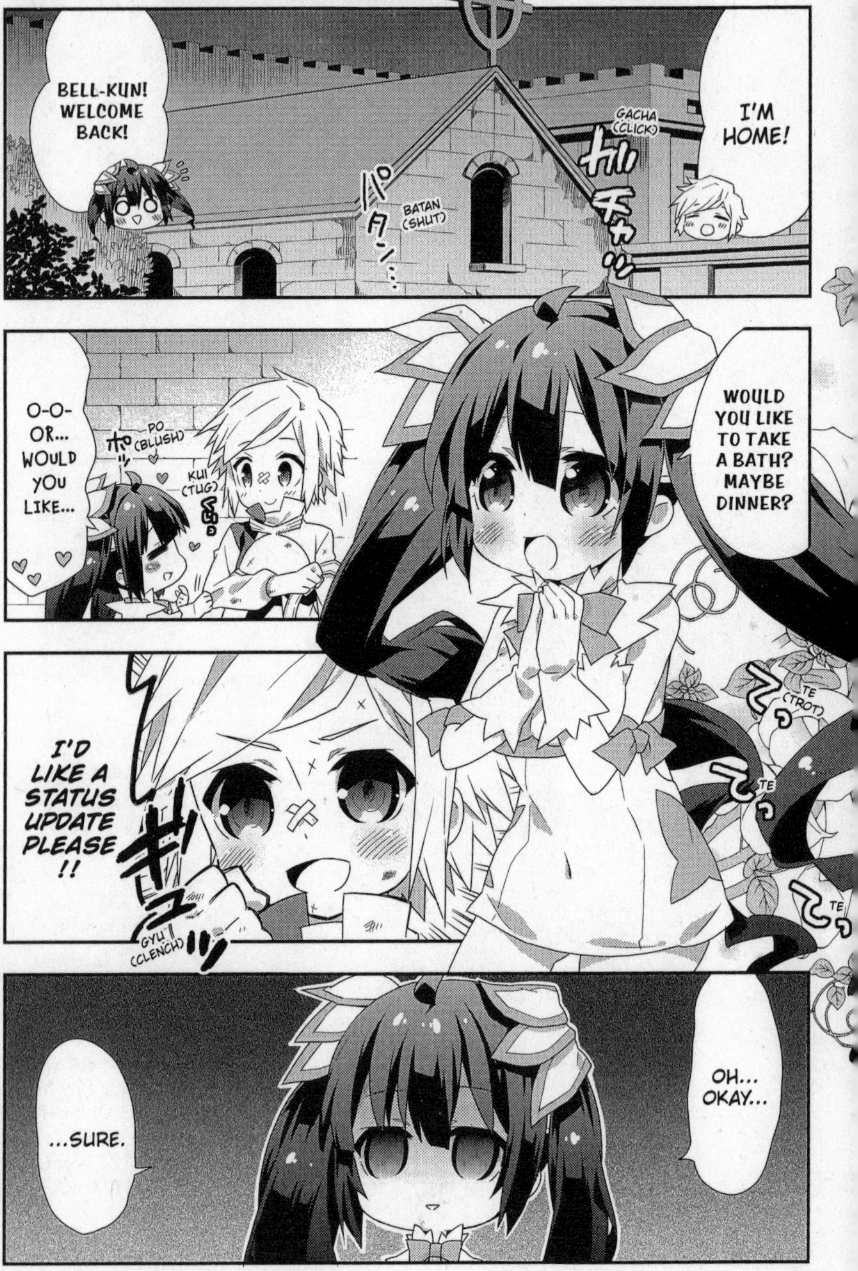
I'M HOME!
GACHA (CLICK)
BATAN (SHUT)
BELL-KUN! WELCOME BACK!
WOULD YOU LIKE TO TAKE A BATH? MAYBE DINNER?
TE (TROT)
TE
TE
O-O-OR... WOULD YOU LIKE...
PO (BLUSH)
KUI (TUG)
I'D LIKE A STATUS UPDATE PLEASE!!
GYU (CLENCH)
OH... OKAY...
...SURE.

READ BETWEEN THE LINES!!

STATUS UPDATE!

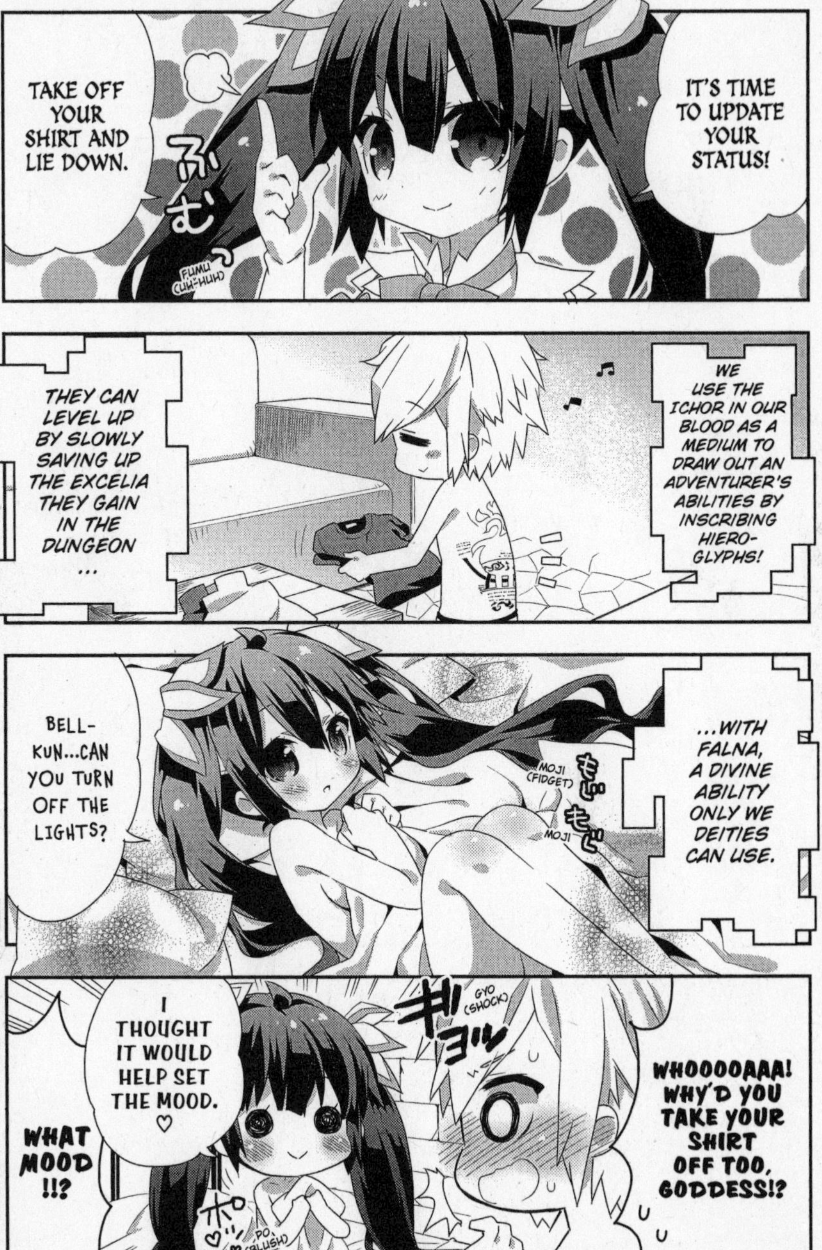

IT'S TIME TO UPDATE YOUR STATUS!
TAKE OFF YOUR SHIRT AND LIE DOWN.
ふむっ
FUMU (UH-HUH)
WE USE THE ICHOR IN OUR BLOOD AS A MEDIUM TO DRAW OUT AN ADVENTURER'S ABILITIES BY INSCRIBING HIERO-GLYPHS!
THEY CAN LEVEL UP BY SLOWLY SAVING UP THE EXCELIA THEY GAIN IN THE DUNGEON ...
...WITH FALNA, A DIVINE ABILITY ONLY WE DEITIES CAN USE.
もじもじ
MOJI (FIDGET) MOJI
BELL-KUN...CAN YOU TURN OFF THE LIGHTS?
WHOOOOAAA! WHY'D YOU TAKE YOUR SHIRT OFF TOO, GODDESS!?
ギョッ
GYO (SHOCK)
I THOUGHT IT WOULD HELP SET THE MOOD. ♡
WHAT MOOD!!?
ポッ
PO (BLUSH)

PREDATORY GODDESS!?

STATUS EFFECT!!

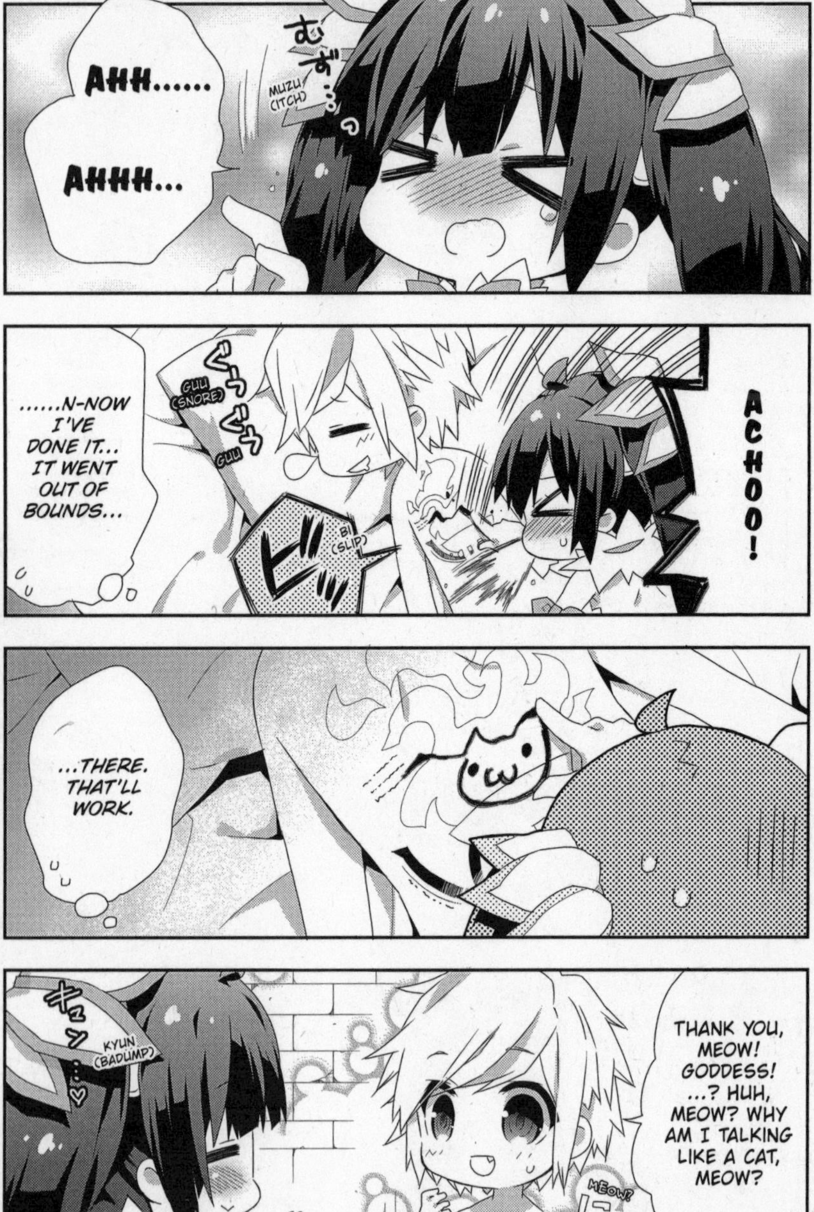
MUZU (ITCH)
AHH......
AHHH...
ACHOO!
GUU (SNORE)
GUU
BI (SLIP)
......N-NOW I'VE DONE IT... IT WENT OUT OF BOUNDS...
...THERE. THAT'LL WORK.
THANK YOU, MEOW! GODDESS! ...? HUH, MEOW? WHY AM I TALKING LIKE A CAT, MEOW?
MEOW?
KYUN (BADUMP)
SO CUTE.

THIS MIGHT BE GOOD IN ITS OWN WAY, MEOW. ♡

A SKILL ACTIVATES!!!

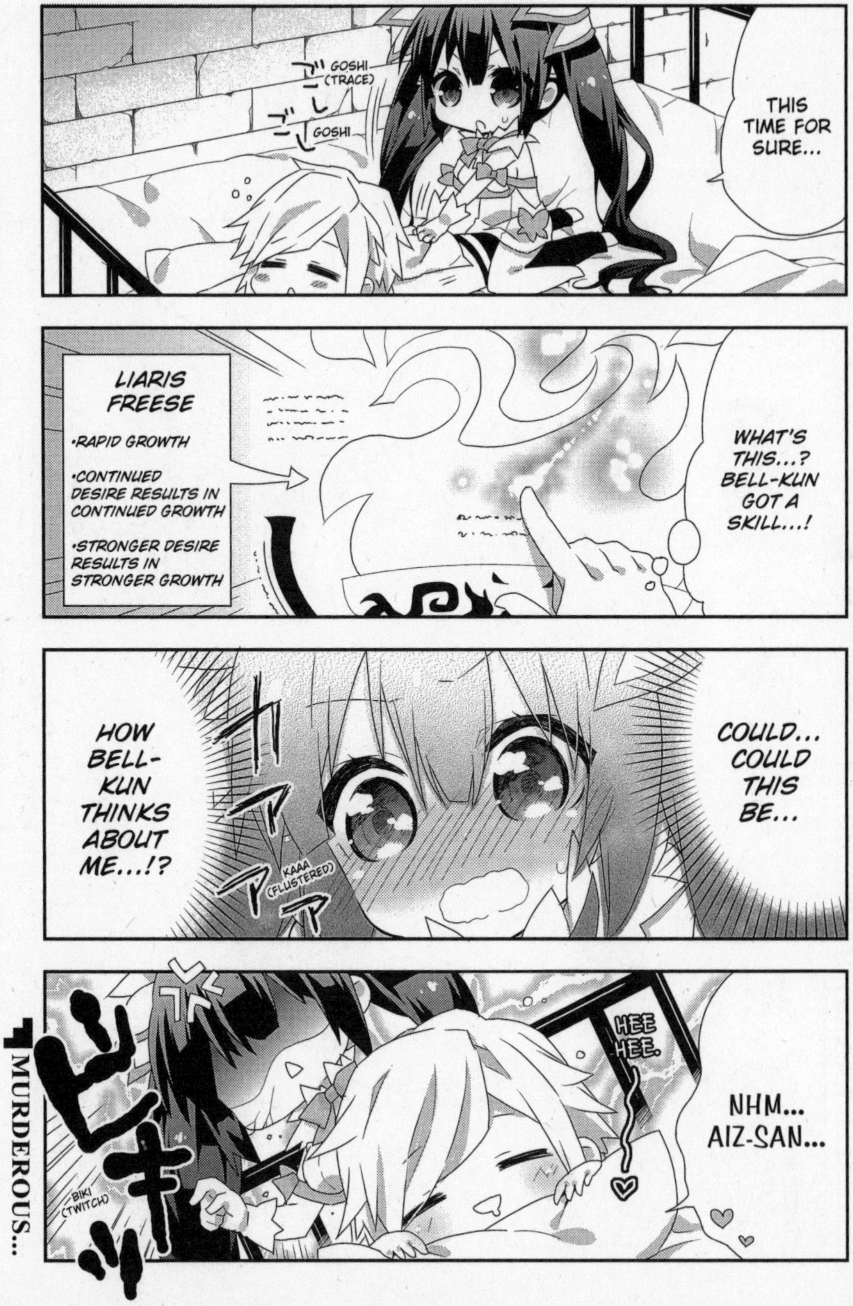
THIS TIME FOR SURE...
GOSHI (TRACE)
GOSHI
WHAT'S THIS...? BELL-KUN GOT A SKILL...!
LIARIS FREESE
•RAPID GROWTH
•CONTINUED DESIRE RESULTS IN CONTINUED GROWTH
•STRONGER DESIRE RESULTS IN STRONGER GROWTH
COULD... COULD THIS BE...
HOW BELL-KUN THINKS ABOUT ME...!?
KAAA (FLUSTERED)
NHM... AIZ-SAN...
HEE HEE.
BIKI (TWITCH)

MURDEROUS...

NEVER HAPPENED!?

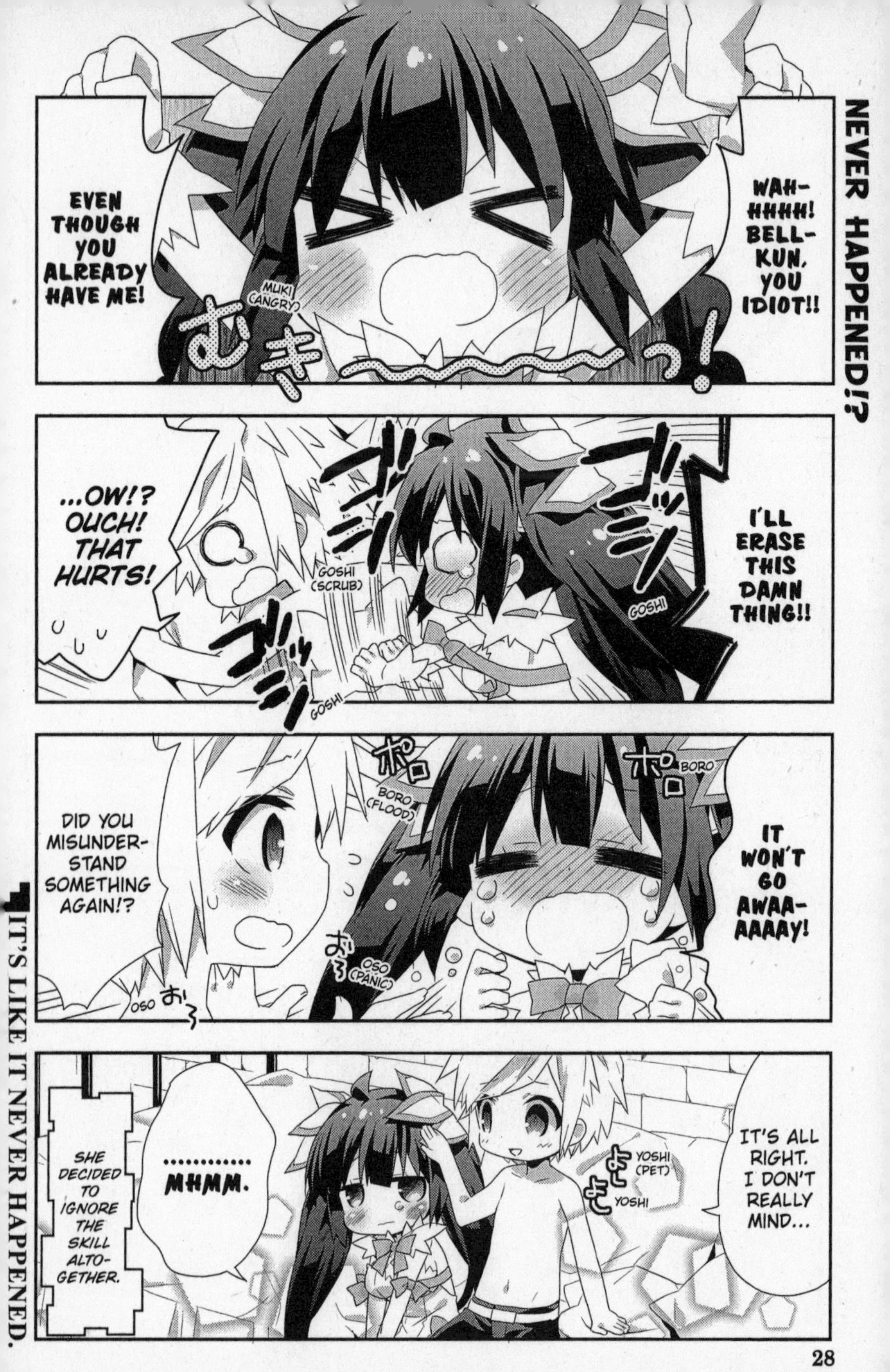
WAH-HHHH! BELL-KUN, YOU IDIOT!!
EVEN THOUGH YOU ALREADY HAVE ME!
MUKI (ANGRY)
I'LL ERASE THIS DAMN THING!!
GOSHI
...OW!? OUCH! THAT HURTS!
GOSHI (SCRUB)
GOSHI
BORO
IT WON'T GO AWAA-AAAAY!
BORO (FLOOD)
DID YOU MISUNDERSTAND SOMETHING AGAIN!?
OSO (PANIC)
OSO
IT'S ALL RIGHT. I DON'T REALLY MIND...
YOSHI (PET)
YOSHI
.... MHMM.
SHE DECIDED TO IGNORE THE SKILL ALTOGETHER.

IT'S LIKE IT NEVER HAPPENED.

LOKI-SAMA DRESSES UP! ♡

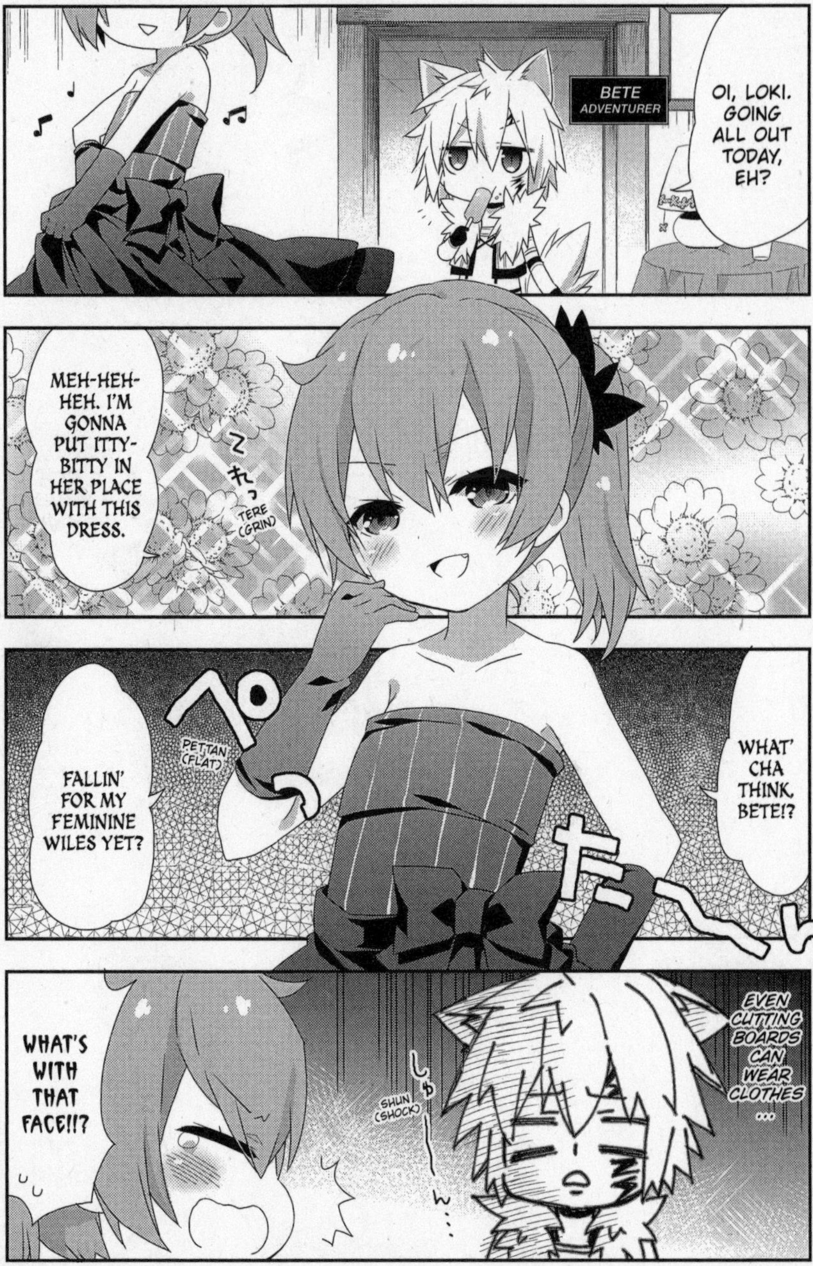
OI, LOKI. GOING ALL OUT TODAY, EH?
BETE
ADVENTURER
TERE (GRIN)
MEH-HEH-HEH. I'M GONNA PUT ITTY-BITTY IN HER PLACE WITH THIS DRESS.
WHAT' CHA THINK, BETE!?
PETTAN (FLAT)
FALLIN' FOR MY FEMININE WILES YET?
EVEN CUTTING BOARDS CAN WEAR CLOTHES...
SHUN (SHOCK)
WHAT'S WITH THAT FACE!!?

NO BITS.

BATTLE OF THE GODS

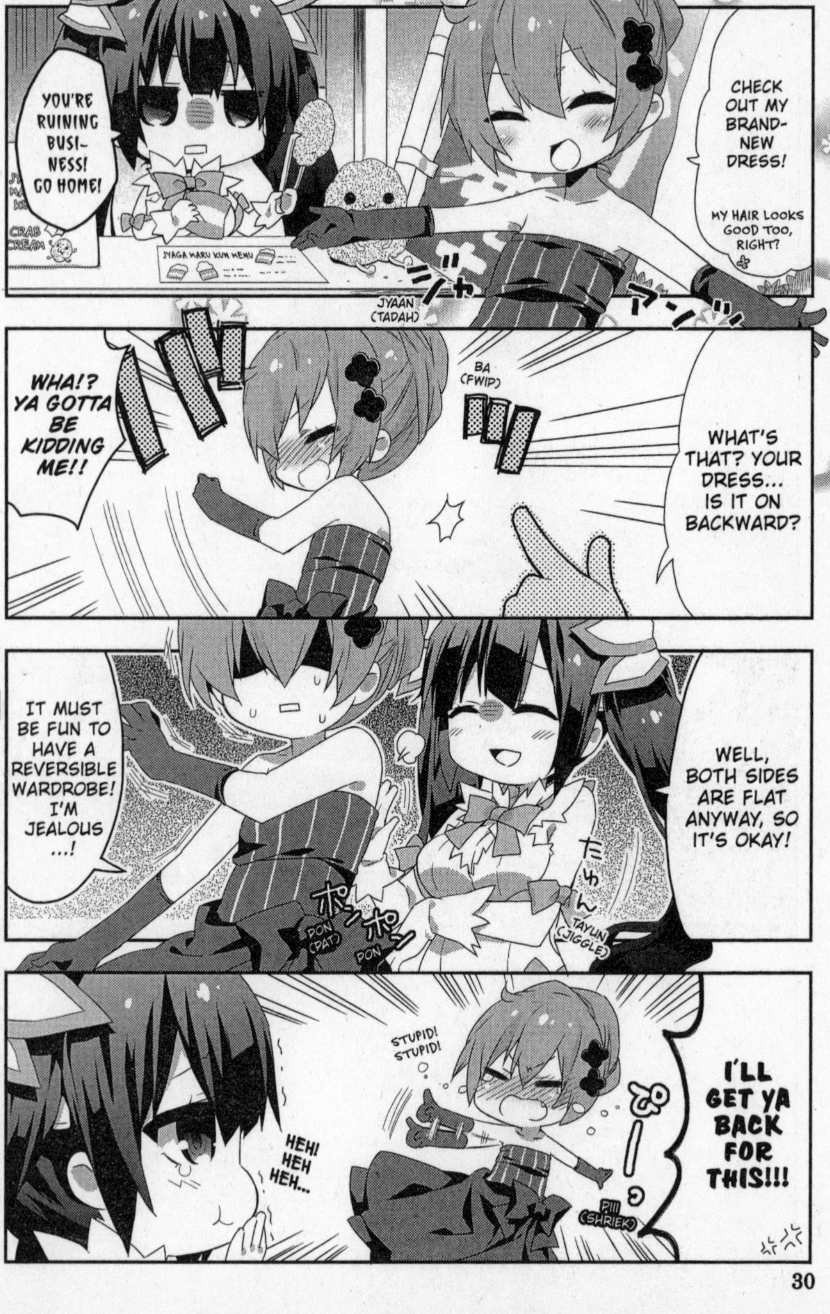

CHECK OUT MY BRAND-NEW DRESS!
MY HAIR LOOKS GOOD TOO, RIGHT?
JYAAN (TADAH)
YOU'RE RUINING BUSI-NESS! GO HOME!
JYAGA MARU KUN MENU
CRAB CREAM
WHAT'S THAT? YOUR DRESS... IS IT ON BACKWARD?
BA (FWIP)
WHA!? YA GOTTA BE KIDDING ME!!
WELL, BOTH SIDES ARE FLAT ANYWAY, SO IT'S OKAY!
たゆん
TAYUN (JIGGLE)
ポンポン
PON (PAT) PON
IT MUST BE FUN TO HAVE A REVERSIBLE WARDROBE! I'M JEALOUS ...!
I'LL GET YA BACK FOR THIS!!!
ぴーっ
PIII (SHRIEK)
STUPID! STUPID!
HEH! HEH HEH...

BIG TALK FOR SOMETHING SO SMALL.

AIZ'S STATUS

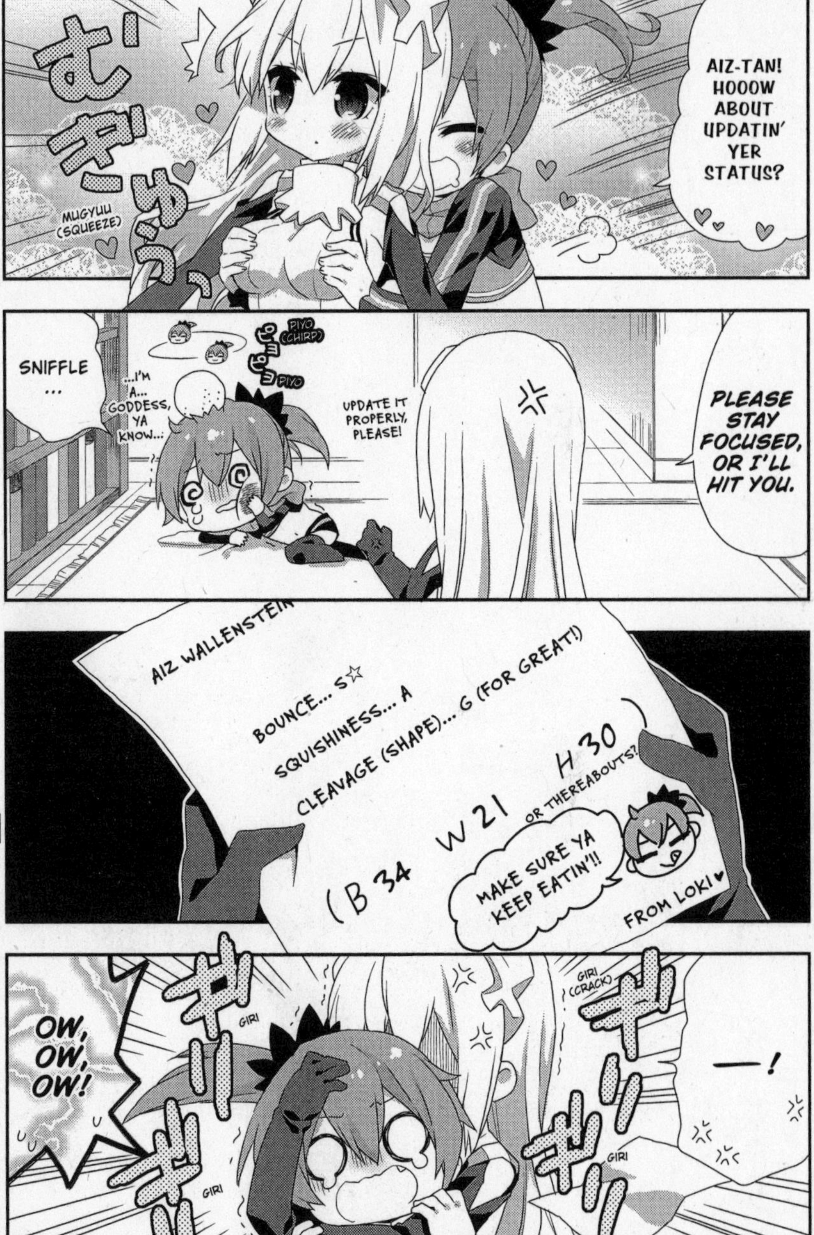
AIZ-TAN! HOOOW ABOUT UPDATIN' YER STATUS?
MUGYUU (SQUEEZE)
PLEASE STAY FOCUSED, OR I'LL HIT YOU.
UPDATE IT PROPERLY, PLEASE!
PIYO (CHIRP)
PIYO
...I'M A... GODDESS, YA KNOW...:
SNIFFLE ...
AIZ WALLENSTEIN
BOUNCE... S☆
SQUISHINESS... A
CLEAVAGE (SHAPE)... G (FOR GREAT!)
(B 34 W 21 H 30)
OR THEREABOUTS?
MAKE SURE YA KEEP EATIN'!!
FROM LOKI♥
—!
GIRI (CRACK)
GIRI
GIRI
GIRI
OW, OW, OW!

"NICE AN' PLUMP!!" —LOKI

NOT OFFICIALLY AUTHORIZED BY FUJINO OMORI-SENSEI!!

☆DEITY STATUS☆
THIRD ENTRY

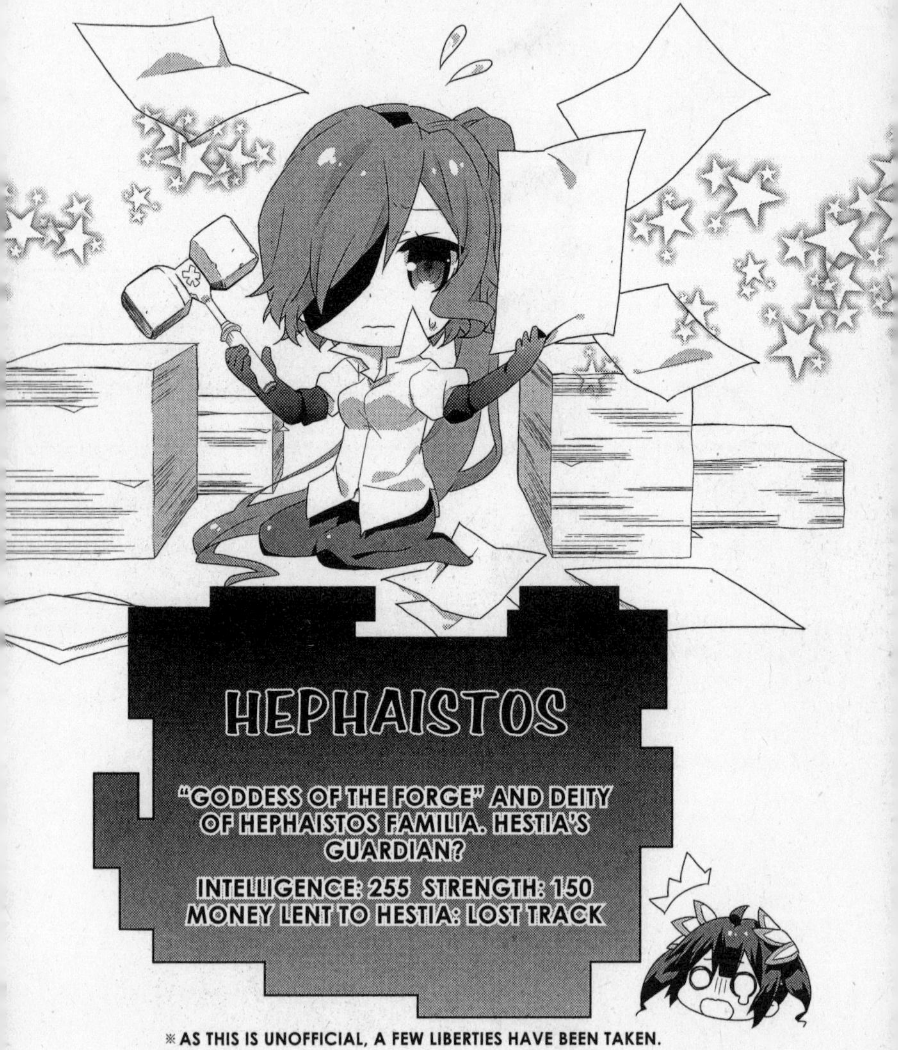
HEPHAISTOS
"GODDESS OF THE FORGE" AND DEITY OF HEPHAISTOS FAMILIA. HESTIA'S GUARDIAN?
INTELLIGENCE: 255 STRENGTH: 150
MONEY LENT TO HESTIA: LOST TRACK

※ AS THIS IS UNOFFICIAL, A FEW LIBERTIES HAVE BEEN TAKEN.

STEP 04

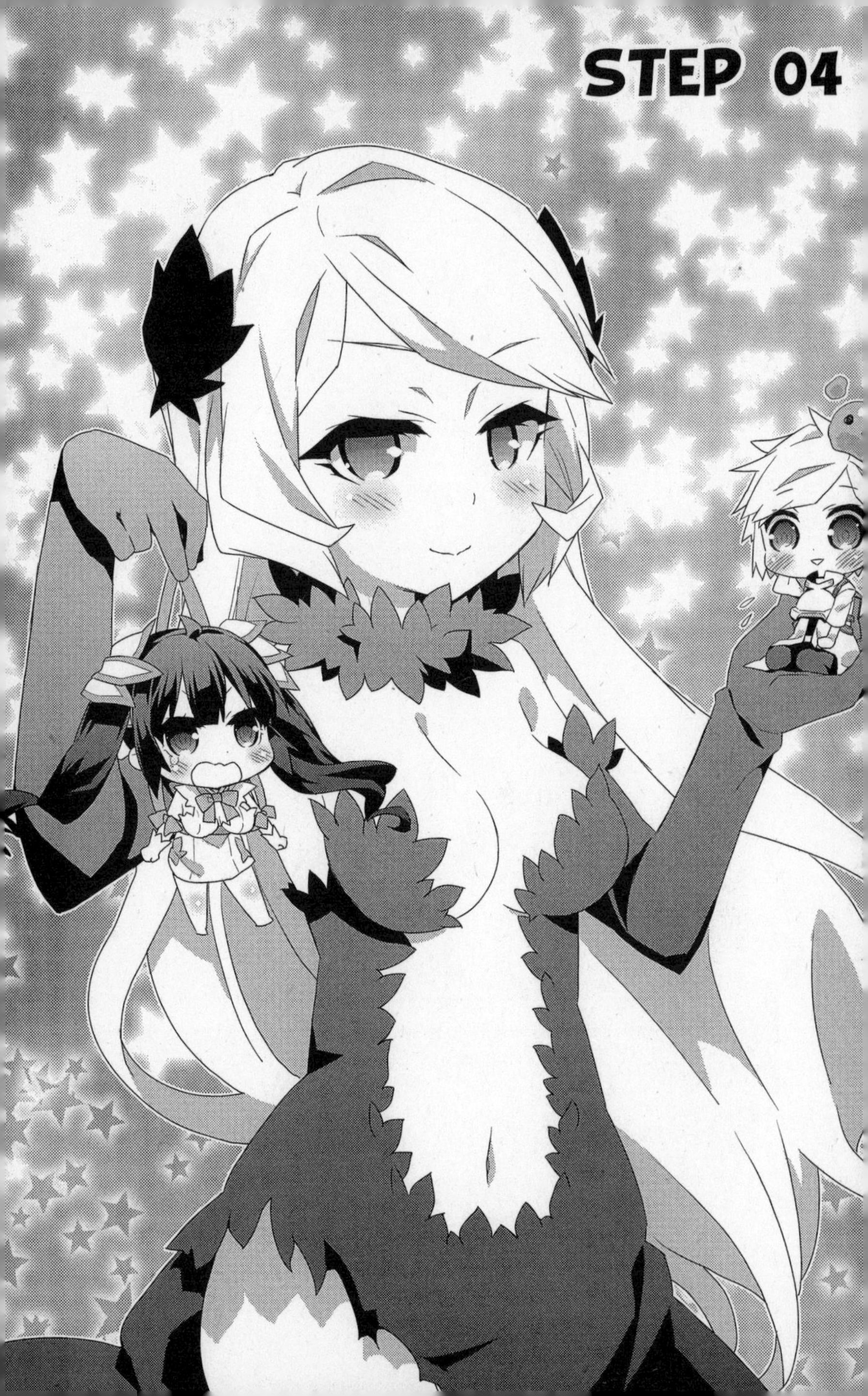

EVER-CHANGING GODDESS?

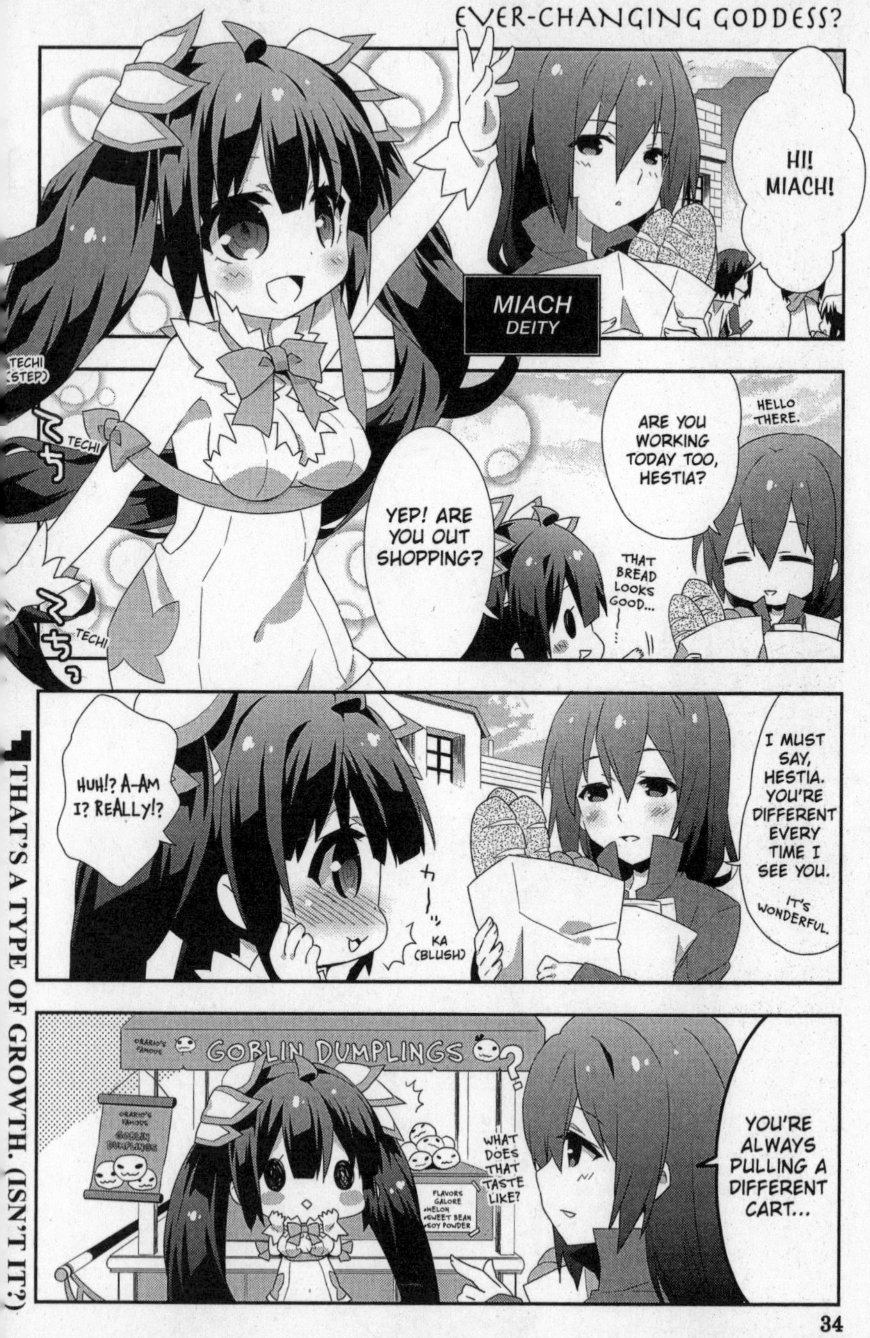
HI! MIACH!
MIACH
DEITY
TECHI (STEP)
TECHI
TECHI
HELLO THERE.
ARE YOU WORKING TODAY TOO, HESTIA?
THAT BREAD LOOKS GOOD...
YEP! ARE YOU OUT SHOPPING?
I MUST SAY, HESTIA. YOU'RE DIFFERENT EVERY TIME I SEE YOU.
IT'S WONDERFUL.
KA (BLUSH)
HUH!? A-AM I? REALLY!?
YOU'RE ALWAYS PULLING A DIFFERENT CART...
WHAT DOES THAT TASTE LIKE?
FLAVORS GALORE •MELON •SWEET BEAN •SOY POWDER
ORARIO'S FAMOUS GOBLIN DUMPLINGS
ORARIO'S FAMOUS GOBLIN DUMPLINGS

THAT'S A TYPE OF GROWTH. (ISN'T IT?)

HESTIA'S GRATITUDE

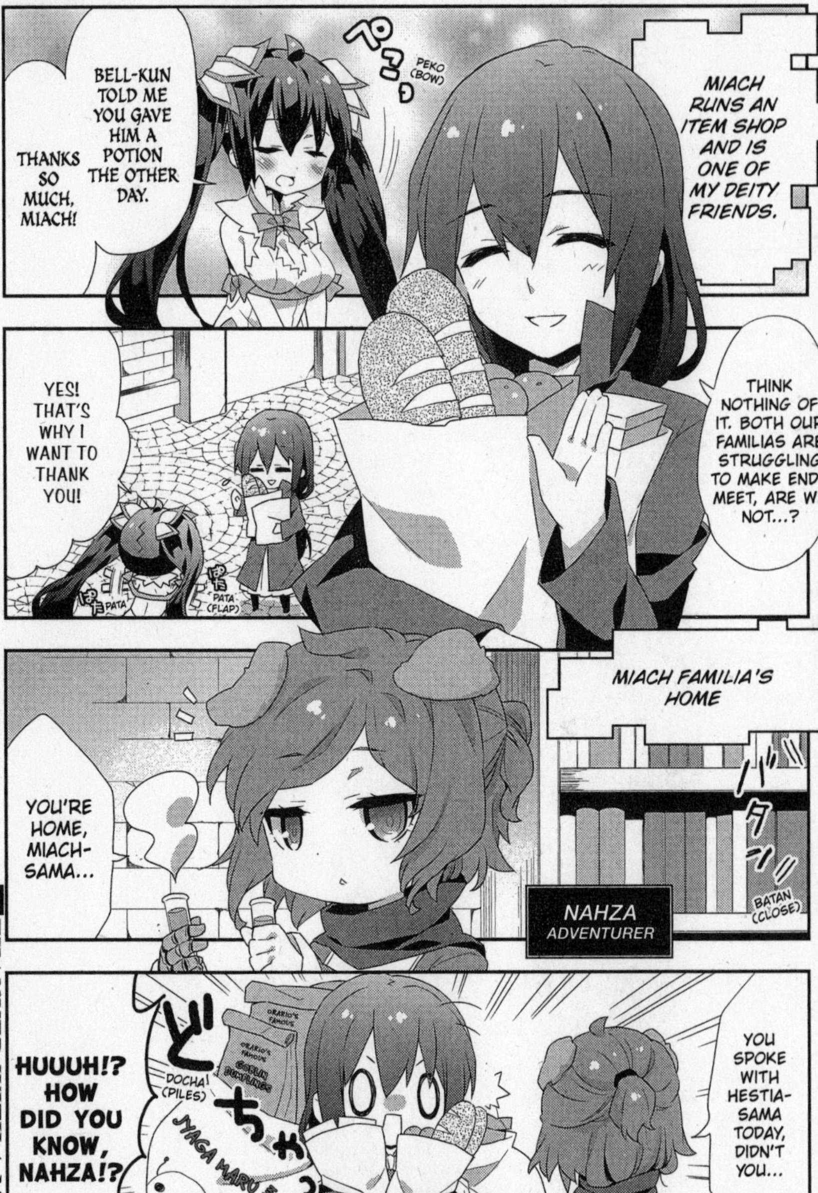

MIACH RUNS AN ITEM SHOP AND IS ONE OF MY DEITY FRIENDS.
PEKO (BOW)
BELL-KUN TOLD ME YOU GAVE HIM A POTION THE OTHER DAY.
THANKS SO MUCH, MIACH!
THINK NOTHING OF IT. BOTH OUR FAMILIAS ARE STRUGGLING TO MAKE ENDS MEET, ARE WE NOT...?
YES! THAT'S WHY I WANT TO THANK YOU!
PATA (FLAP)
PATA
MIACH FAMILIA'S HOME
BATAN (CLOSE)
NAHZA ADVENTURER
YOU'RE HOME, MIACH-SAMA...
YOU SPOKE WITH HESTIA-SAMA TODAY, DIDN'T YOU...
JYAGA MARU
ORARIO'S FAMOUS GOBLIN DUMPLINGS
DOCHA! (PILES)
JYAGA MARU KUN
ORARIO'S FAMOUS GOBLIN
HUUUH!? HOW DID YOU KNOW, NAHZA!?

THANKED WITH A MEAL.

IS MILK AN INGREDIENT?

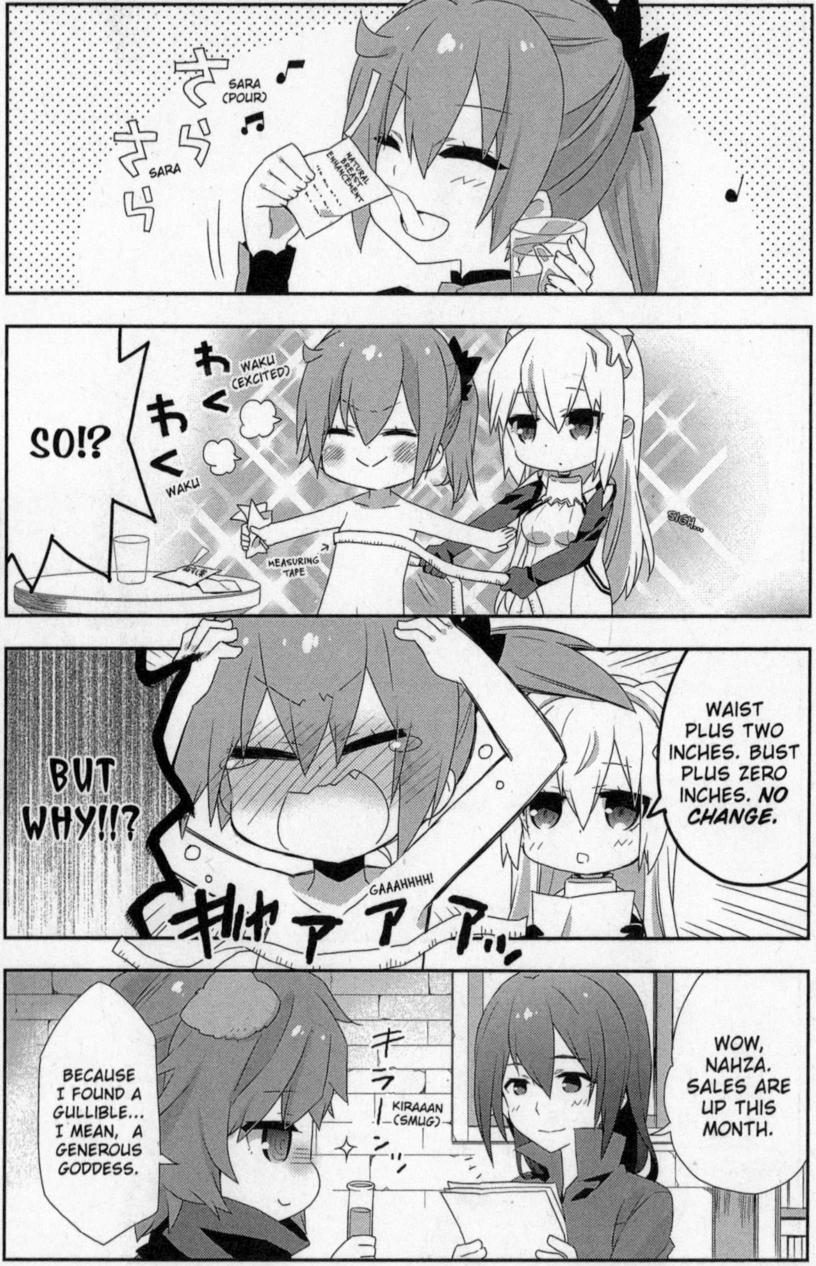
NATURAL BREAST ENHANCEMENT
さらさら
SARA (POUR)
SARA
SIGH...
わくわく
WAKU (EXCITED)
WAKU
MEASURING TAPE
SO!?
WAIST PLUS TWO INCHES. BUST PLUS ZERO INCHES. *NO CHANGE.*
ギャアアッ
GAAAHHHH!
BUT WHY!!?
WOW, NAHZA. SALES ARE UP THIS MONTH.
キラーン
KIRAAAN (SMUG)
BECAUSE I FOUND A GULLIBLE... I MEAN, A GENEROUS GODDESS.

ZERO CHANGE TO BUST (IT'S IMPORTANT, SO IT BEARS REPEATING).

GODDESS OF BEAUTY! FREYA ON THE SCENE!

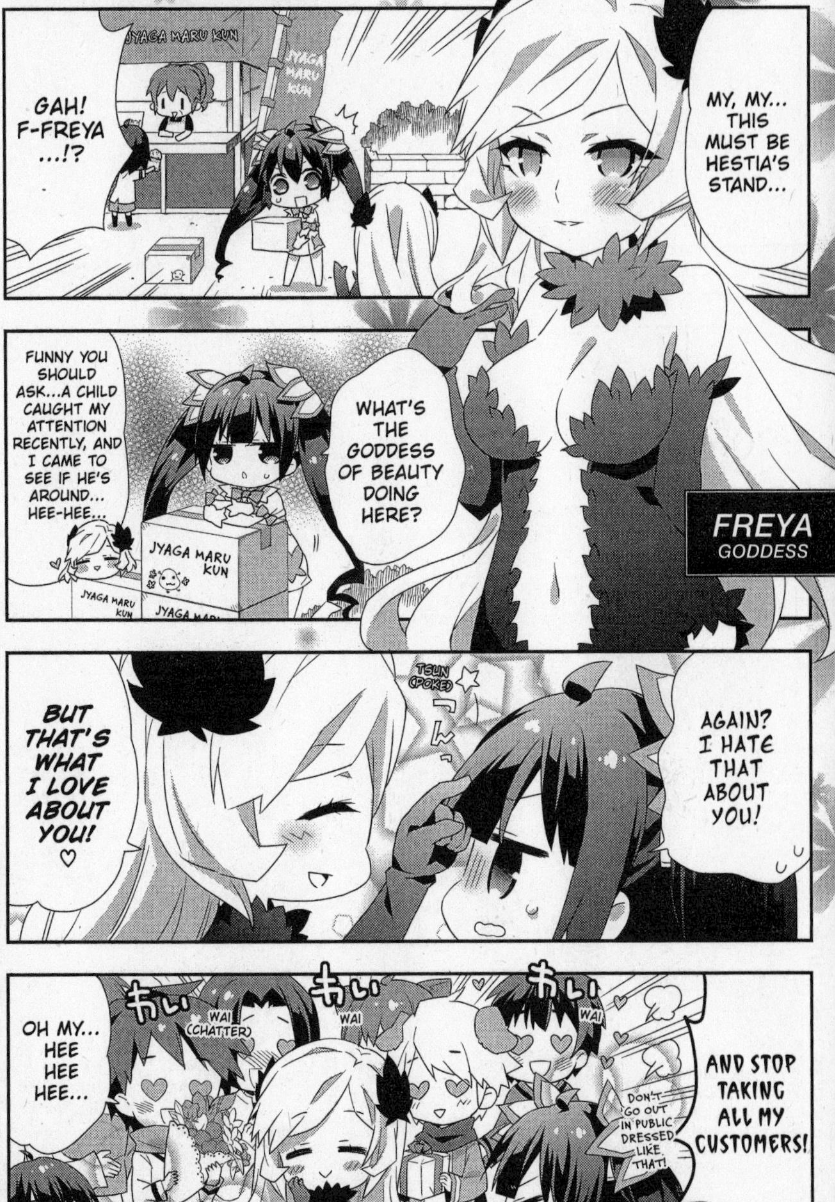
JYAGA MARU KUN
JYAGA MARU KUN
MY, MY... THIS MUST BE HESTIA'S STAND...
GAH! F-FREYA ...!?
WHAT'S THE GODDESS OF BEAUTY DOING HERE?
FUNNY YOU SHOULD ASK...A CHILD CAUGHT MY ATTENTION RECENTLY, AND I CAME TO SEE IF HE'S AROUND... HEE-HEE...
JYAGA MARU KUN
JYAGA MARU KUN
FREYA
GODDESS
AGAIN? I HATE THAT ABOUT YOU!
TSUN (POKED)
BUT THAT'S WHAT I LOVE ABOUT YOU! ♡
AND STOP TAKING ALL MY CUSTOMERS!
DON'T GO OUT IN PUBLIC DRESSED LIKE THAT!
WAI
WAI
WAI (CHATTER)
OH MY... HEE HEE HEE...

SHE WANTS TO GET POKED.

SMELLS GOOD ♡

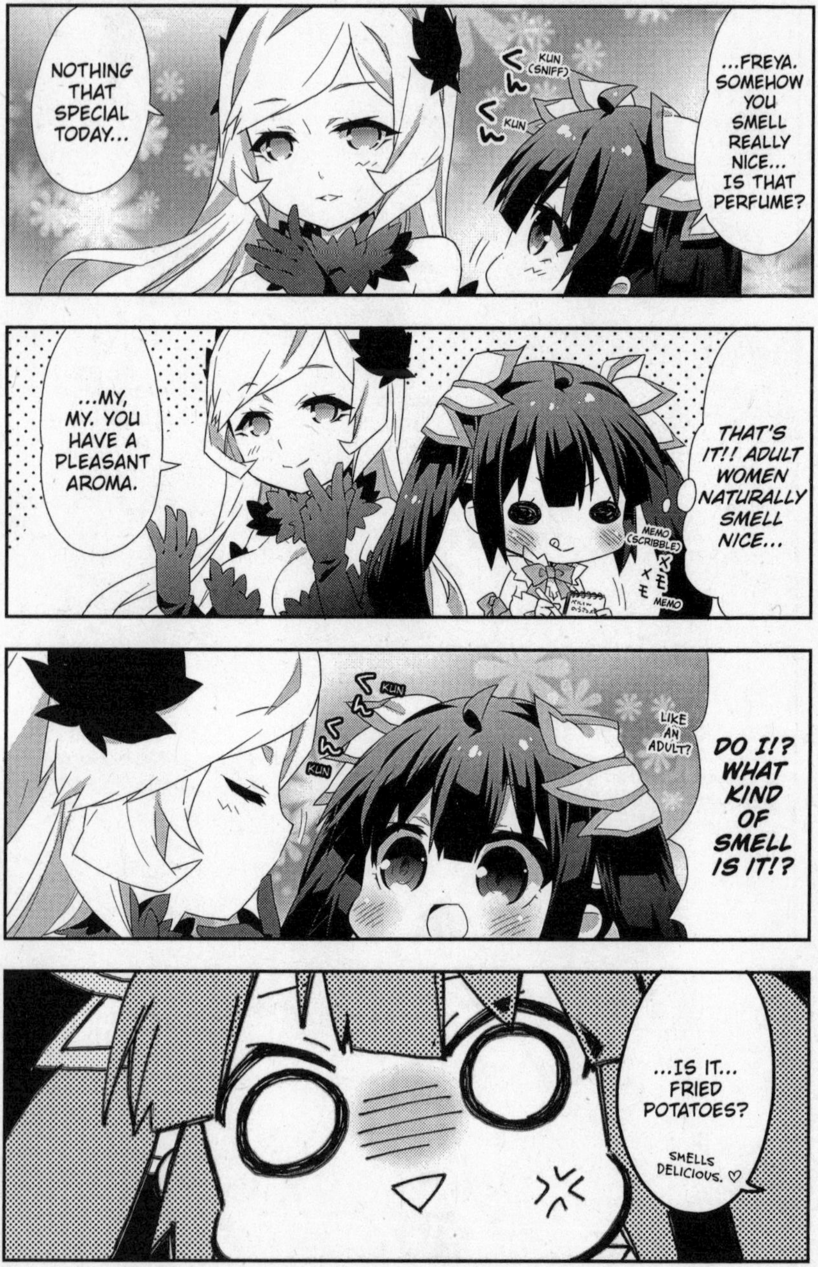
...FREYA. SOMEHOW YOU SMELL REALLY NICE... IS THAT PERFUME?
KUN (SNIFF)
KUN
NOTHING THAT SPECIAL TODAY...
THAT'S IT!! ADULT WOMEN NATURALLY SMELL NICE...
MEMO (SCRIBBLE)
MEMO
...MY, MY. YOU HAVE A PLEASANT AROMA.
DO I!? WHAT KIND OF SMELL IS IT!?
LIKE AN ADULT?
KUN
KUN
...IS IT... FRIED POTATOES?
SMELLS DELICIOUS. ♡

FRIED POTATOES = HESTIA.

FREYA'S SECRET

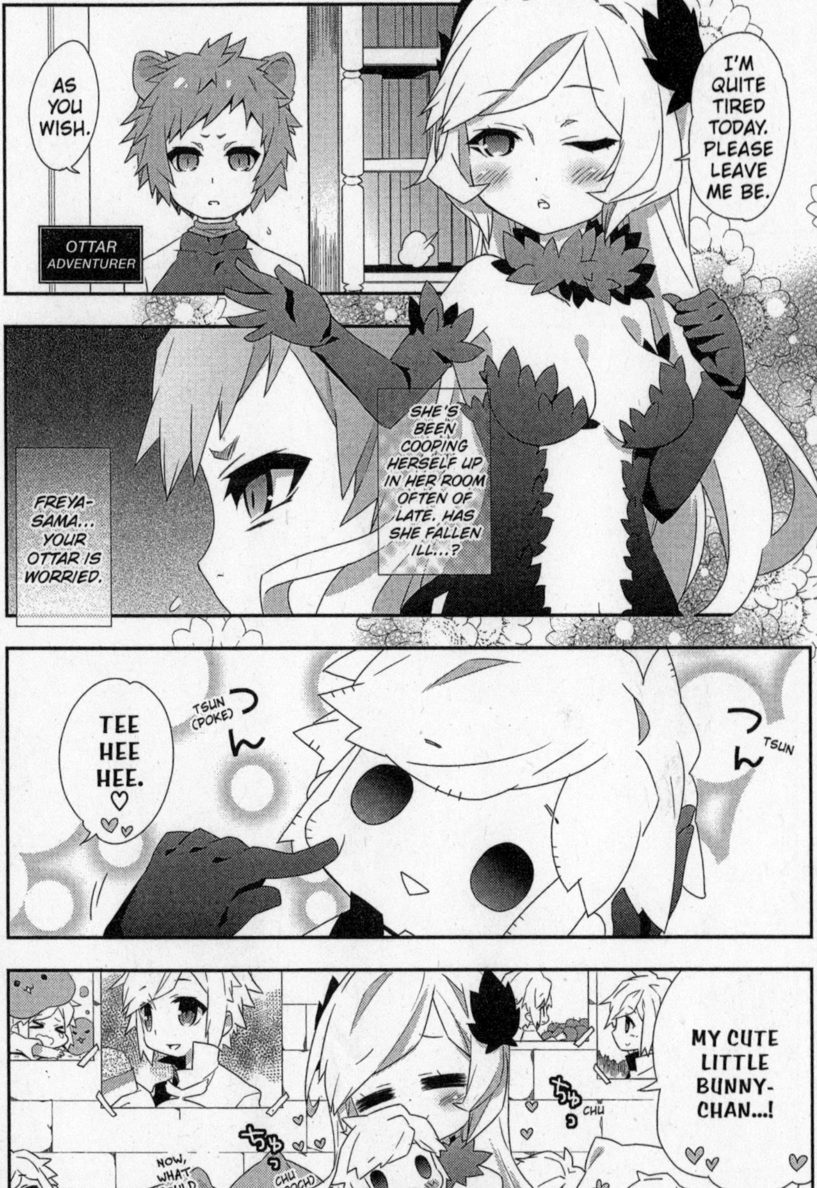
I'M QUITE TIRED TODAY. PLEASE LEAVE ME BE.
AS YOU WISH.
OTTAR ADVENTURER
SHE'S BEEN COOPING HERSELF UP IN HER ROOM OFTEN OF LATE. HAS SHE FALLEN ILL...?
FREYA-SAMA... YOUR OTTAR IS WORRIED.
TSUN
TSUN (POKE)
TEE HEE HEE. ♡
MY CUTE LITTLE BUNNY-CHAN...!
CHU
CHU (SMOOCH)
NOW, WHAT COULD YOUR NAME BE...? ♡

JUST A STALKER, PLAIN AND SIMPLE.

OTTAR'S OUTFIT COORDINATION

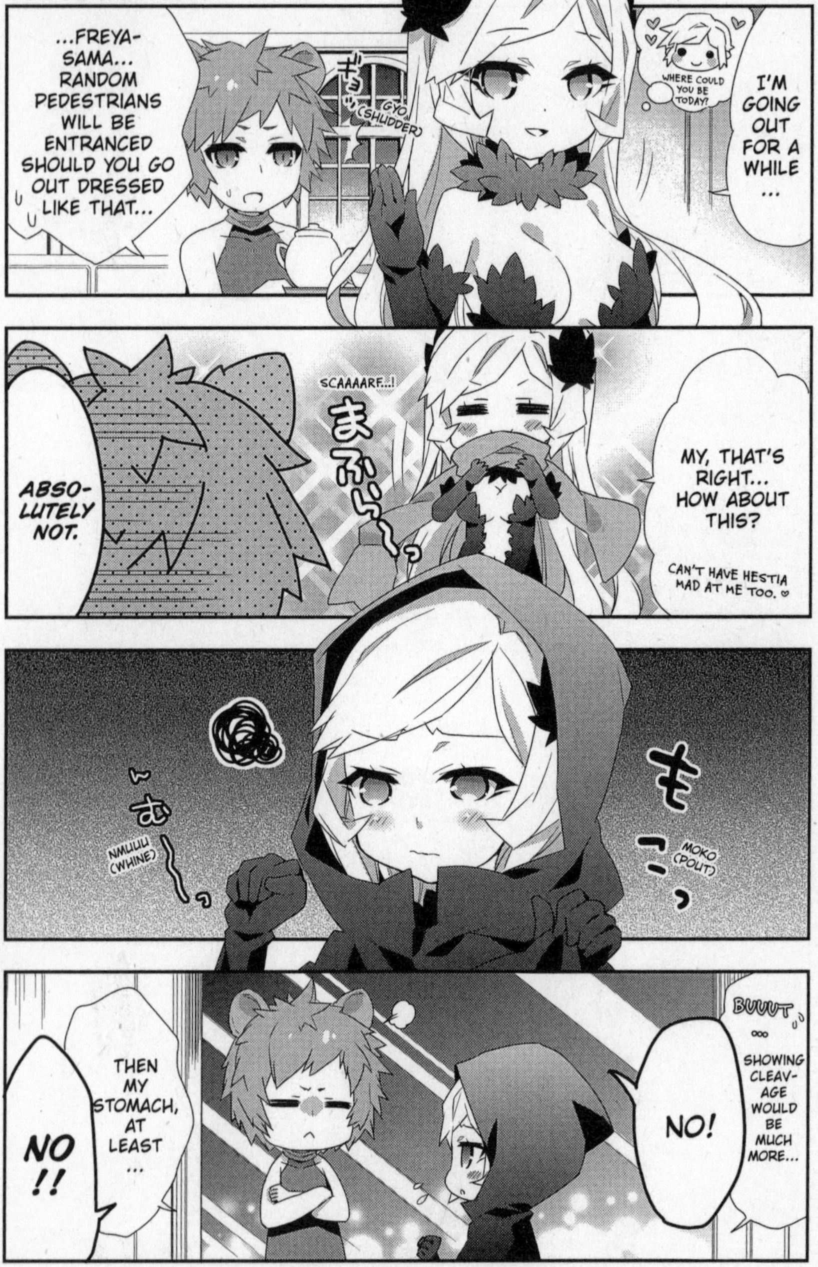
I'M GOING OUT FOR A WHILE ...
WHERE COULD YOU BE TODAY?
ギョッ
GYO (SHUDDER)
...FREYA-SAMA... RANDOM PEDESTRIANS WILL BE ENTRANCED SHOULD YOU GO OUT DRESSED LIKE THAT...
MY, THAT'S RIGHT... HOW ABOUT THIS?
CAN'T HAVE HESTIA MAD AT ME TOO. ♡
まふら〜っ
SCAAAARF...!
ABSO-LUTELY NOT.
もこっ
MOKO (POUT)
んむ〜〜っ
NMUUU (WHINE)
BUUUT... SHOWING CLEAV-AGE WOULD BE MUCH MORE...
NO!
THEN MY STOMACH, AT LEAST ...
NO!!

HOW TO ACT LIKE A LADY.

FREYA-SAMA, PULL YOURSELF TOGETHER!

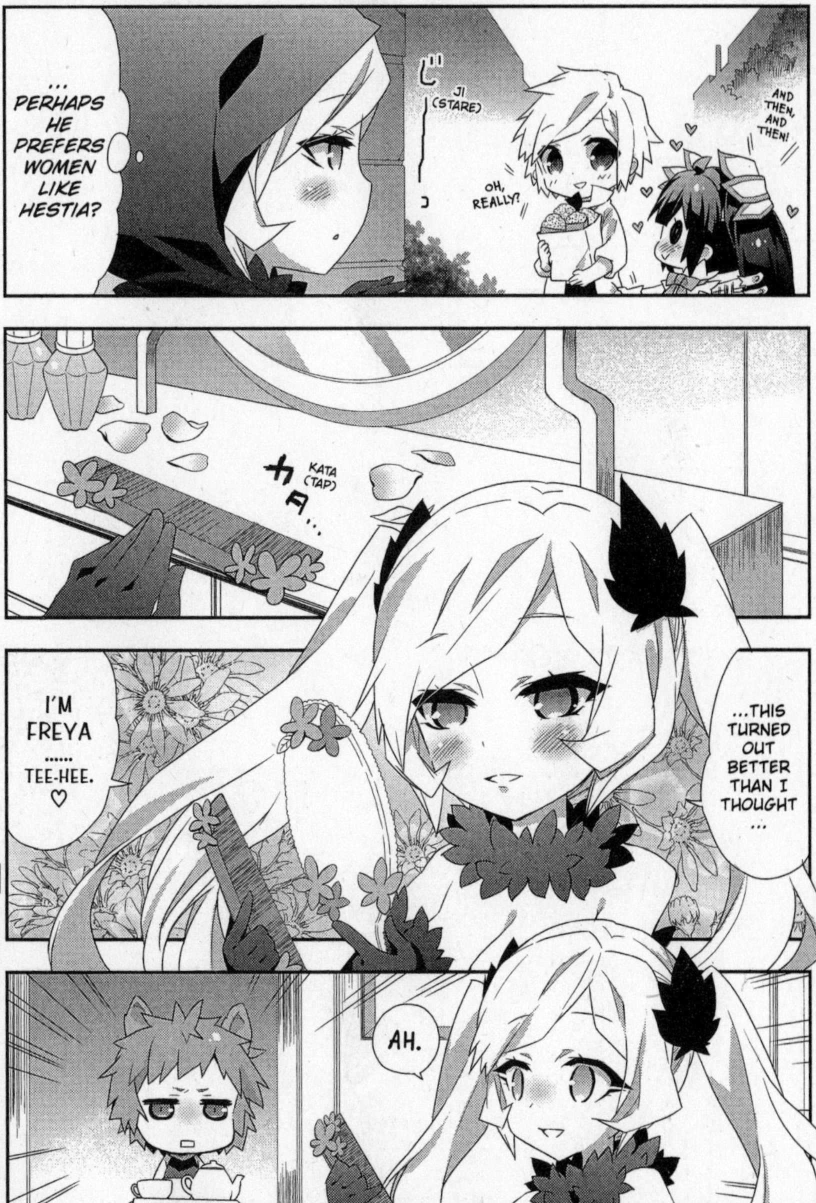
AND THEN, AND THEN!
JI (STARE)
OH, REALLY?
...PERHAPS HE PREFERS WOMEN LIKE HESTIA?
KATA (TAP)
...THIS TURNED OUT BETTER THAN I THOUGHT...
I'M FREYA...... TEE-HEE. ♡
AH.

OTTAR SAW EVERYTHING.

NOT OFFICIALLY AUTHORIZED BY FUJINO OMORI-SENSEI!!

☆DEITY STATUS☆
FOURTH ENTRY

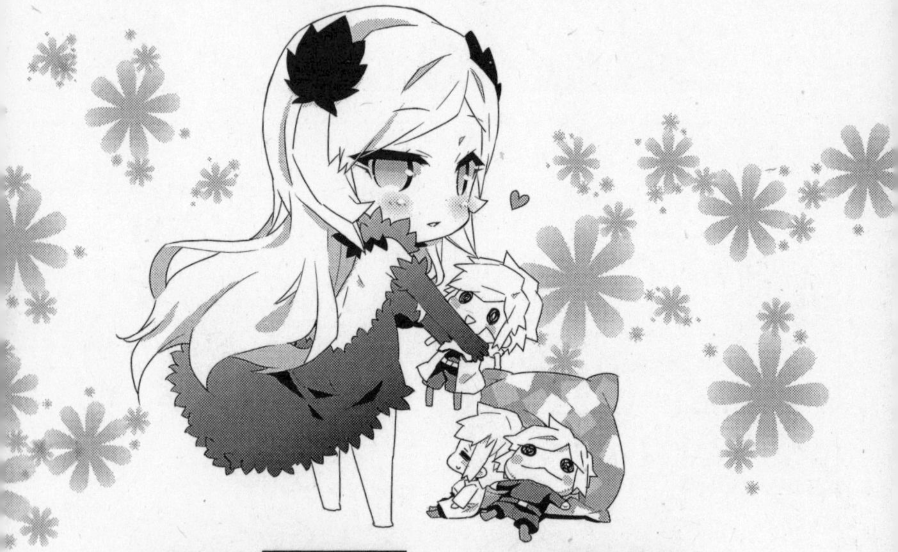

FREYA

FREYA FAMILIA'S PATRON DEITY. GODDESS OF BEAUTY. EVERYONE WHO SEES HER BECOMES ENTRANCED. VERY INTERESTED IN A "WHITE RABBIT" (BELL) SHE HAPPENED TO SEE IN TOWN.

APPEAL: 999 NICE AROMA: 999
EQUIPMENT: SCARF – EXPOSURE: –10
EQUIPMENT: OTTAR'S RECOMMENDED COAT – EXPOSURE: –980
(EXPOSURE BEFORE EQUIPPING: 999)

※ AS THIS IS UNOFFICIAL, A FEW LIBERTIES HAVE BEEN TAKEN.

STEP 05

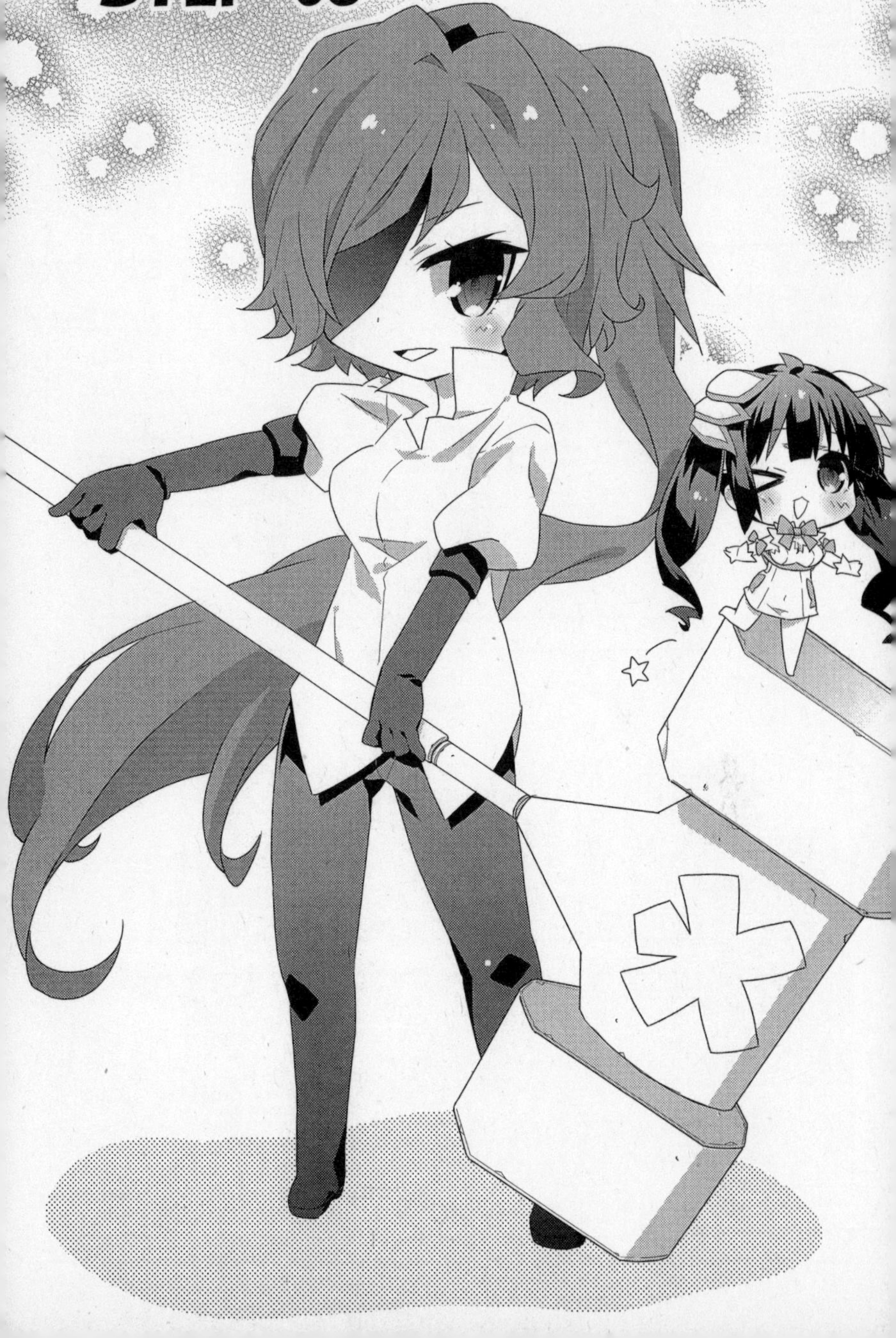

HEPHAISTOS' DIARY

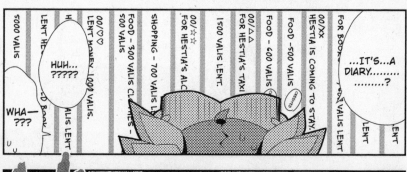

JI (STARE)

HMMM...

NISHISHI (SNEAK)

JUST WHAT IS HEPHAISTOS ALWAYS WRITING...?

...IT'S...A DIARY............?

HUH... ?????

WHA—???

00/XX HESTIA IS COMING TO STAY. FOR BOOK— 700 VALIS LENT

FOOD —500 VALIS — LENT

FOOD - 600 VALIS — LENT

00/△△ FOR HESTIA'S TAXI 1500 VALIS LENT.

00/☆☆ FOR HESTIA'S ALC— SHOPPING - 700 VALIS LENT

FOOD - 300 VALIS CLOTHES — 500 VALIS

00/♡♡ LENT MONEY 1000 VALIS.

H... LENT HE...ED BOOK ALIS LENT

5000 VALIS

BIKU (JOLT)

RETURN WHAT YOU BORROW, OKAY...?

AND OF COURSE, THE INTEREST TOO.

44

IT WAS IN A BOOK!!

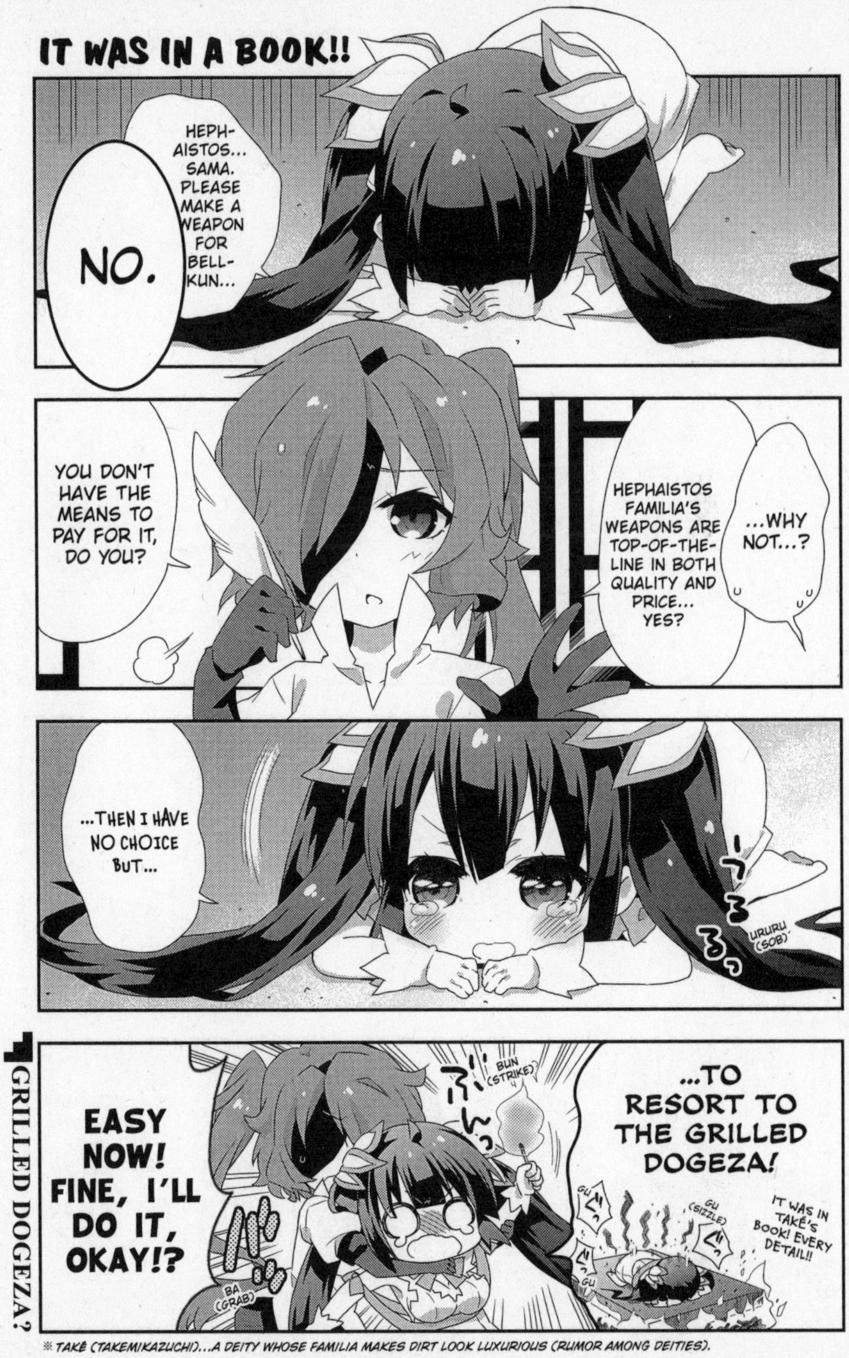
HEPHAISTOS... SAMA. PLEASE MAKE A WEAPON FOR BELL-KUN...
NO.
...WHY NOT...?
HEPHAISTOS FAMILIA'S WEAPONS ARE TOP-OF-THE-LINE IN BOTH QUALITY AND PRICE... YES?
YOU DON'T HAVE THE MEANS TO PAY FOR IT, DO YOU?
URURU (SOB)
...THEN I HAVE NO CHOICE BUT...
...TO RESORT TO THE GRILLED DOGEZA!
IT WAS IN TAKÉ'S BOOK! EVERY DETAIL!!
GU (SIZZLE)
GU
GU
BUN (STRIKE)
EASY NOW! FINE, I'LL DO IT, OKAY!?
BA (GRAB)

4 GRILLED DOGEZA?

※ TAKÉ (TAKEMIKAZUCHI)...A DEITY WHOSE FAMILIA MAKES DIRT LOOK LUXURIOUS (RUMOR AMONG DEITIES).

HEPHAISTOS CAN DO IT!

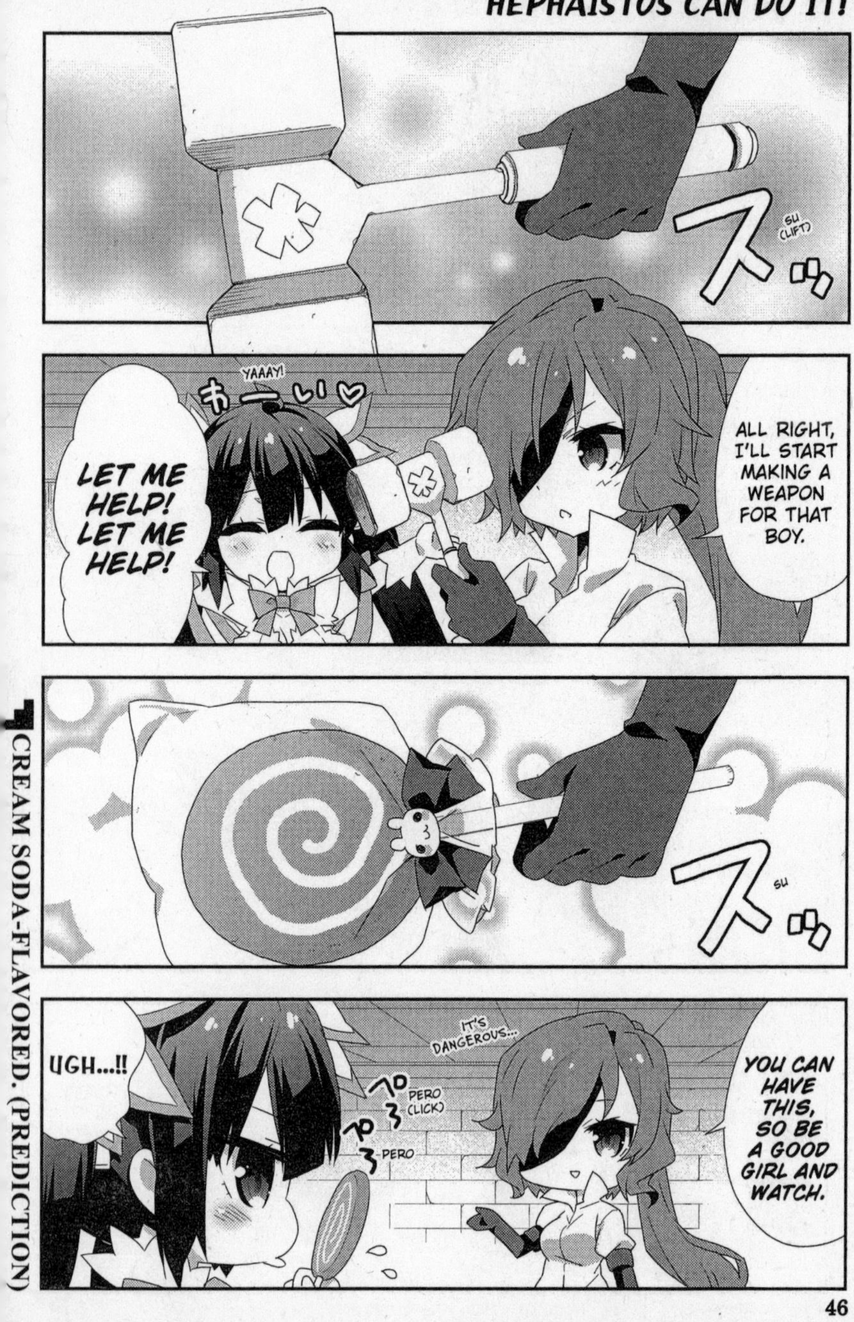

スッ
SU (LIFT)
ALL RIGHT, I'LL START MAKING A WEAPON FOR THAT BOY.
ホーい!♡
YAAAY!
LET ME HELP! LET ME HELP!
スッ
SU
YOU CAN HAVE THIS, SO BE A GOOD GIRL AND WATCH.
IT'S DANGEROUS...
ペロ
PERO (CLICK)
ペロ
PERO
UGH...!!

CREAM SODA-FLAVORED. (PREDICTION)

BE SURE TO READ THE USER MANUAL!

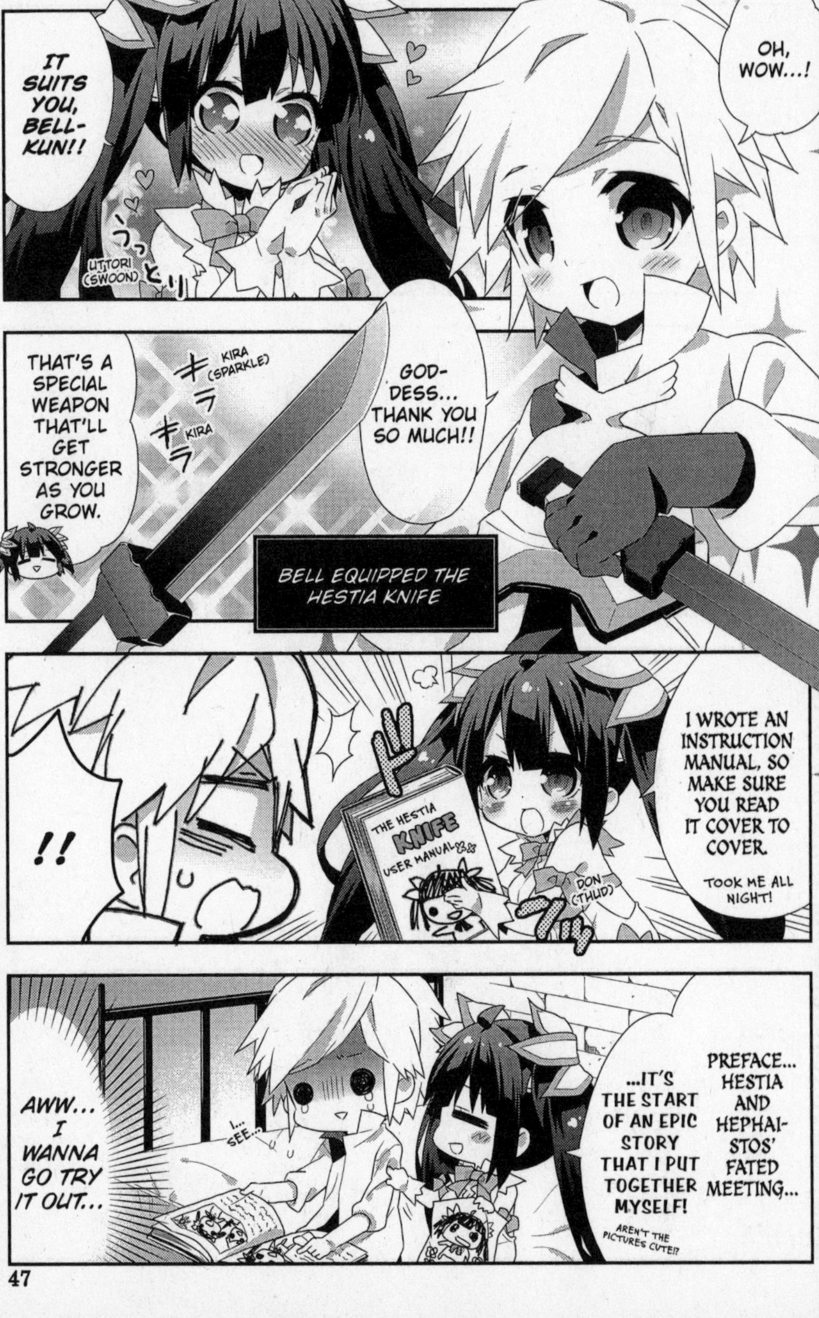

OH, WOW...!
IT SUITS YOU, BELL-KUN!!
UTTORI (SWOON)
GOD-DESS... THANK YOU SO MUCH!!
KIRA (SPARKLE)
KIRA
THAT'S A SPECIAL WEAPON THAT'LL GET STRONGER AS YOU GROW.
BELL EQUIPPED THE HESTIA KNIFE
I WROTE AN INSTRUCTION MANUAL, SO MAKE SURE YOU READ IT COVER TO COVER.
TOOK ME ALL NIGHT!
DON (THUD)
THE HESTIA KNIFE USER MANUAL
!!
PREFACE... HESTIA AND HEPHAISTOS' FATED MEETING...
...IT'S THE START OF AN EPIC STORY THAT I PUT TOGETHER MYSELF!
AREN'T THE PICTURES CUTE!?
I... SEE...
AWW... I WANNA GO TRY IT OUT...

HESTIA'S SPECIAL SKILL

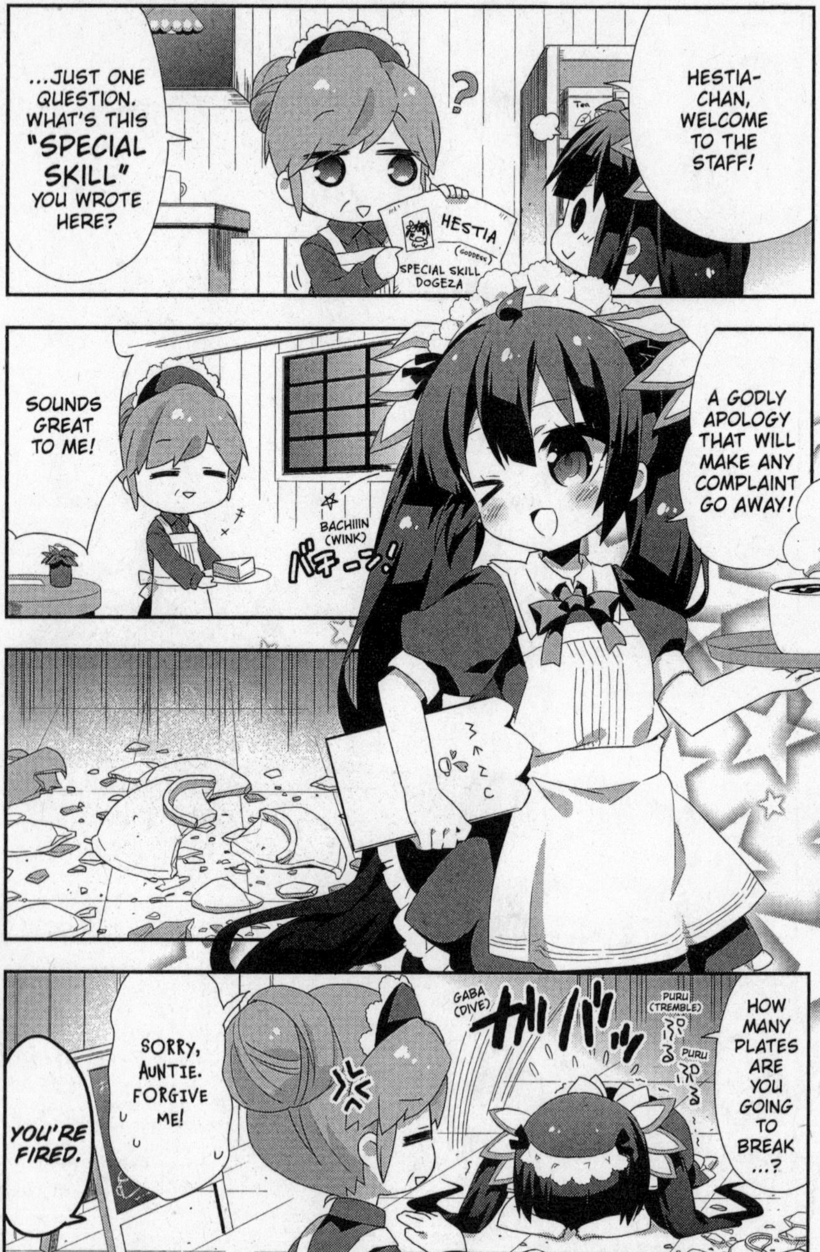
HESTIA-CHAN, WELCOME TO THE STAFF!
...JUST ONE QUESTION. WHAT'S THIS "SPECIAL SKILL" YOU WROTE HERE?
HESTIA
(GODDESS)
SPECIAL SKILL DOGEZA
A GODLY APOLOGY THAT WILL MAKE ANY COMPLAINT GO AWAY!
BACHIIIN (WINK)
バチーン!
SOUNDS GREAT TO ME!
HOW MANY PLATES ARE YOU GOING TO BREAK ...?
PURU (TREMBLE)
ぷる
PURU
ぷる
GABA (DIVE)
ガバッ
SORRY, AUNTIE. FORGIVE ME!
YOU'RE FIRED.

WEAKNESS – CLUMSY

LOKI'S PRESENT

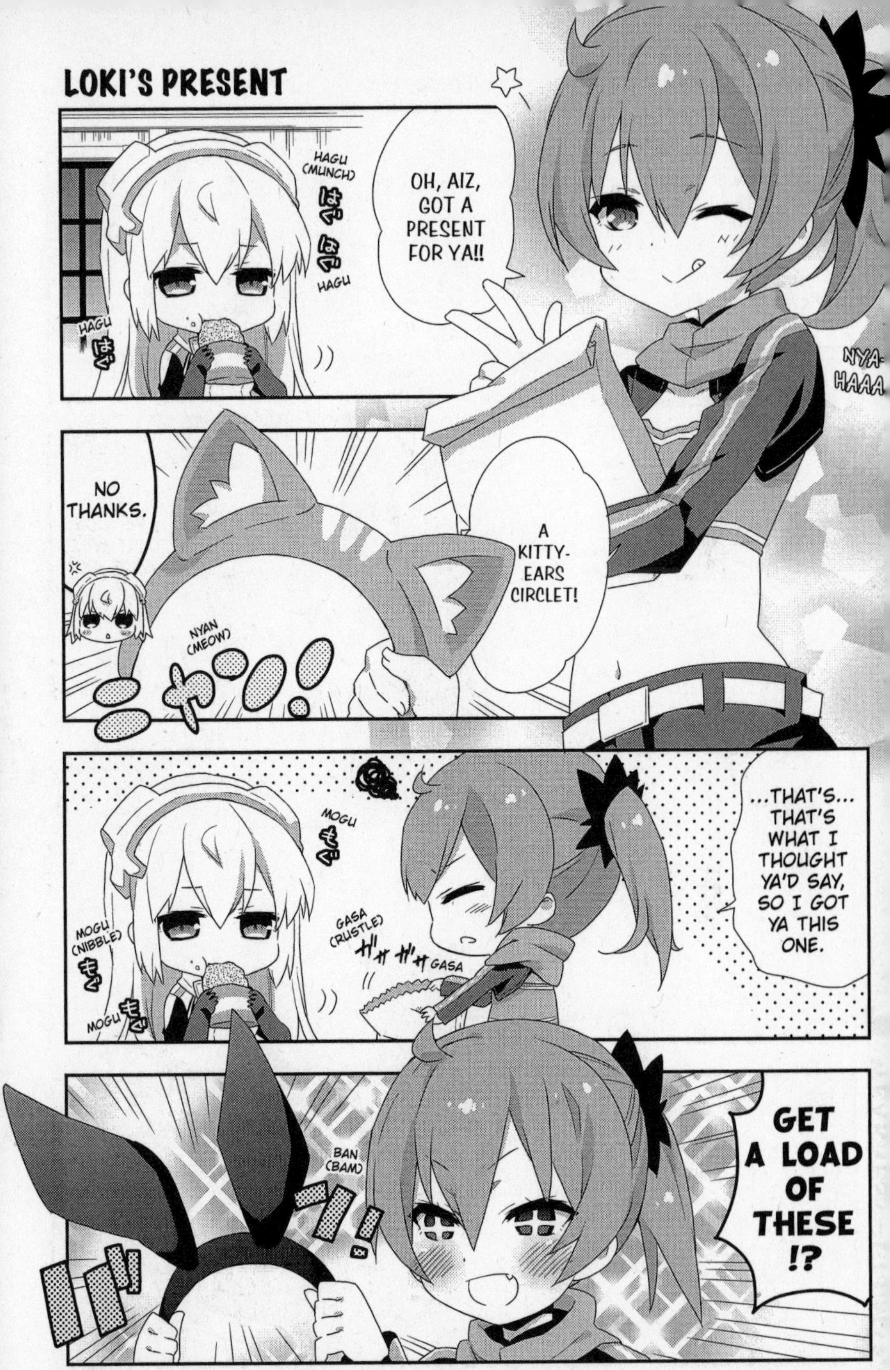
OH, AIZ, GOT A PRESENT FOR YA!!
HAGU (MUNCH)
HAGU
HAGU
NYA-HAAA
A KITTY-EARS CIRCLET!
NYAN (MEOW)
NO THANKS.
...THAT'S... THAT'S WHAT I THOUGHT YA'D SAY, SO I GOT YA THIS ONE.
GASA (RUSTLE)
GASA
MOGU
MOGU (NIBBLE)
MOGU
GET A LOAD OF THESE!?
BAN (BAM)

NO THANKS. (SECOND TIME)

LOKI'S STRATEGY

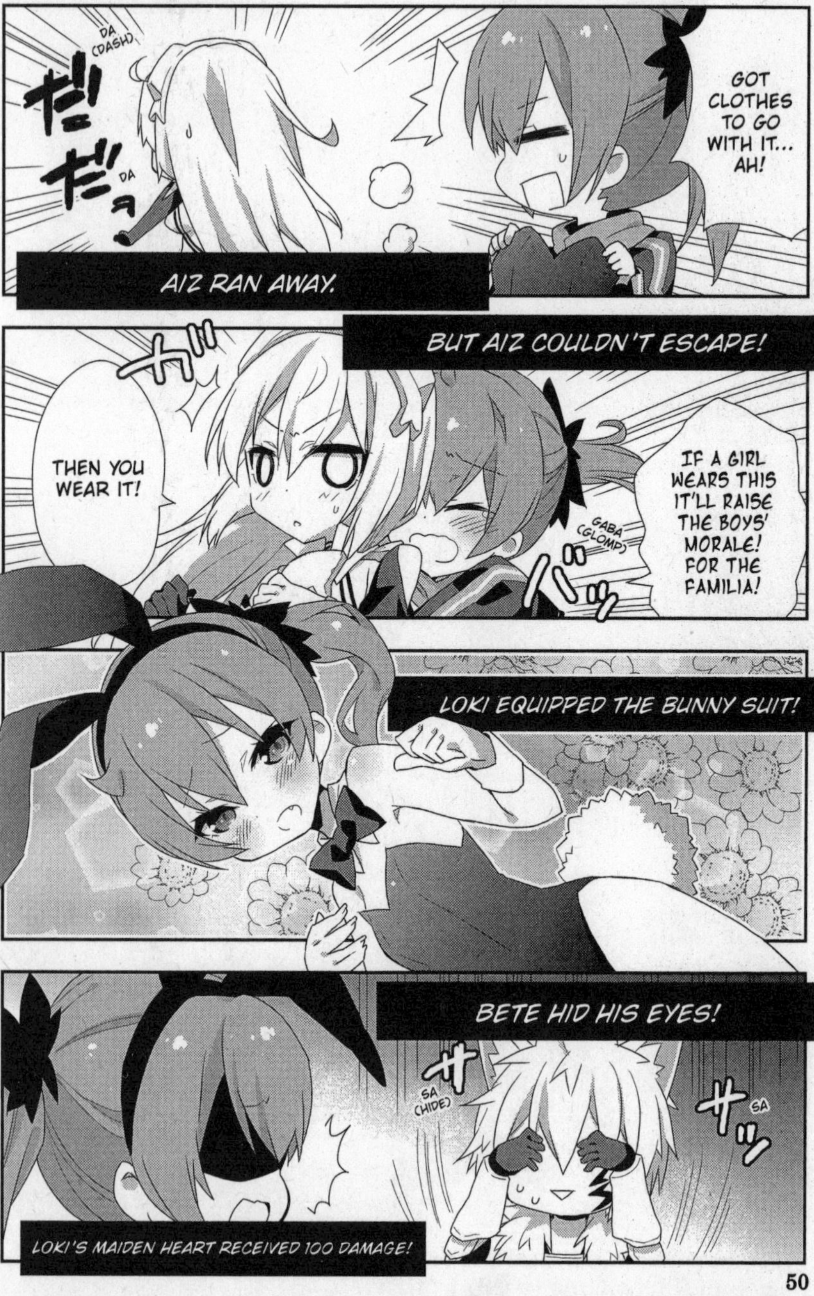
GOT CLOTHES TO GO WITH IT... AH!
DA (DASH)
DA
AIZ RAN AWAY.
BUT AIZ COULDN'T ESCAPE!
IF A GIRL WEARS THIS IT'LL RAISE THE BOYS' MORALE! FOR THE FAMILIA!
GABA (GLOMP)
THEN YOU WEAR IT!
LOKI EQUIPPED THE BUNNY SUIT!
BETE HID HIS EYES!
SA
SA (HIDE)
LOKI'S MAIDEN HEART RECEIVED 100 DAMAGE!

SURPRISINGLY DELICATE.

LOKI'S GRAND PLAN!

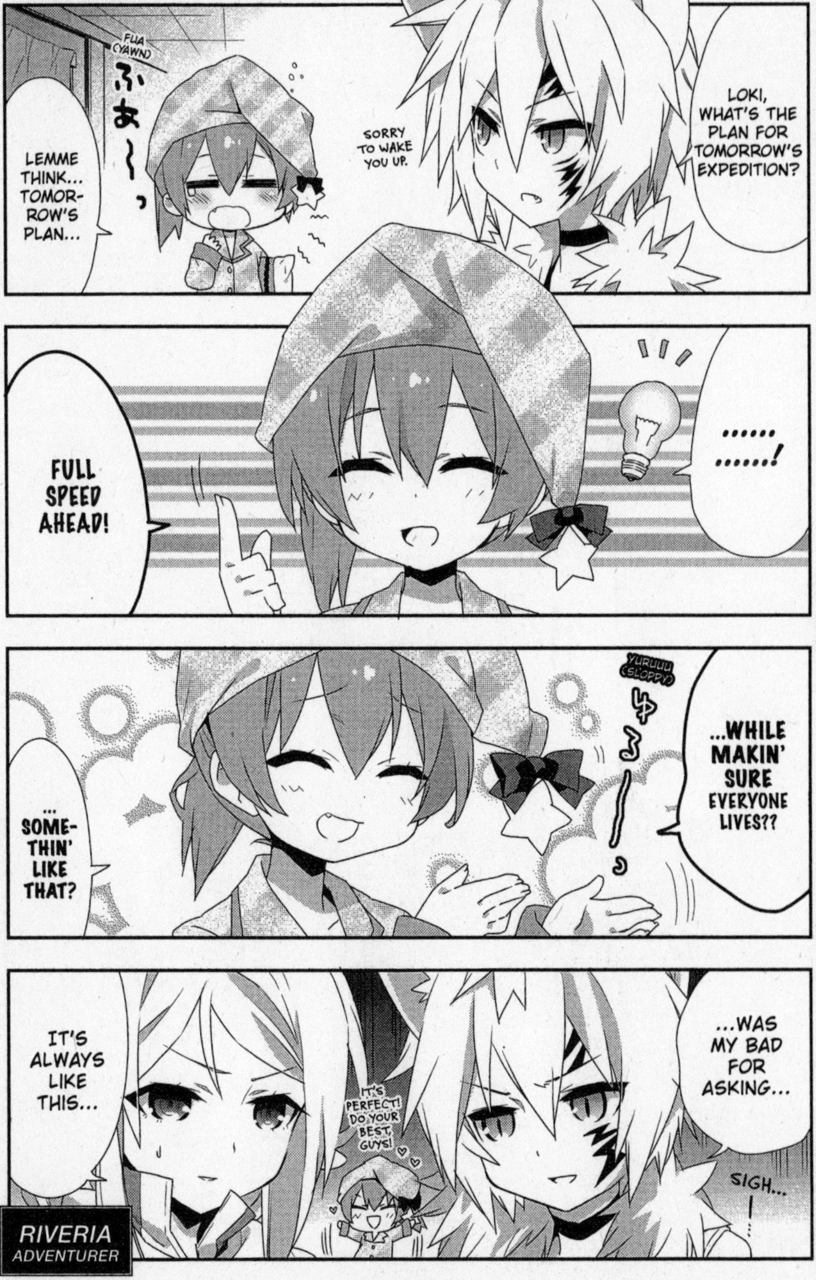
LOKI, WHAT'S THE PLAN FOR TOMORROW'S EXPEDITION?
SORRY TO WAKE YOU UP.
FUA (YAWN)
ふあ～っ
LEMME THINK... TOMORROW'S PLAN...
......!
FULL SPEED AHEAD!
...WHILE MAKIN' SURE EVERYONE LIVES??
YURUUU (SLOPPY)
ゆる～～っ
...SOMETHIN' LIKE THAT?
...WAS MY BAD FOR ASKING...
SIGH...!
IT'S PERFECT! DO YOUR BEST, GUYS!
IT'S ALWAYS LIKE THIS...
RIVERIA
ADVENTURER

GOOD LUCK, EVERYBODY.

NOT OFFICIALLY AUTHORIZED BY FUJINO OMORI-SENSEI!!

☆DEITY STATUS☆
FIFTH ENTRY

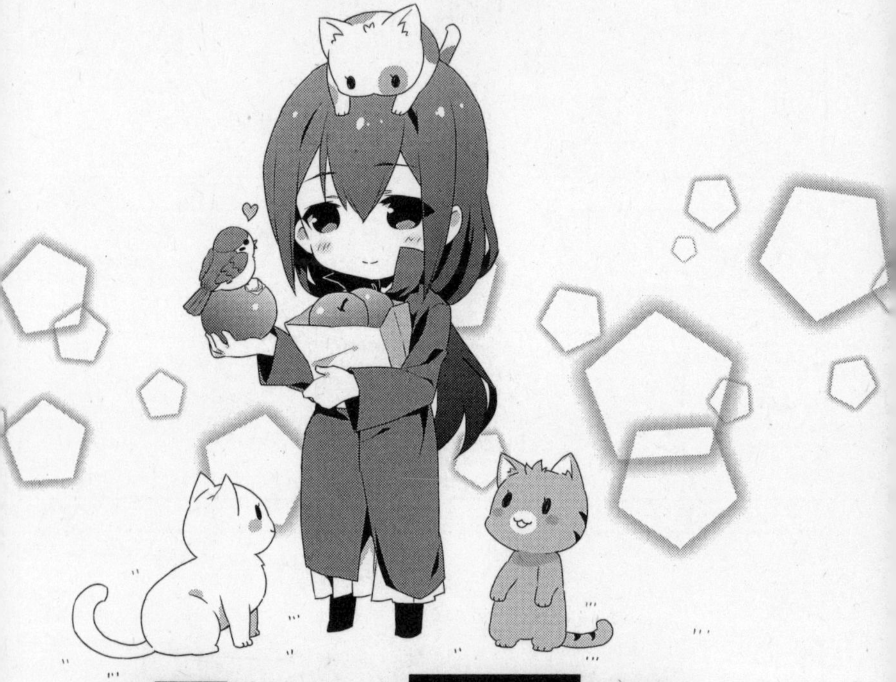

MIACH

HEAD OF THE MERCANTILE MIACH FAMILIA. JUST AS POOR AS HESTIA. WOMEN OFTEN MISTAKE HIS KINDNESS FOR FLIRTING, BUT HE IS COMPLETELY OBLIVIOUS.

KINDNESS: 255 INTELLECT: 255
BUSINESS SENSE: 5

※ AS THIS IS UNOFFICIAL, A FEW LIBERTIES HAVE BEEN TAKEN.

STEP 06

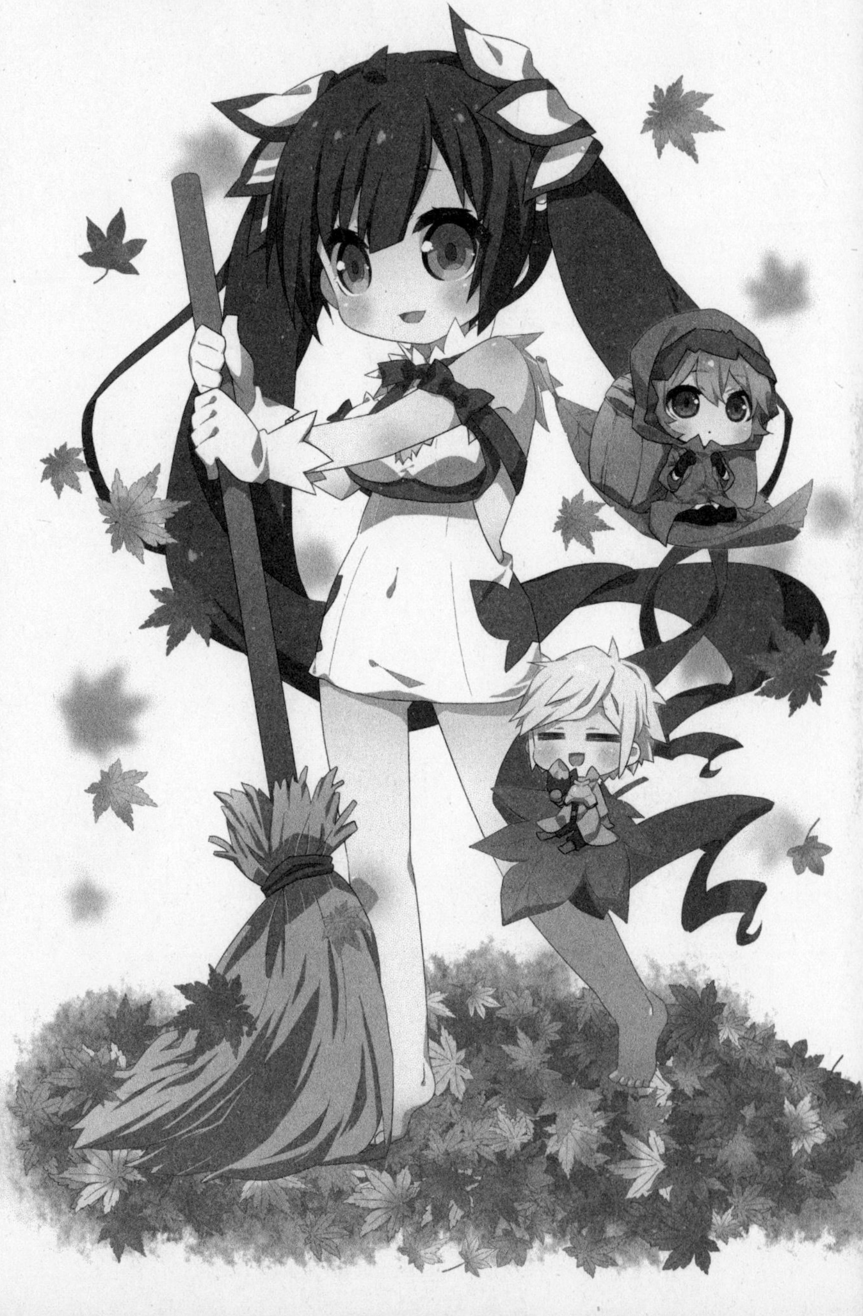

WHAT BELL-KUN DROPPED

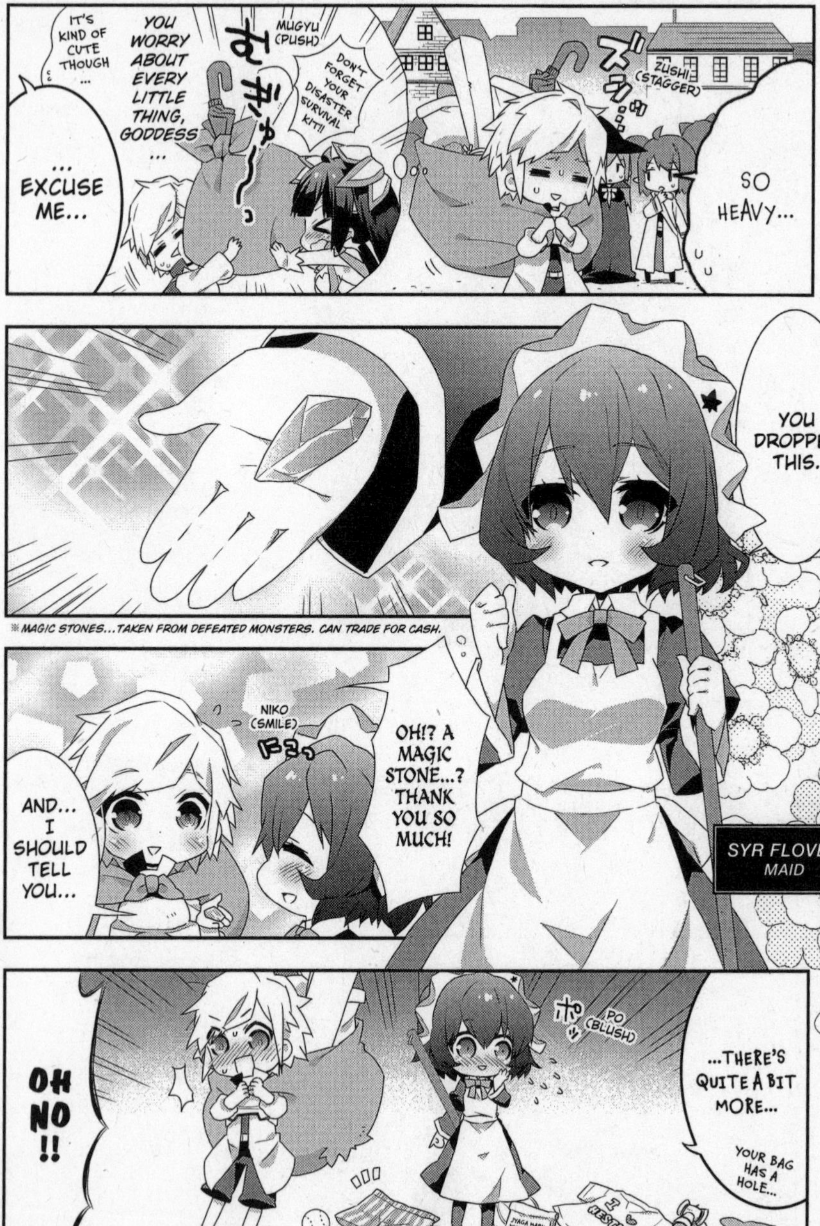
SO HEAVY...
ZUSHI (STAGGER)
DON'T FORGET YOUR DISASTER SURVIVAL KIT!!
MUGYU (PUSH)
YOU WORRY ABOUT EVERY LITTLE THING, GODDESS...
IT'S KIND OF CUTE THOUGH...
...EXCUSE ME...
YOU DROPPED THIS.
SYR FLOVER
MAID
OH!? A MAGIC STONE...? THANK YOU SO MUCH!
NIKO (SMILE)
AND... I SHOULD TELL YOU...
...THERE'S QUITE A BIT MORE...
YOUR BAG HAS A HOLE...
PO (BLUSH)
OH NO!!
JYAGA MARU KUN CHEESE FLAVOR

※MAGIC STONES...TAKEN FROM DEFEATED MONSTERS. CAN TRADE FOR CASH.

TOO MUCH TO PICK UP.

STAFF MEAL MADE BY A MAID?

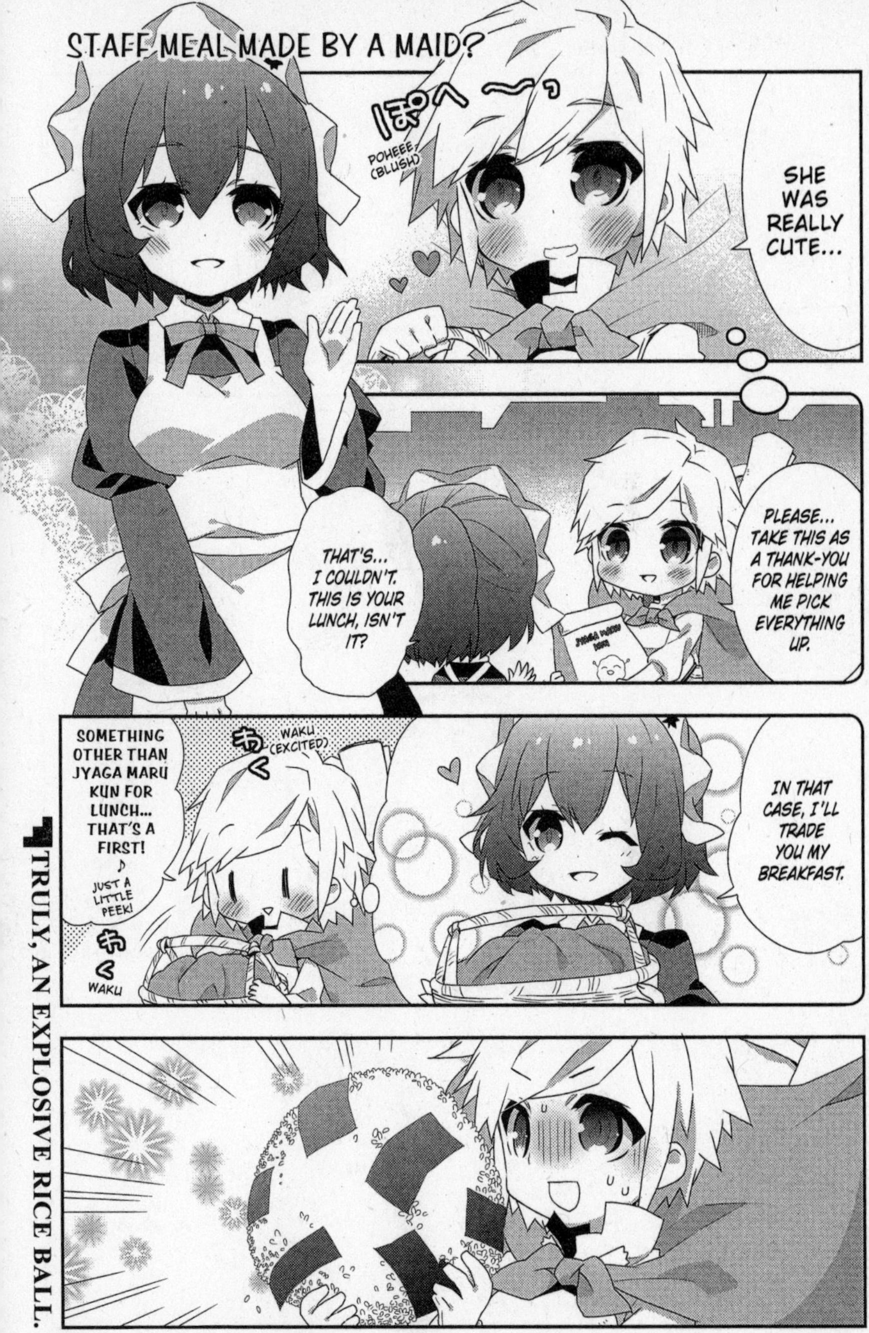
SHE WAS REALLY CUTE...
ぽへ～っ
POHEEE (BLUSH)
PLEASE... TAKE THIS AS A THANK-YOU FOR HELPING ME PICK EVERYTHING UP.
JYAGA MARU KUN
THAT'S... I COULDN'T. THIS IS YOUR LUNCH, ISN'T IT?
IN THAT CASE, I'LL TRADE YOU MY BREAKFAST.
わく
WAKU (EXCITED)
SOMETHING OTHER THAN JYAGA MARU KUN FOR LUNCH... THAT'S A FIRST! ♪
JUST A LITTLE PEEK!
わく
WAKU

TRULY, AN EXPLOSIVE RICE BALL.

BELL-KUN'S FIRST SUPPORTER

IF NOTHING ELSE, LET ME CARRY THOSE...

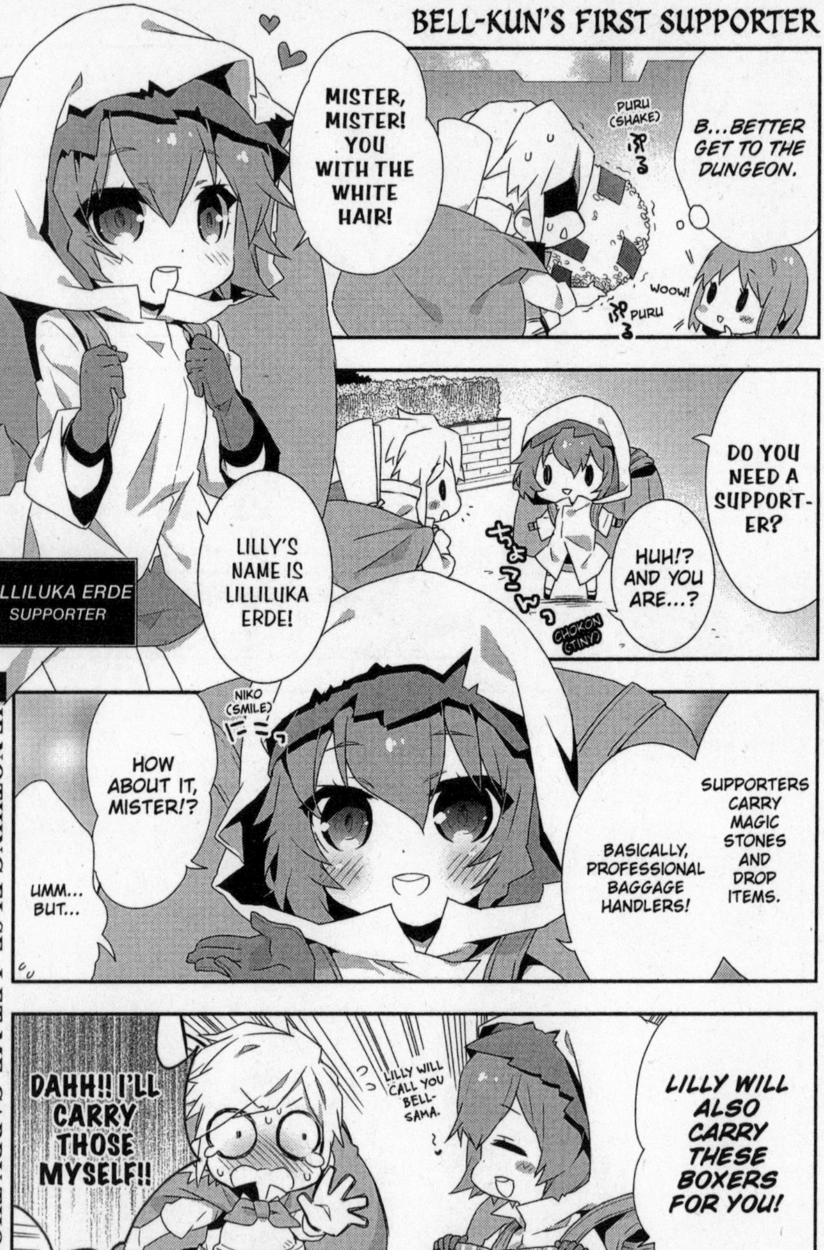
B...BETTER GET TO THE DUNGEON.
PURU (SHAKE)
WOOW!
PURU
DO YOU NEED A SUPPORT-ER?
HUH!? AND YOU ARE...?
CHOKON (TINY)
MISTER, MISTER! YOU WITH THE WHITE HAIR!
LILLY'S NAME IS LILLILUKA ERDE!
LILLILUKA ERDE
SUPPORTER
SUPPORTERS CARRY MAGIC STONES AND DROP ITEMS.
BASICALLY, PROFESSIONAL BAGGAGE HANDLERS!
NIKO (SMILE)
HOW ABOUT IT, MISTER!?
UMM... BUT...
LILLY WILL ALSO CARRY THESE BOXERS FOR YOU!
LILLY WILL CALL YOU BELL-SAMA.
BELL
DAHH!! I'LL CARRY THOSE MYSELF!!

LILLY'S TRUE IDENTITY

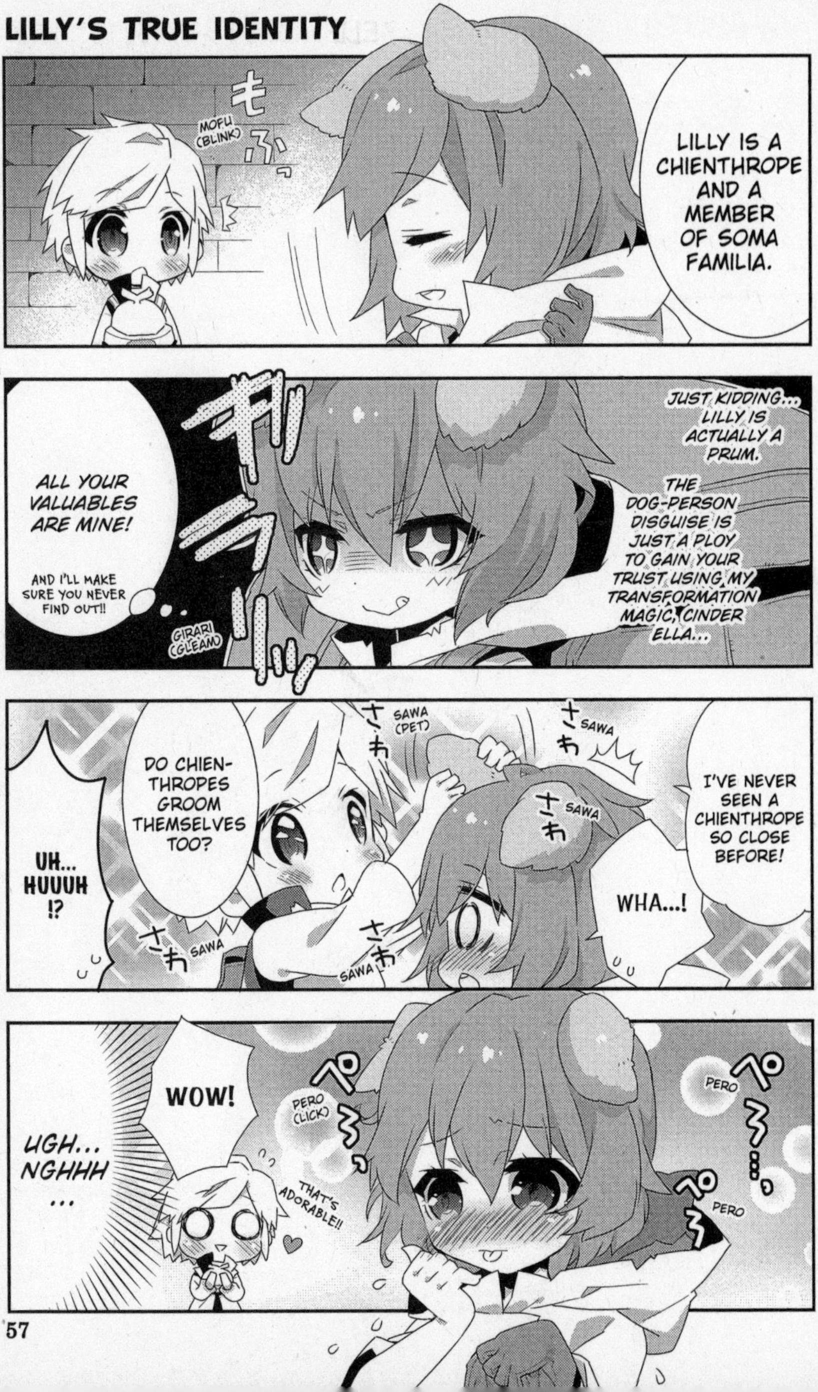

LILLY IS A CHIENTHROPE AND A MEMBER OF SOMA FAMILIA.
MOFU (BLINK)
JUST KIDDING... LILLY IS ACTUALLY A PRUM.
THE DOG-PERSON DISGUISE IS JUST A PLOY TO GAIN YOUR TRUST USING MY TRANSFORMATION MAGIC, CINDER ELLA...
GIRARI (GLEAM)
ALL YOUR VALUABLES ARE MINE!
AND I'LL MAKE SURE YOU NEVER FIND OUT!!
I'VE NEVER SEEN A CHIENTHROPE SO CLOSE BEFORE!
WHA...!
SAWA
SAWA
SAWA (PET)
DO CHIEN-THROPES GROOM THEMSELVES TOO?
SAWA
SAWA
UH... HUUUH!?
PERO
PERO
PERO (LICK)
WOW!
THAT'S ADORABLE!!
UGH... NGHHH ...

OBLIVIOUS BELL'S DESTRUCTIVE POWER.

AFTER THE KNIFE

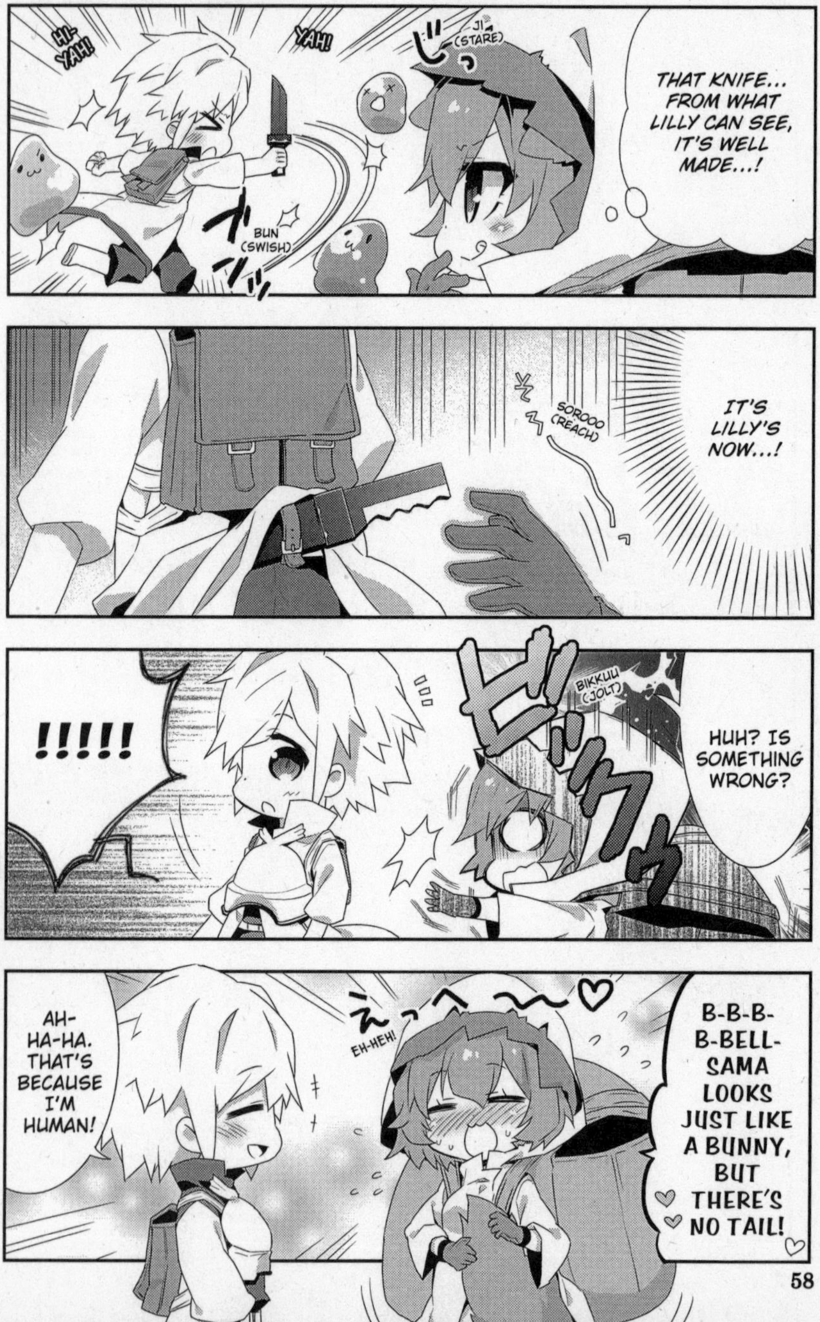
THAT KNIFE... FROM WHAT LILLY CAN SEE, IT'S WELL MADE...!
JI (STARE)
YAH!
HI-YAH!
BUN (SWISH)
IT'S LILLY'S NOW...!
SOROOO (REACH)
HUH? IS SOMETHING WRONG?
BIKKUU (JOLT)
!!!!!
B-B-B-B-BELL-SAMA LOOKS JUST LIKE A BUNNY, BUT THERE'S NO TAIL!
EH-HEH!
AH-HA-HA. THAT'S BECAUSE I'M HUMAN!

FALLS FOR IT EVERY TIME.

A BIG MISUNDERSTANDING

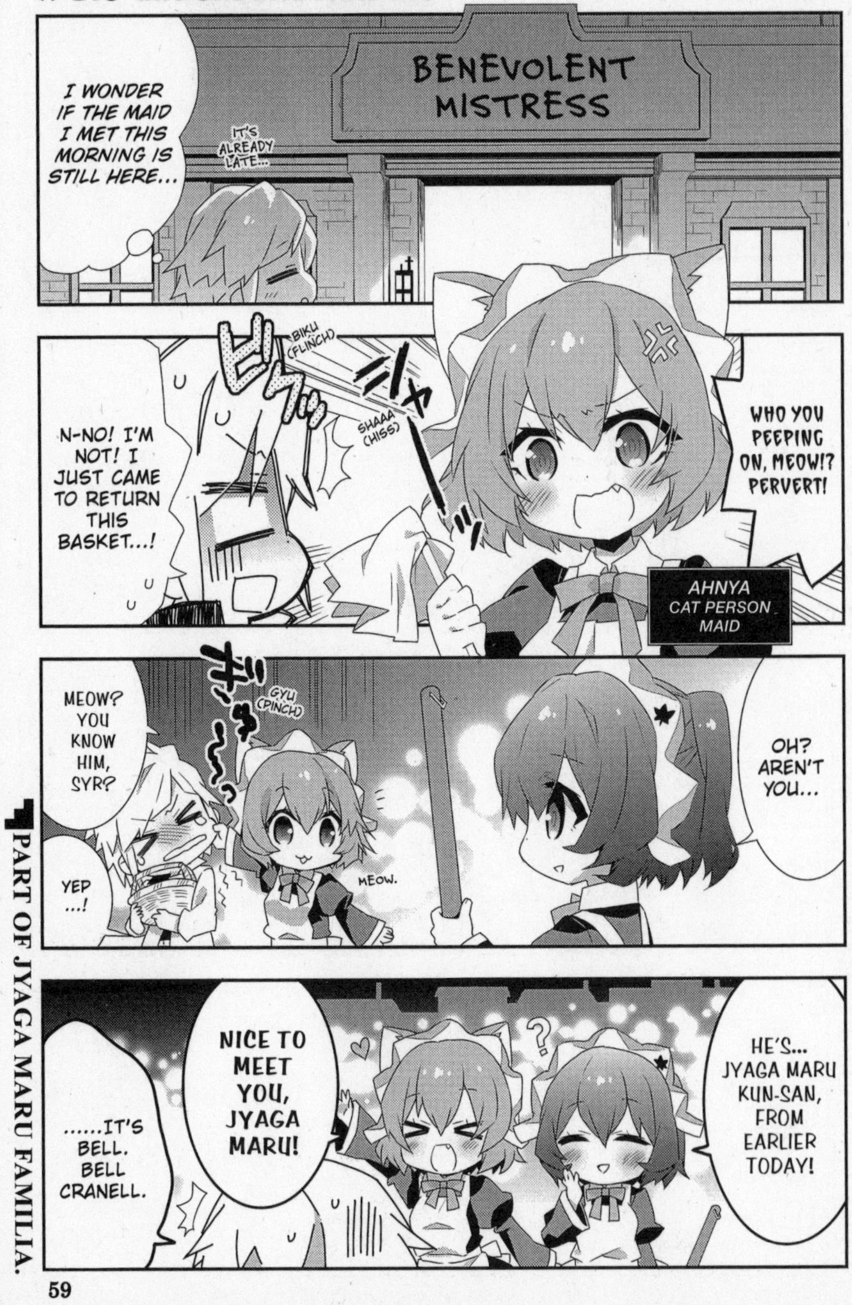
BENEVOLENT MISTRESS
I WONDER IF THE MAID I MET THIS MORNING IS STILL HERE...
IT'S ALREADY LATE...
WHO YOU PEEPING ON, MEOW!? PERVERT!
AHNYA CAT PERSON MAID
SHAAA (HISS)
BIKU (FLINCH)
N-NO! I'M NOT! I JUST CAME TO RETURN THIS BASKET...!
OH? AREN'T YOU...
MEOW.
GYU (PINCH)
MEOW? YOU KNOW HIM, SYR?
YEP ...!
HE'S... JYAGA MARU KUN-SAN, FROM EARLIER TODAY!
NICE TO MEET YOU, JYAGA MARU!
......IT'S BELL. BELL CRANELL.

PART OF JYAGA MARU FAMILIA.

AND THE OBSERVER IS...?

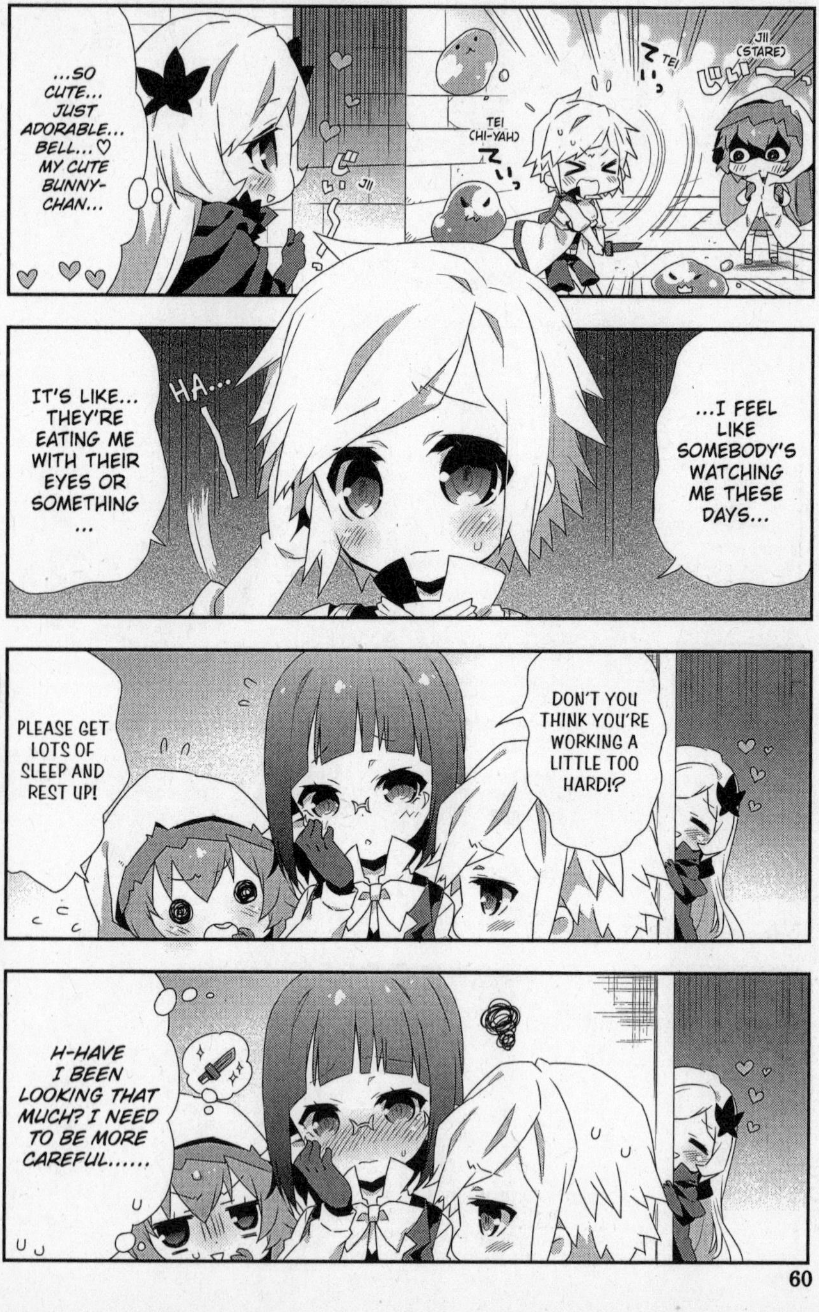
JII (STARE)
TEI
TEI (CHI-YAH)
JII
...SO CUTE... JUST ADORABLE... BELL...♡ MY CUTE BUNNY-CHAN...
...I FEEL LIKE SOMEBODY'S WATCHING ME THESE DAYS...
HA...
IT'S LIKE... THEY'RE EATING ME WITH THEIR EYES OR SOMETHING...
DON'T YOU THINK YOU'RE WORKING A LITTLE TOO HARD!?
PLEASE GET LOTS OF SLEEP AND REST UP!
H-HAVE I BEEN LOOKING THAT MUCH? I NEED TO BE MORE CAREFUL......

WOMEN WHO KNOW WHAT THEY WANT.

BELL-KUN'S AFFAIR!?

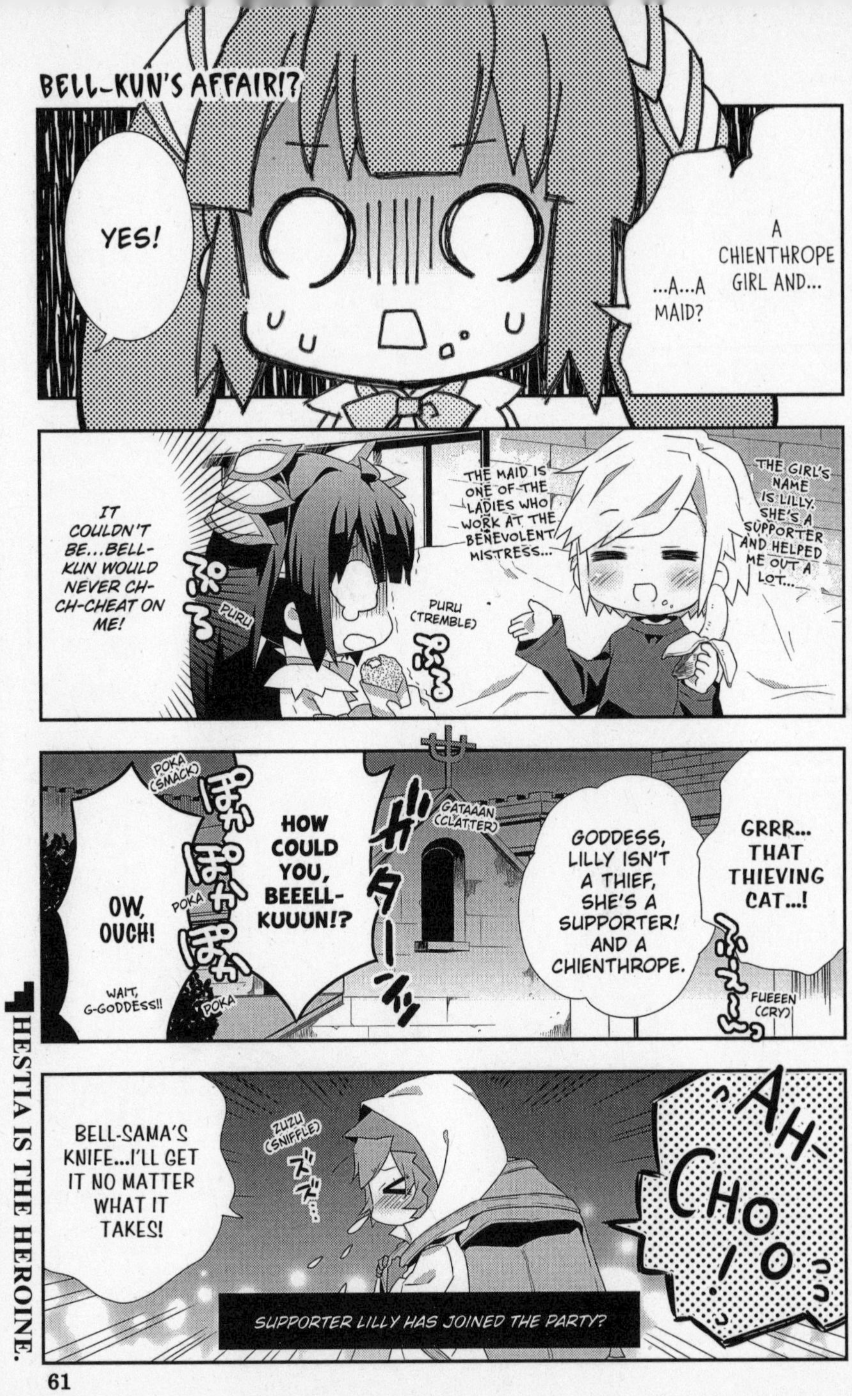
A CHIENTHROPE GIRL AND...
...A...A MAID?
YES!
THE GIRL'S NAME IS LILLY. SHE'S A SUPPORTER AND HELPED ME OUT A LOT...
THE MAID IS ONE OF THE LADIES WHO WORK AT THE BENEVOLENT MISTRESS...
PURU (TREMBLE)
PURU
IT COULDN'T BE...BELL-KUN WOULD NEVER CH-CH-CHEAT ON ME!
GRRR... THAT THIEVING CAT...!
FUEEEN (CRY)
GODDESS, LILLY ISN'T A THIEF, SHE'S A SUPPORTER! AND A CHIENTHROPE.
GATAAAN (CLATTER)
HOW COULD YOU, BEEELL-KUUUN!?
POKA (SMACK)
POKA
OW, OUCH!
POKA
WAIT, G-GODDESS!!
AH-CHOO!
ZUZU (SNIFFLE)
BELL-SAMA'S KNIFE...I'LL GET IT NO MATTER WHAT IT TAKES!
SUPPORTER LILLY HAS JOINED THE PARTY?

HESTIA IS THE HEROINE.

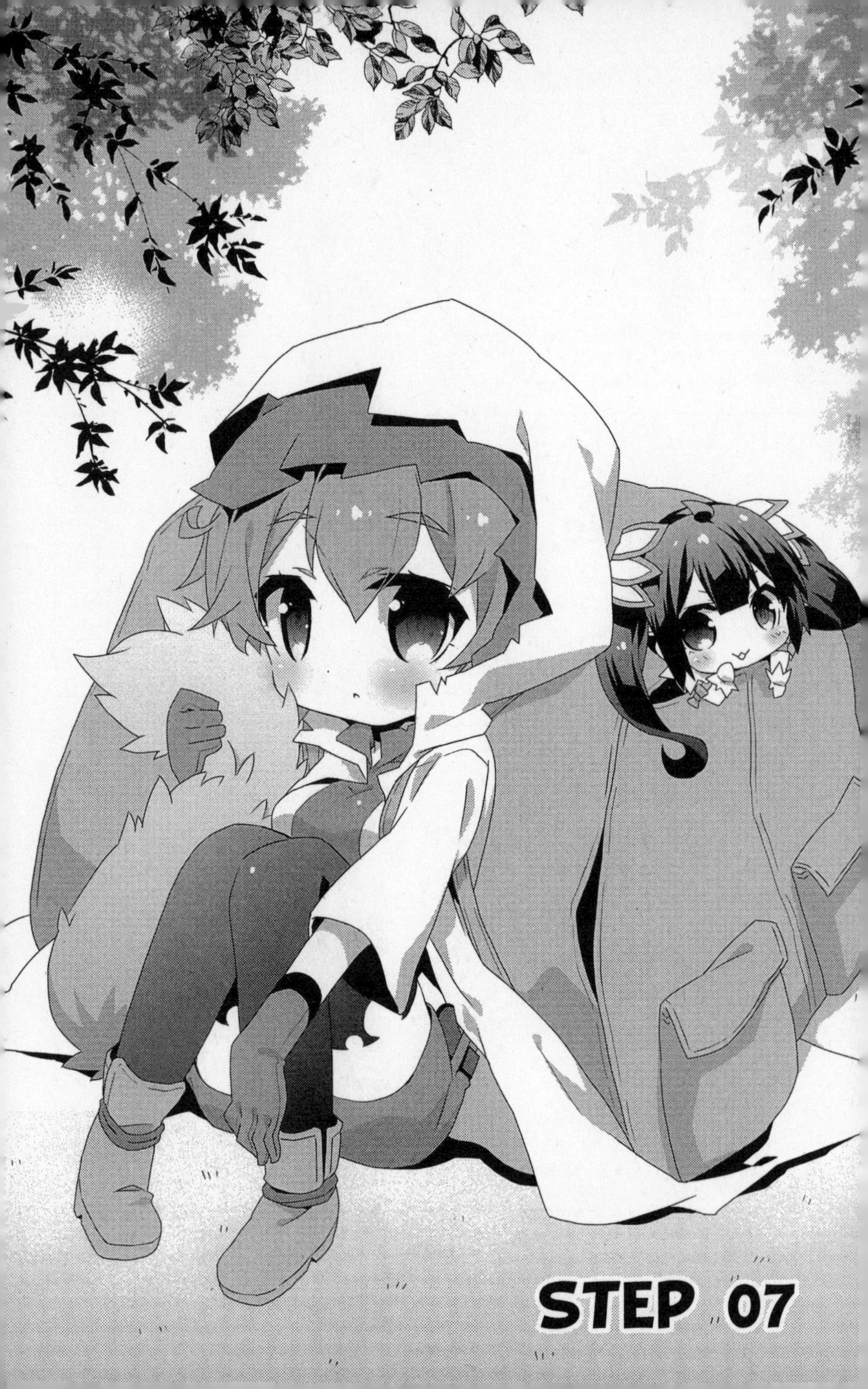
STEP 07

MISUNDERSTANDING?

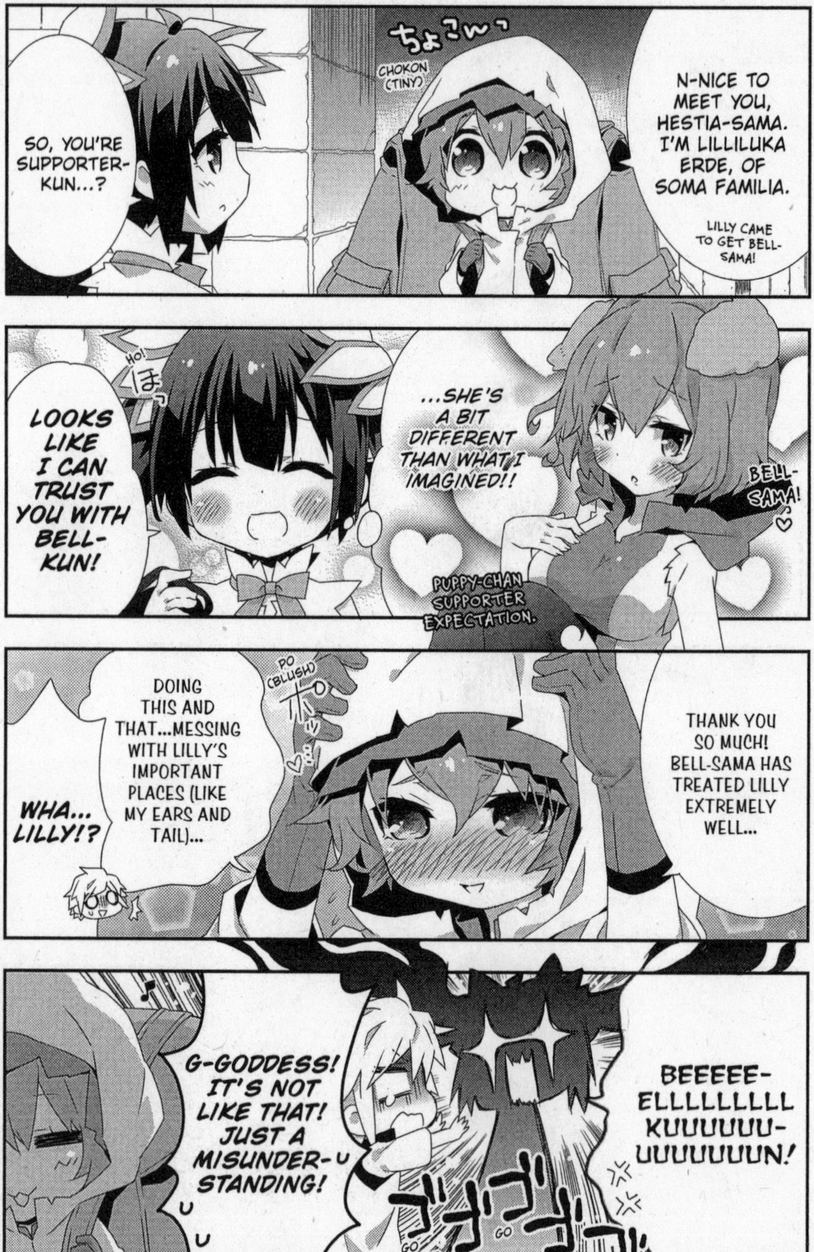
N-NICE TO MEET YOU, HESTIA-SAMA. I'M LILLILUKA ERDE, OF SOMA FAMILIA.
LILLY CAME TO GET BELL-SAMA!
ちょこん
CHOKON (TINY)
SO, YOU'RE SUPPORTER-KUN...?
BELL-SAMA!
PUPPY-CHAN SUPPORTER EXPECTATION.
...SHE'S A BIT DIFFERENT THAN WHAT I IMAGINED!!
HO!
ほっ
LOOKS LIKE I CAN TRUST YOU WITH BELL-KUN!
THANK YOU SO MUCH! BELL-SAMA HAS TREATED LILLY EXTREMELY WELL...
PO (BLUSH)
DOING THIS AND THAT...MESSING WITH LILLY'S IMPORTANT PLACES (LIKE MY EARS AND TAIL)...
WHA... LILLY!?
BEEEEE-ELLLLLLLLL KUUUUUU-UUUUUUUN!
GO (RUMBLE) GO GO GO GO
G-GODDESS! IT'S NOT LIKE THAT! JUST A MISUNDER-STANDING!

WHAT LILLILUKA WANTS

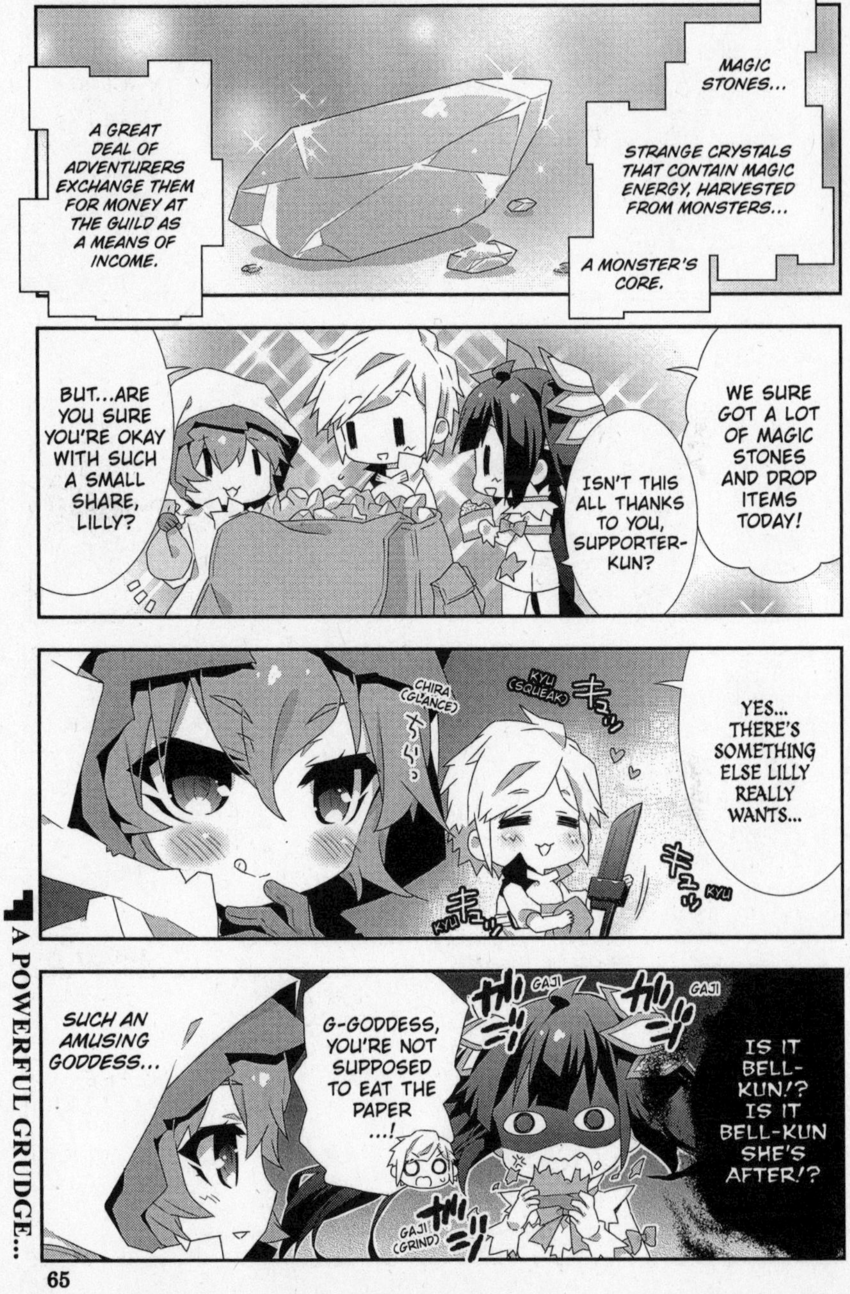
MAGIC STONES...
STRANGE CRYSTALS THAT CONTAIN MAGIC ENERGY, HARVESTED FROM MONSTERS...
A MONSTER'S CORE.
A GREAT DEAL OF ADVENTURERS EXCHANGE THEM FOR MONEY AT THE GUILD AS A MEANS OF INCOME.
WE SURE GOT A LOT OF MAGIC STONES AND DROP ITEMS TODAY!
ISN'T THIS ALL THANKS TO YOU, SUPPORTER-KUN?
BUT...ARE YOU SURE YOU'RE OKAY WITH SUCH A SMALL SHARE, LILLY?
YES... THERE'S SOMETHING ELSE LILLY REALLY WANTS...
KYU (SQUEAK)
CHIRA (GLANCE)
KYU
KYU
IS IT BELL-KUN!? IS IT BELL-KUN SHE'S AFTER!?
GAJI
GAJI
G-GODDESS, YOU'RE NOT SUPPOSED TO EAT THE PAPER ...!
SUCH AN AMUSING GODDESS...
GAJI (GRIND)

A POWERFUL GRUDGE...

WHAT HESTIA IS MADE OF

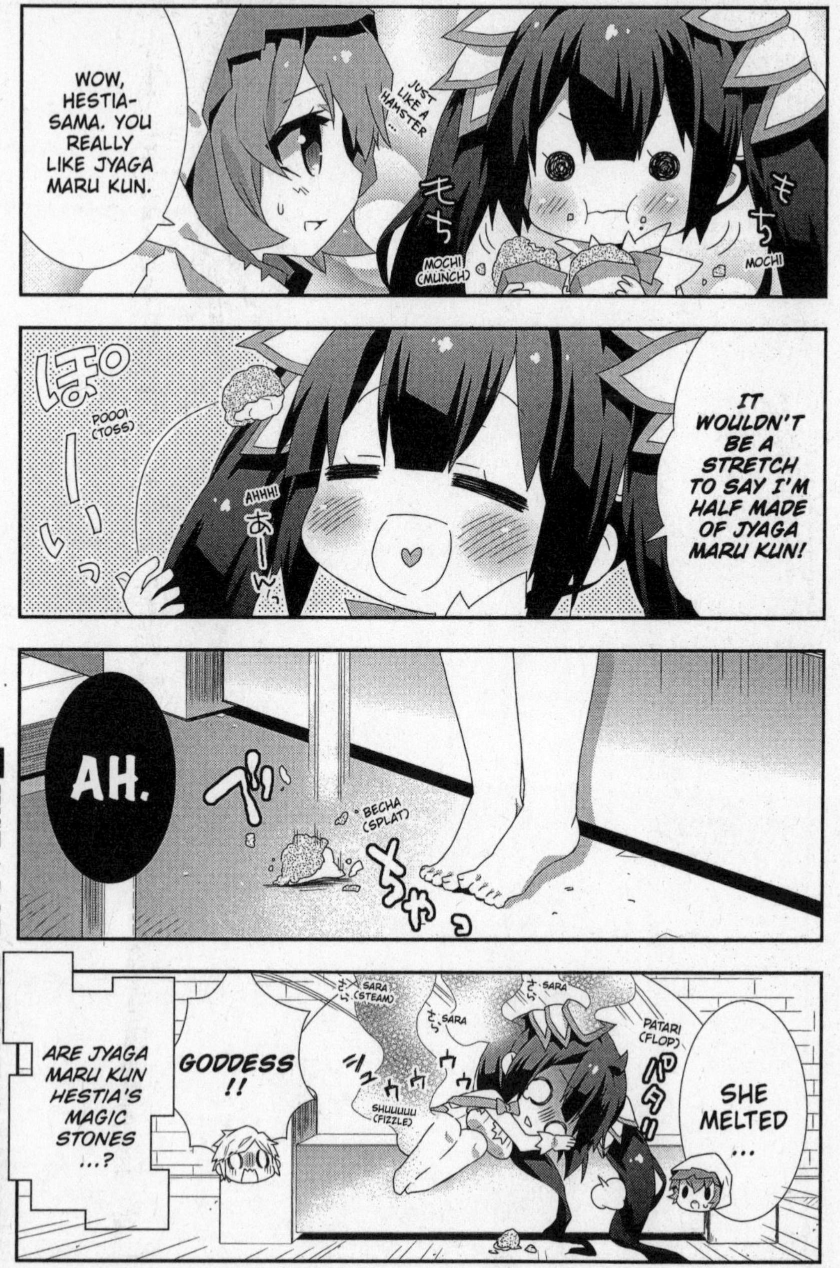
MOCHI
JUST LIKE A HAMSTER ...
MOCHI (MUNCH)
WOW, HESTIA-SAMA. YOU REALLY LIKE JYAGA MARU KUN.
IT WOULDN'T BE A STRETCH TO SAY I'M HALF MADE OF JYAGA MARU KUN!
AHHH!
POOOI (TOSS)
BECHA (SPLAT)
AH.
SHE MELTED ...
PATARI (FLOP)
SARA
SARA
SARA (STEAM)
SHUUUUUU (FIZZLE)
GODDESS !!
ARE JYAGA MARU KUN HESTIA'S MAGIC STONES ...?

JUST A POTATO-LOVING GODDESS.

BELL-KUN'S VEGETABLES

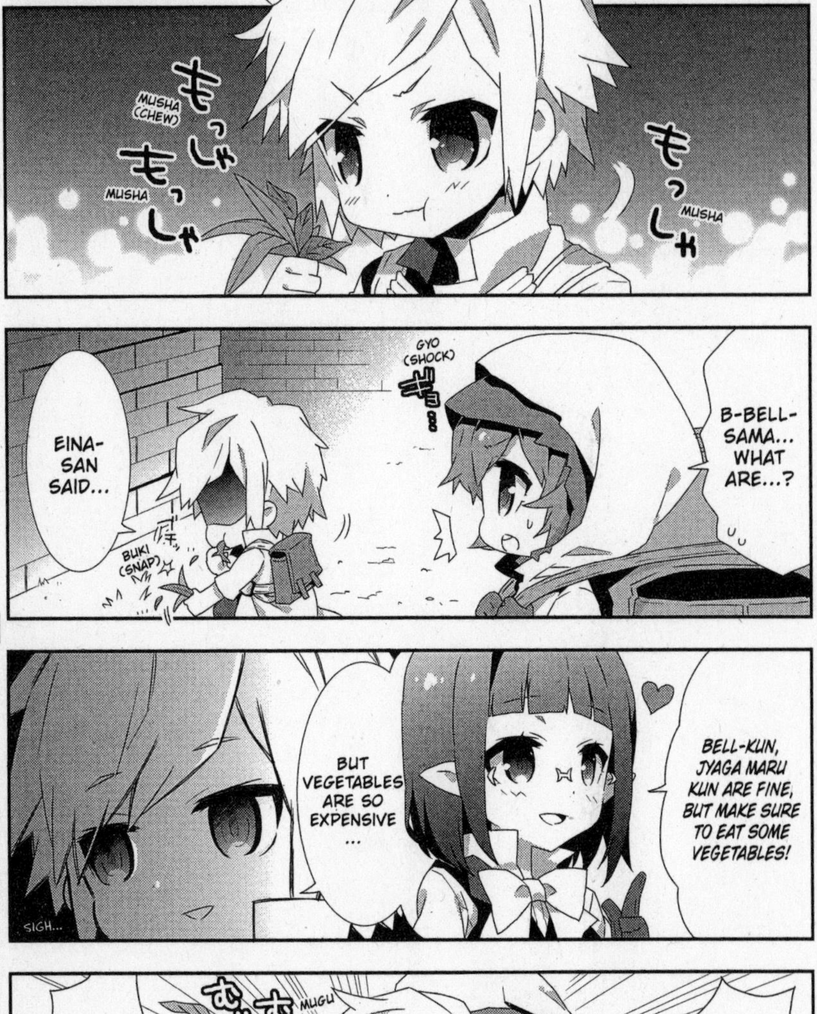
MUSHA
MUSHA (CHEW)
MUSHA
B-BELL-SAMA... WHAT ARE...?
GYO (SHOCK)
EINA-SAN SAID...
BUKI (SNAP)
BELL-KUN, JYAGA MARU KUN ARE FINE, BUT MAKE SURE TO EAT SOME VEGETABLES!
BUT VEGETABLES ARE SO EXPENSIVE ...
SIGH...
STOP, OR YOU'RE GOING TO GET SICK!
GASHI (GRAB)
MUGU
MUGU (NOM)
YOU'LL REALLY BECOME A RABBIT!

BELL=RABBIT THEORY, GAINING TRACTION.

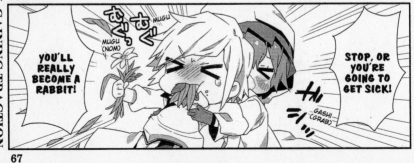

NICE IDEA ★

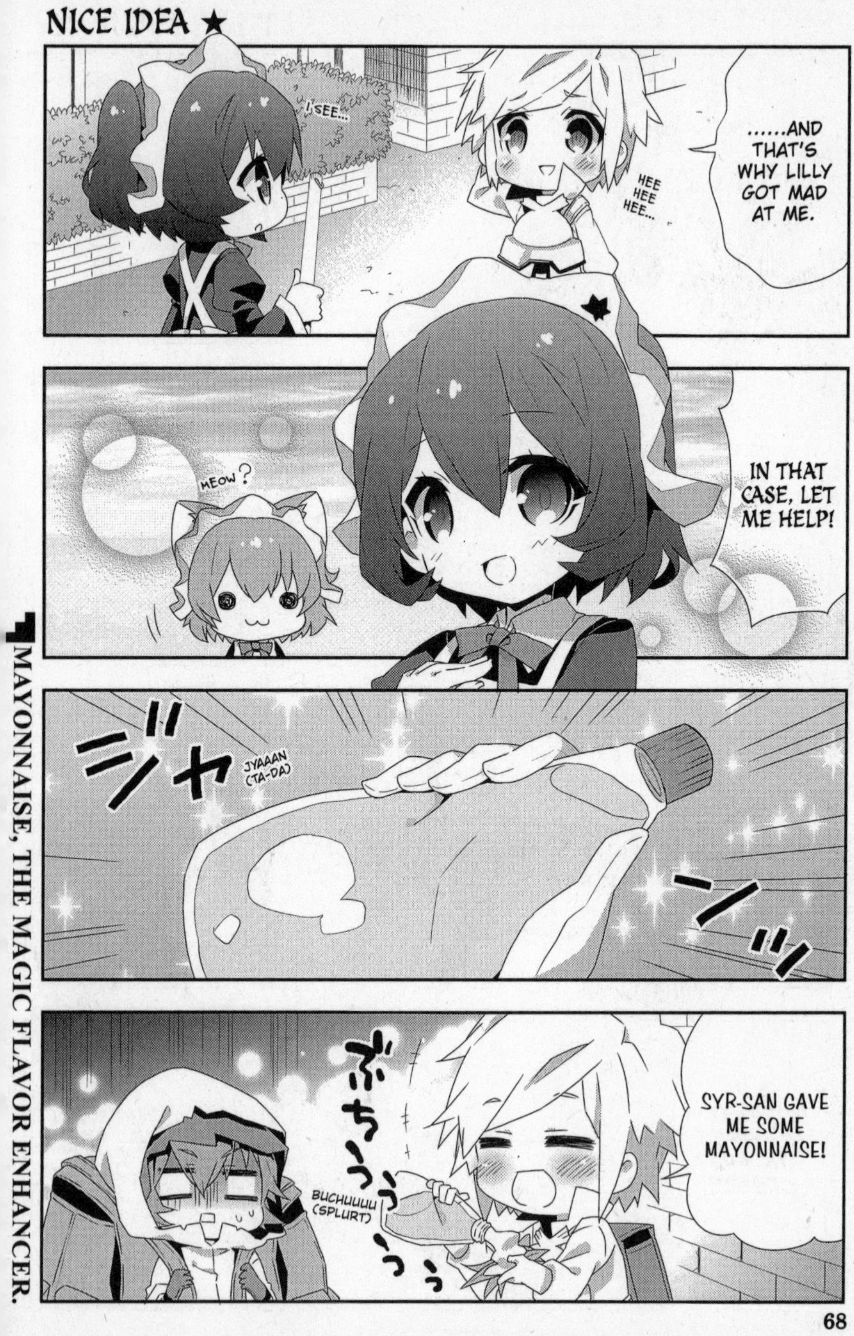
......AND THAT'S WHY LILLY GOT MAD AT ME.
HEE HEE HEE...
I SEE...
IN THAT CASE, LET ME HELP!
MEOW?
ジャーンッ
JYAAAN (TA-DA)
SYR-SAN GAVE ME SOME MAYONNAISE!
ぶちゅううう
BUCHUUUU (SPLURT)

MAYONNAISE, THE MAGIC FLAVOR ENHANCER.

HESTIA'S BUSINESS?

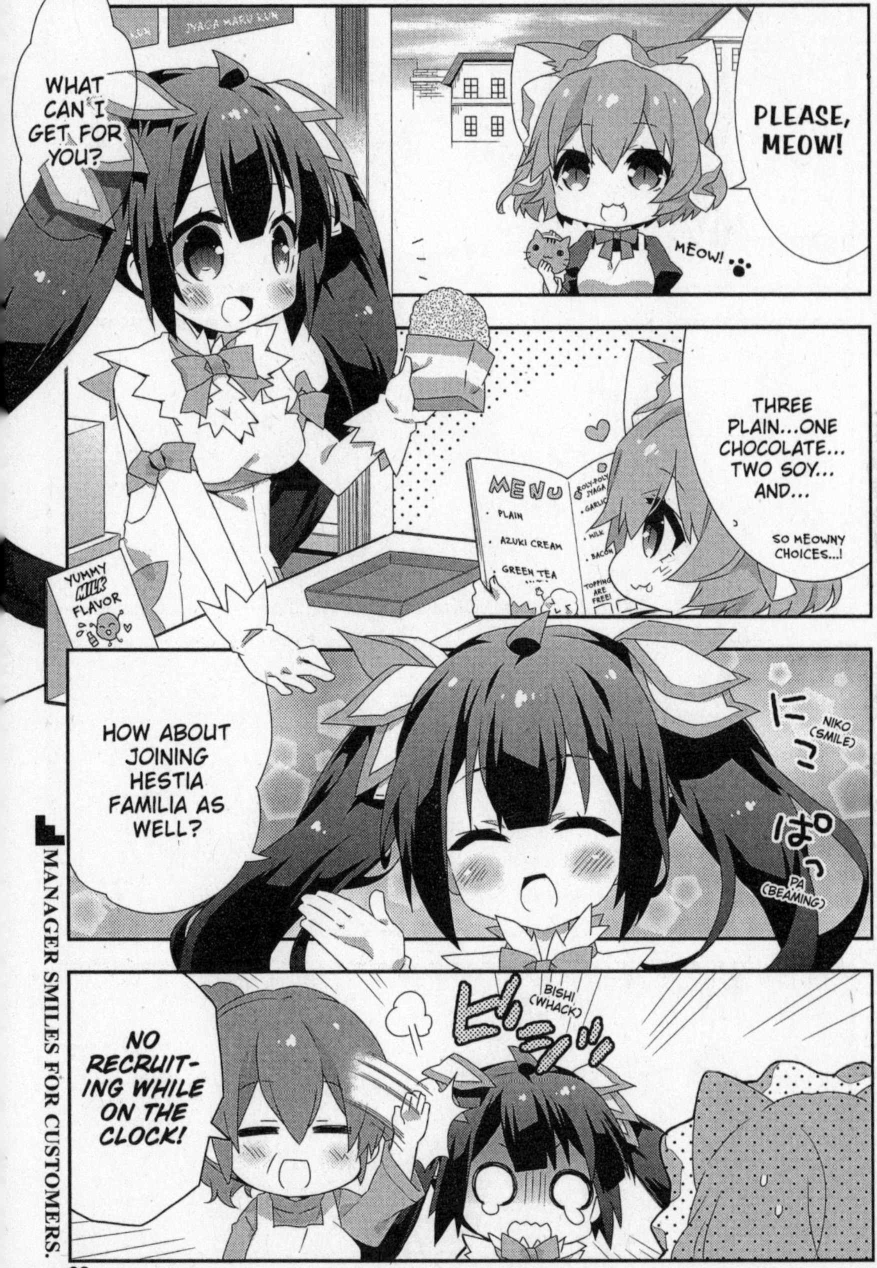
JYAGA MARU KUN
PLEASE, MEOW!
MEOW!
WHAT CAN I GET FOR YOU?
THREE PLAIN...ONE CHOCOLATE... TWO SOY... AND...
SO MEOWNY CHOICES...!
MENU
PLAIN
AZUKI CREAM
GREEN TEA
ROLY-POLY JYAGA
GARLIC
MILK
BACON
TOPPING ARE FREE!
YUMMY MILK FLAVOR
にこ
NIKO (SMILE)
ぱっ
PA (BEAMING)
HOW ABOUT JOINING HESTIA FAMILIA AS WELL?
BISHI (WHACK)
NO RECRUITING WHILE ON THE CLOCK!

MANAGER SMILES FOR CUSTOMERS.

LEAVE IT TO AHNYA

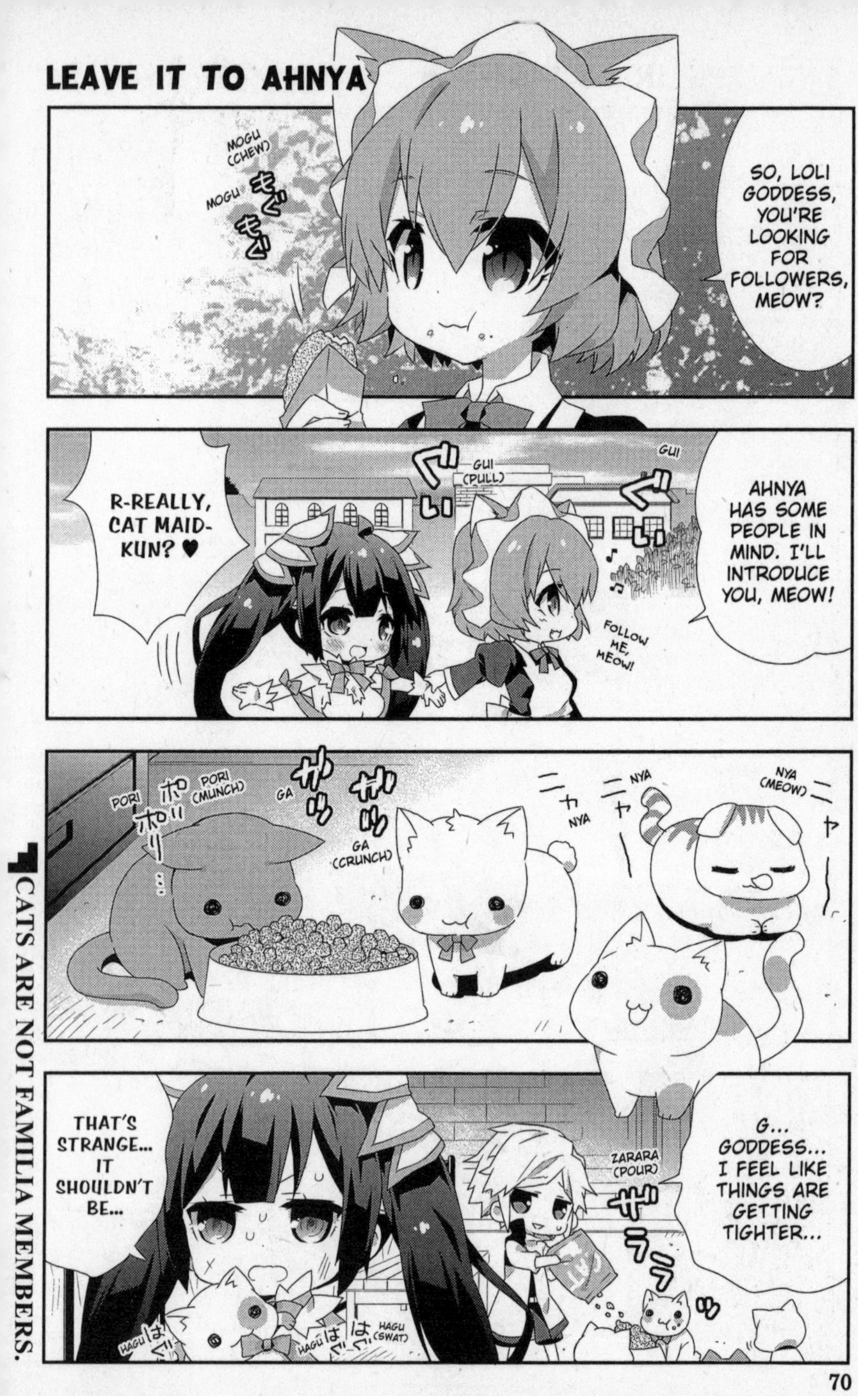
SO, LOLI GODDESS, YOU'RE LOOKING FOR FOLLOWERS, MEOW?
MOGU (CHEW)
MOGU
もぐもぐ
AHNYA HAS SOME PEOPLE IN MIND. I'LL INTRODUCE YOU, MEOW!
GUI
ぐい
GUI (PULL)
ぐい
FOLLOW ME, MEOW!
R-REALLY, CAT MAID-KUN? ♥
NYA (MEOW)
ニャー
NYA
ニャー
NYA
ニャー
GA (CRUNCH)
ガッ
GA
ガッ
PORI (MUNCH)
PORI
ポリポリ…
G… GODDESS… I FEEL LIKE THINGS ARE GETTING TIGHTER…
ZARARA (POUR)
ザラララッ
HAGU (SWAT)
HAGU
はぐはぐ
HAGU
THAT'S STRANGE… IT SHOULDN'T BE…

CATS ARE NOT FAMILIA MEMBERS.

SNEAKING IN AT NIGHT ♥

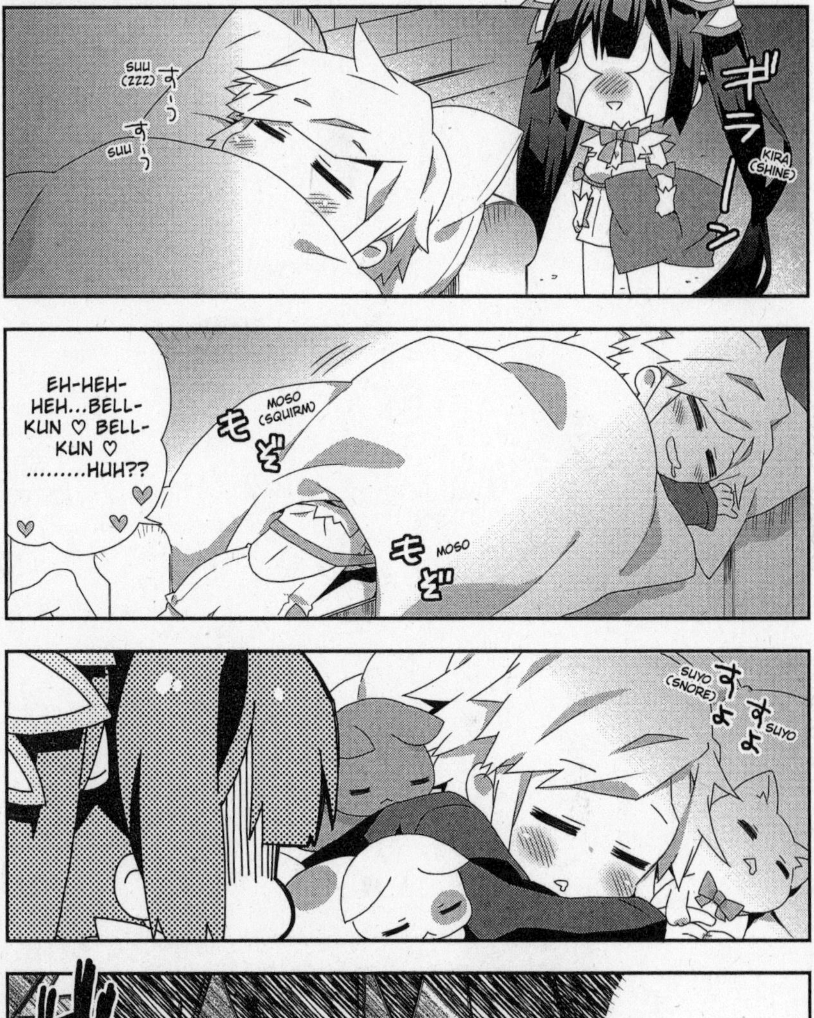
ギラーン
KIRA (SHINE)
SUU (ZZZ)
SUU
MOSO (SQUIRM)
EH-HEH-HEH...BELL-KUN ♡ BELL-KUN ♡ ....HUH??
MOSO
SUYO (SNORE)
SUYO
MY SPOT!!
GAAAN (SHOCK)

YES, CATS ARE PETS.

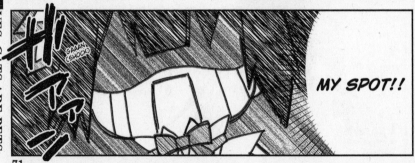

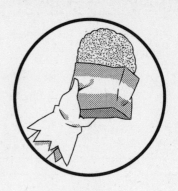

STEP 08

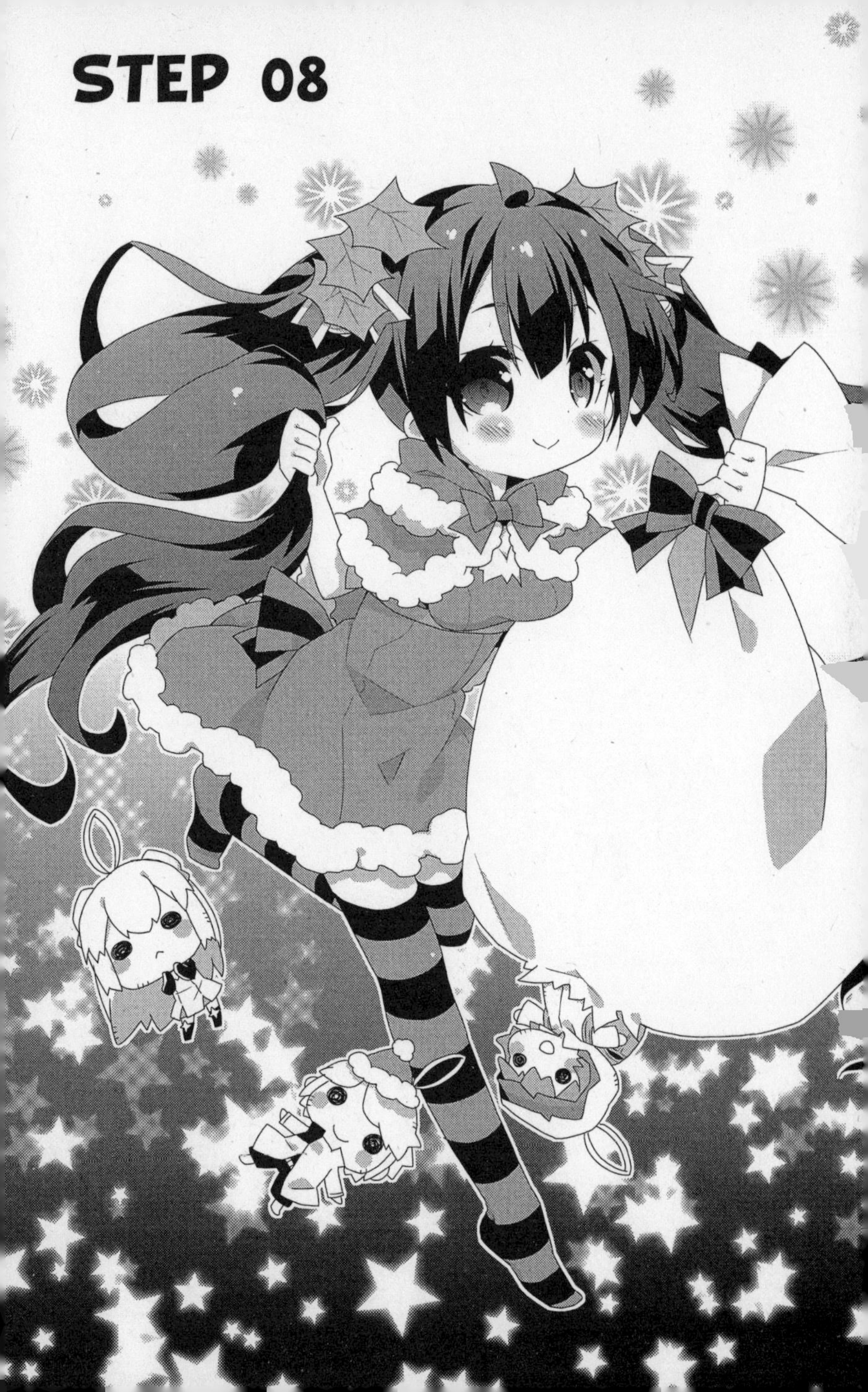

CHRISTMAS IN ORARIO

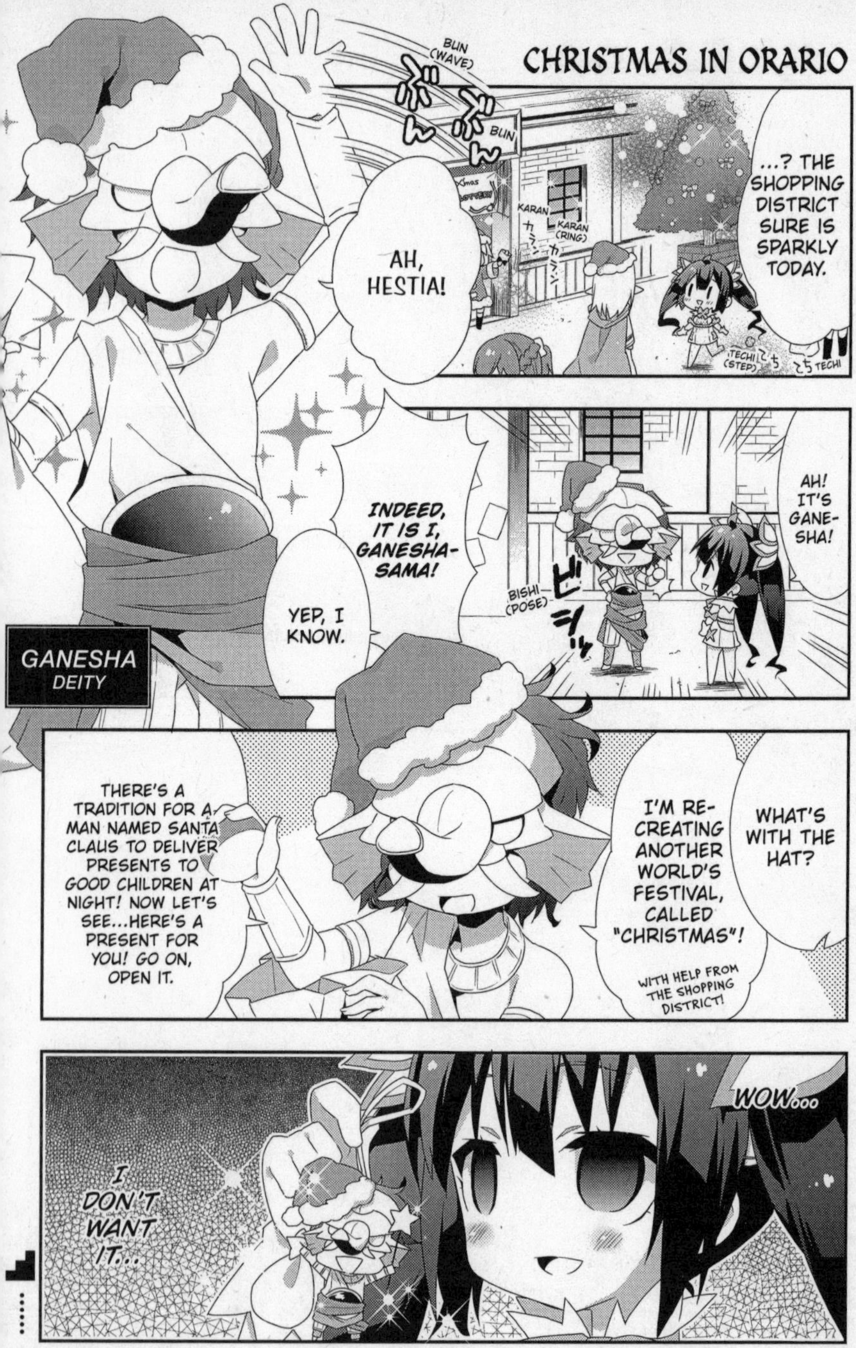
...? THE SHOPPING DISTRICT SURE IS SPARKLY TODAY.
TECHI (STEP) TECHI
KARAN (RING) KARAN
BUN (WAVE) BUN
AH, HESTIA!
AH! IT'S GANE-SHA!
INDEED, IT IS I, GANESHA-SAMA!
BISHI (POSE)
YEP, I KNOW.
GANESHA
DEITY
WHAT'S WITH THE HAT?
I'M RE-CREATING ANOTHER WORLD'S FESTIVAL, CALLED "CHRISTMAS"!
WITH HELP FROM THE SHOPPING DISTRICT!
THERE'S A TRADITION FOR A MAN NAMED SANTA CLAUS TO DELIVER PRESENTS TO GOOD CHILDREN AT NIGHT! NOW LET'S SEE...HERE'S A PRESENT FOR YOU! GO ON, OPEN IT.
WOW...
I DON'T WANT IT...

HESTIA'S PRESENT

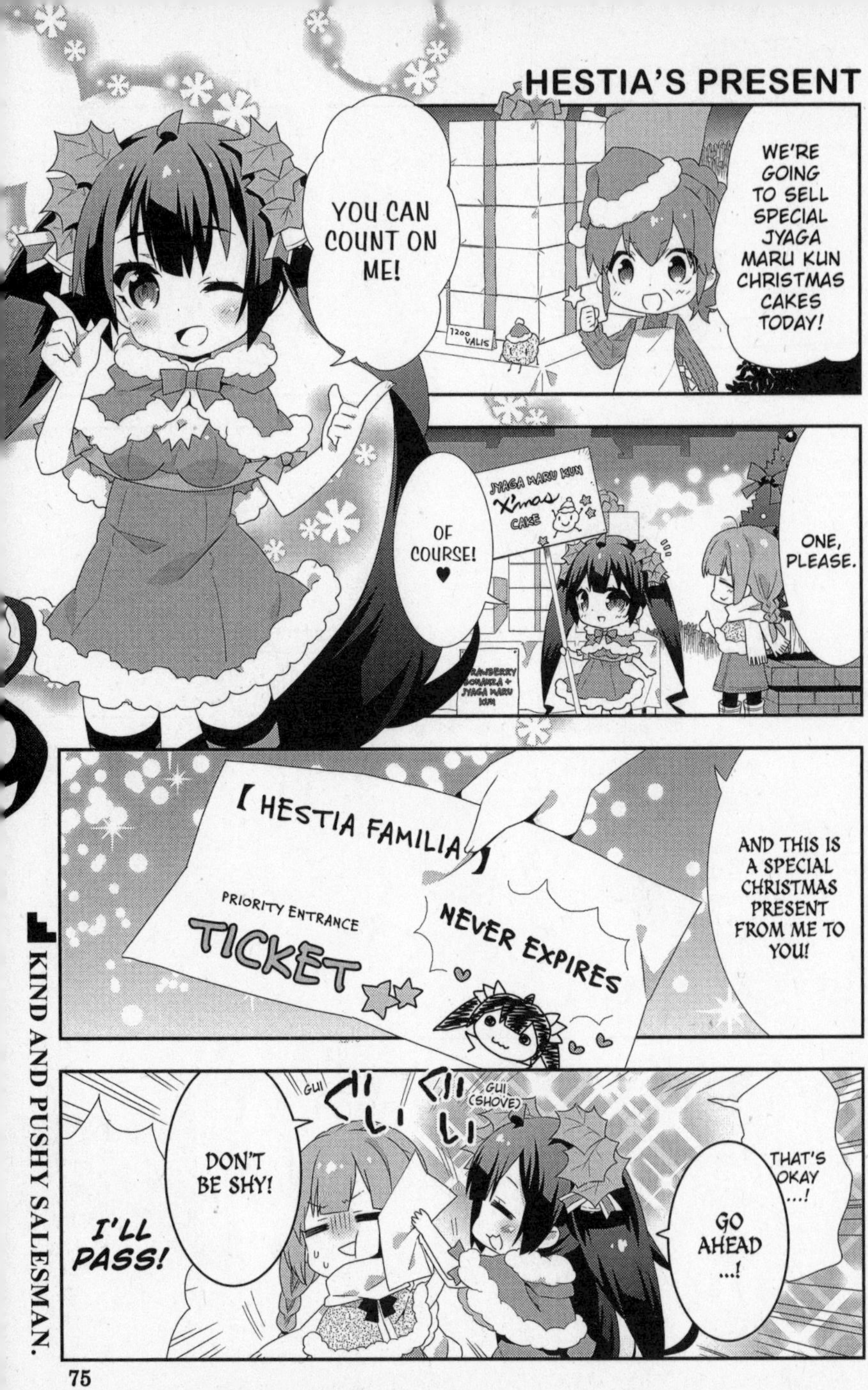
WE'RE GOING TO SELL SPECIAL JYAGA MARU KUN CHRISTMAS CAKES TODAY!
1200 VALIS
ONE, PLEASE.
OF COURSE! ♥
JYAGA MARU KUN X'mas CAKE
RAWBERRY BONANZA + JYAGA MARU KUN
YOU CAN COUNT ON ME!
AND THIS IS A SPECIAL CHRISTMAS PRESENT FROM ME TO YOU!
【HESTIA FAMILIA】
PRIORITY ENTRANCE
TICKET
NEVER EXPIRES
THAT'S OKAY ...!
GO AHEAD ...!
GUI (SHOVE)
GUI
DON'T BE SHY!
I'LL PASS!

KIND AND PUSHY SALESMAN.

SANTA-SAN'S IDENTITY

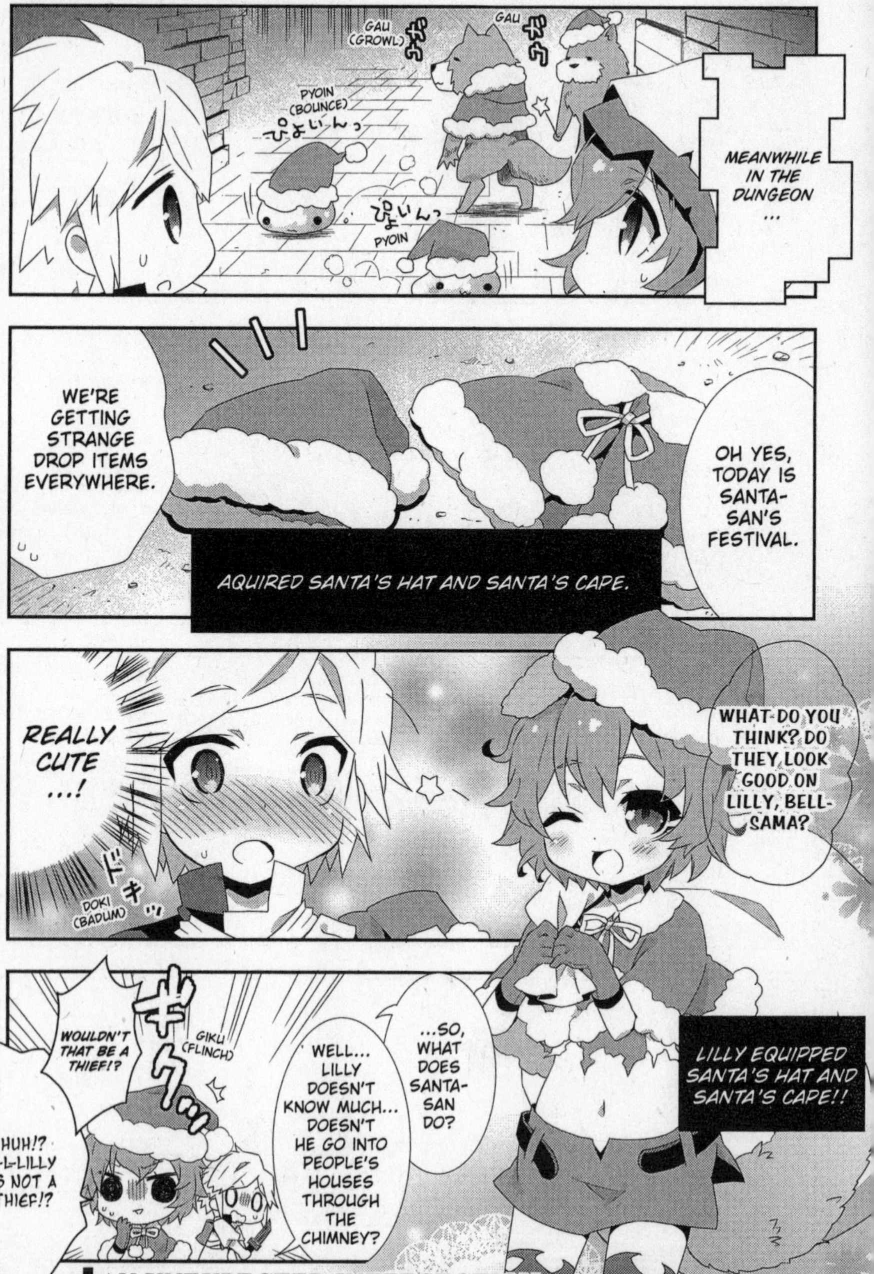
MEANWHILE IN THE DUNGEON ...
GAU
GAU (GROWL)
PYOIN (BOUNCE)
PYOIN
OH YES, TODAY IS SANTA-SAN'S FESTIVAL.
AQUIRED SANTA'S HAT AND SANTA'S CAPE.
WE'RE GETTING STRANGE DROP ITEMS EVERYWHERE.
WHAT DO YOU THINK? DO THEY LOOK GOOD ON LILLY, BELL-SAMA?
REALLY CUTE ...!
DOKI (BADUM)
LILLY EQUIPPED SANTA'S HAT AND SANTA'S CAPE!!
...SO, WHAT DOES SANTA-SAN DO?
WELL... LILLY DOESN'T KNOW MUCH... DOESN'T HE GO INTO PEOPLE'S HOUSES THROUGH THE CHIMNEY?
GIKU (FLINCH)
WOULDN'T THAT BE A THIEF!?
HUH!? L-L-LILLY IS NOT A THIEF!?

AN UNEXPECTED INTERSECTION.

PRACTICALLY A REGULAR

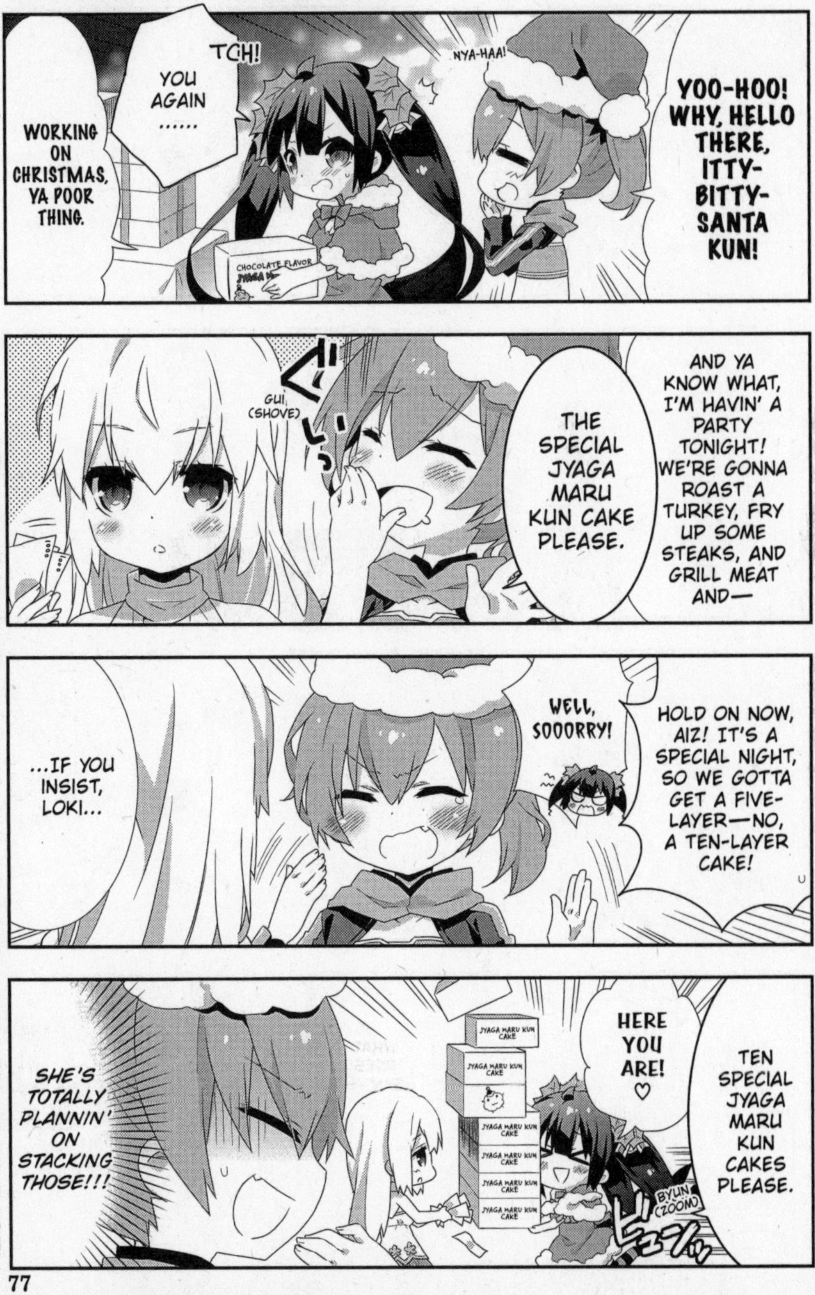

YOO-HOO! WHY, HELLO THERE, ITTY-BITTY-SANTA KUN!
NYA-HAA!
TCH!
YOU AGAIN ......
WORKING ON CHRISTMAS, YA POOR THING.
CHOCOLATE FLAVOR
AND YA KNOW WHAT, I'M HAVIN' A PARTY TONIGHT! WE'RE GONNA ROAST A TURKEY, FRY UP SOME STEAKS, AND GRILL MEAT AND—
THE SPECIAL JYAGA MARU KUN CAKE PLEASE.
GUI (SHOVE)
HOLD ON NOW, AIZ! IT'S A SPECIAL NIGHT, SO WE GOTTA GET A FIVE-LAYER—NO, A TEN-LAYER CAKE!
WELL, SOOORRY!
...IF YOU INSIST, LOKI...
TEN SPECIAL JYAGA MARU KUN CAKES PLEASE.
HERE YOU ARE! ♡
BYUN (ZOOM)
JYAGA MARU KUN CAKE
JYAGA MARU KUN CAKE
JYAGA MARU KUN CAKE
JYAGA MARU KUN CAKE
JYAGA MARU KUN CAKE
JYAGA MARU KUN CAKE
SHE'S TOTALLY PLANNIN' ON STACKING THOSE!!!

LOVE FOR JYAGA MARU KUN UP 30% (FOR THIS RELEASE).

HESTIA'S SALESMANSHIP

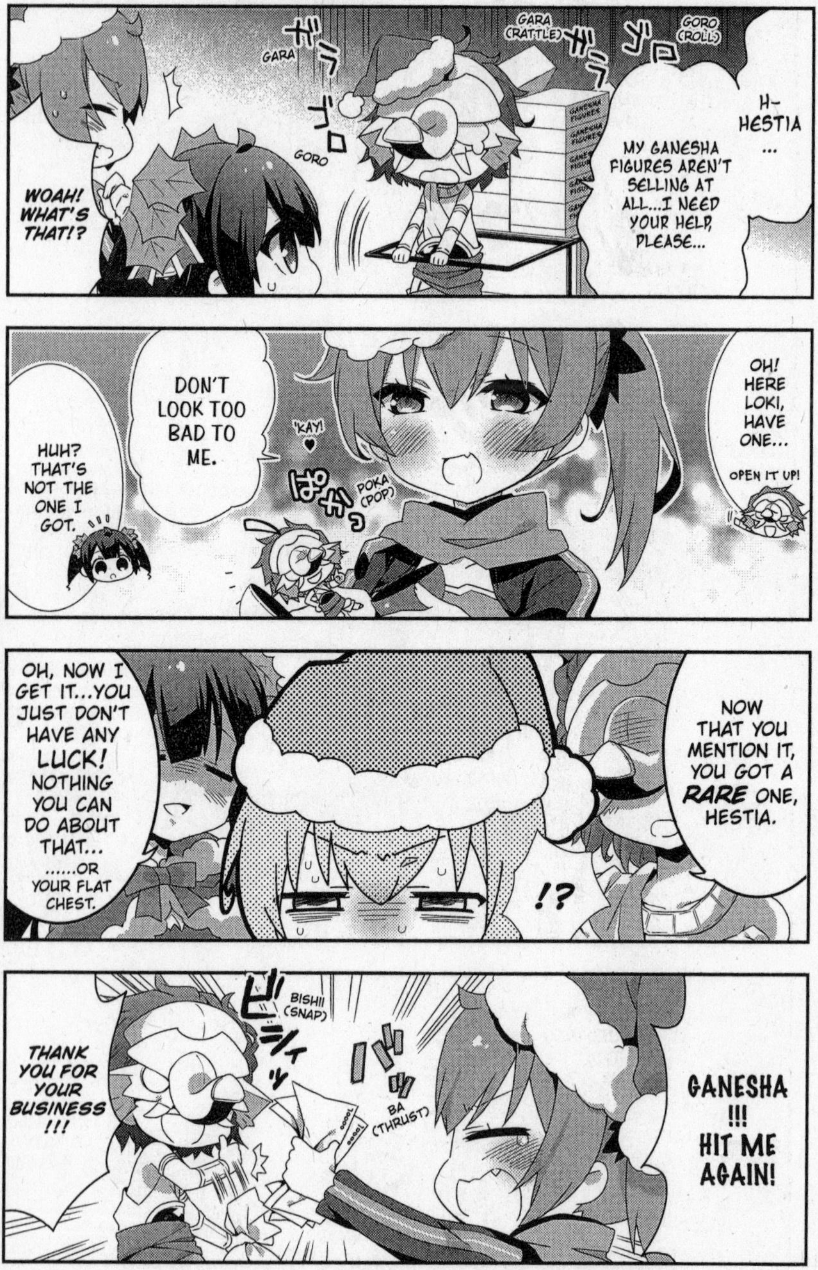
H-HESTIA ...
GORO (ROLL)
GARA (RATTLE)
MY GANESHA FIGURES AREN'T SELLING AT ALL...I NEED YOUR HELP, PLEASE...
GARA
GORO
WOAH! WHAT'S THAT!?
OH! HERE LOKI, HAVE ONE...
OPEN IT UP!
POKA (POP)
'KAY! ♥
DON'T LOOK TOO BAD TO ME.
HUH? THAT'S NOT THE ONE I GOT.
NOW THAT YOU MENTION IT, YOU GOT A RARE ONE, HESTIA.
!?
OH, NOW I GET IT...YOU JUST DON'T HAVE ANY LUCK! NOTHING YOU CAN DO ABOUT THAT... ......OR YOUR FLAT CHEST.
GANESHA!!! HIT ME AGAIN!
BISHI! (SNAP)
BA (THRUST)
THANK YOU FOR YOUR BUSINESS!!!

COULDN'T ASK FOR A BETTER SITTING DUCK.

LOKI FAMILIA'S CRISIS

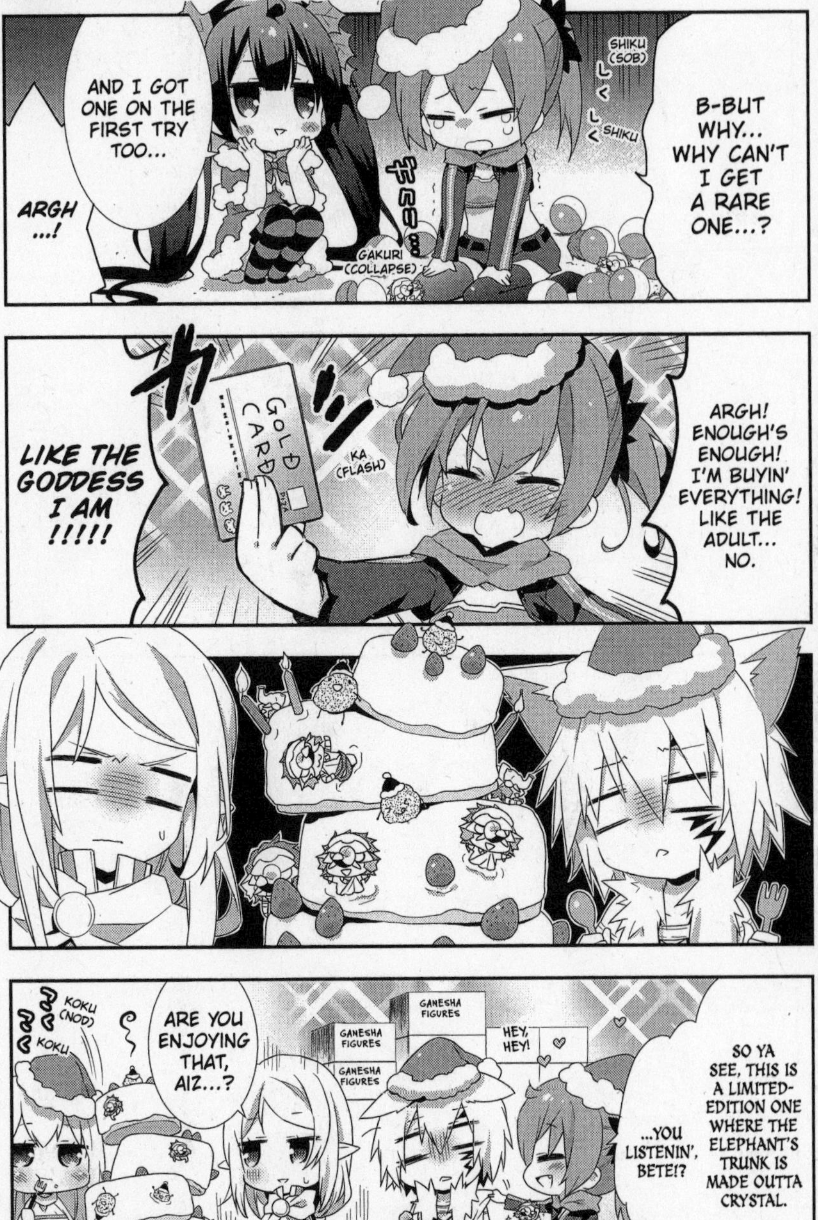

SHIKU (SOB)
B-BUT WHY... WHY CAN'T I GET A RARE ONE...?
SHIKU
GAKURI (COLLAPSE)
AND I GOT ONE ON THE FIRST TRY TOO...
ARGH ...!
ARGH! ENOUGH'S ENOUGH! I'M BUYIN' EVERYTHING! LIKE THE ADULT... NO.
KA (FLASH)
GOLD CARD
LIKE THE GODDESS I AM !!!!!
SO YA SEE, THIS IS A LIMITED-EDITION ONE WHERE THE ELEPHANT'S TRUNK IS MADE OUTTA CRYSTAL.
...YOU LISTENIN', BETE!?
HEY, HEY!
GANESHA FIGURES
GANESHA FIGURES
GANESHA FIGURES
ARE YOU ENJOYING THAT, AIZ...?
KOKU (NOD)
KOKU

A CHRISTMAS TO REMEMBER (DESPAIR).

A FUN CHRISTMAS EVE

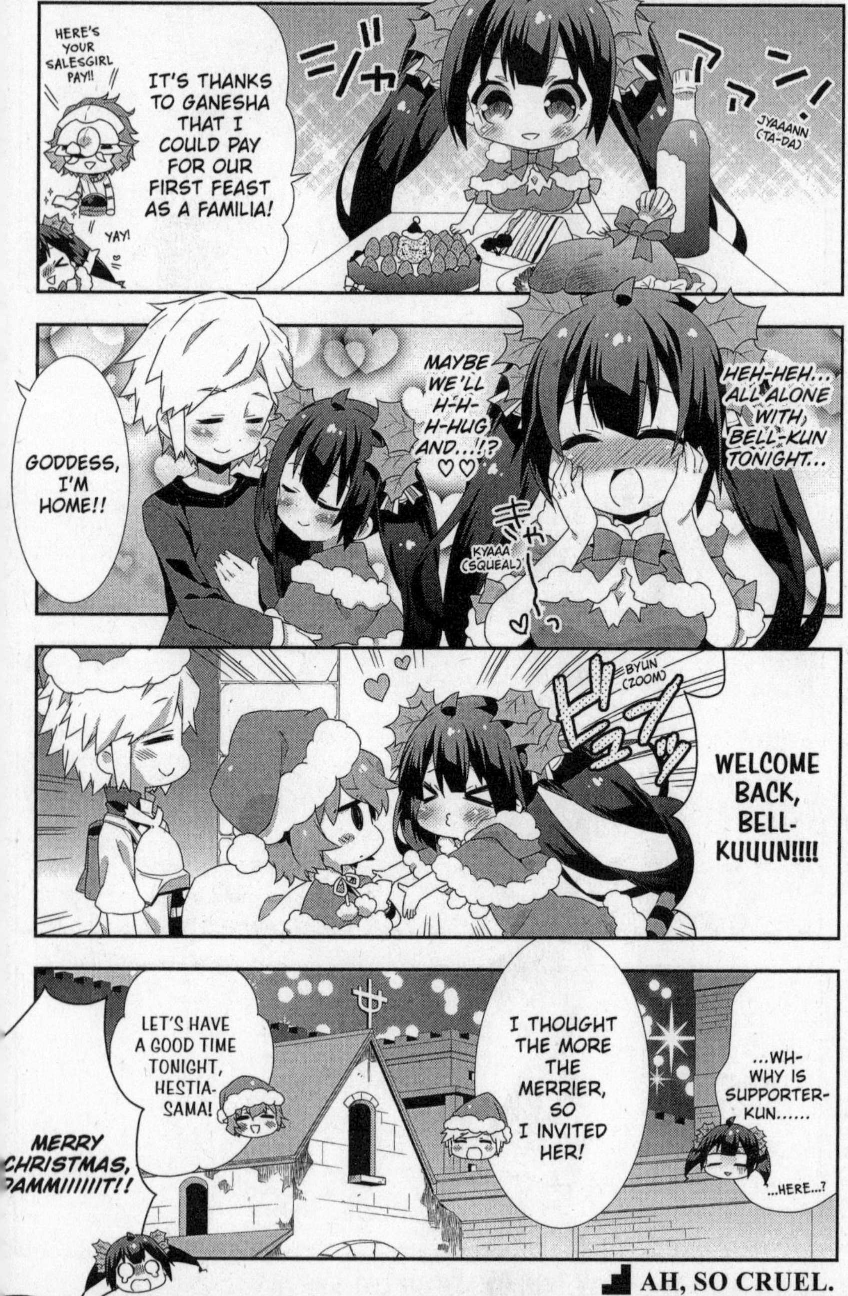
JYAAANN (TA-DA)
IT'S THANKS TO GANESHA THAT I COULD PAY FOR OUR FIRST FEAST AS A FAMILIA!
HERE'S YOUR SALESGIRL PAY!!
YAY!
HEH-HEH... ALL ALONE WITH BELL-KUN TONIGHT...
MAYBE WE'LL H-H-H-HUG AND...!? ♡♡
KYAAA (SQUEAL)
GODDESS, I'M HOME!!
WELCOME BACK, BELL-KUUUN!!!!
BYUN (ZOOM)
...WH- WHY IS SUPPORTER-KUN......
...HERE...?
I THOUGHT THE MORE THE MERRIER, SO I INVITED HER!
LET'S HAVE A GOOD TIME TONIGHT, HESTIA-SAMA!
MERRY CHRISTMAS, DAMMIIIIIIT!!

AH, SO CRUEL.

A PRESENT FROM HESTIA?

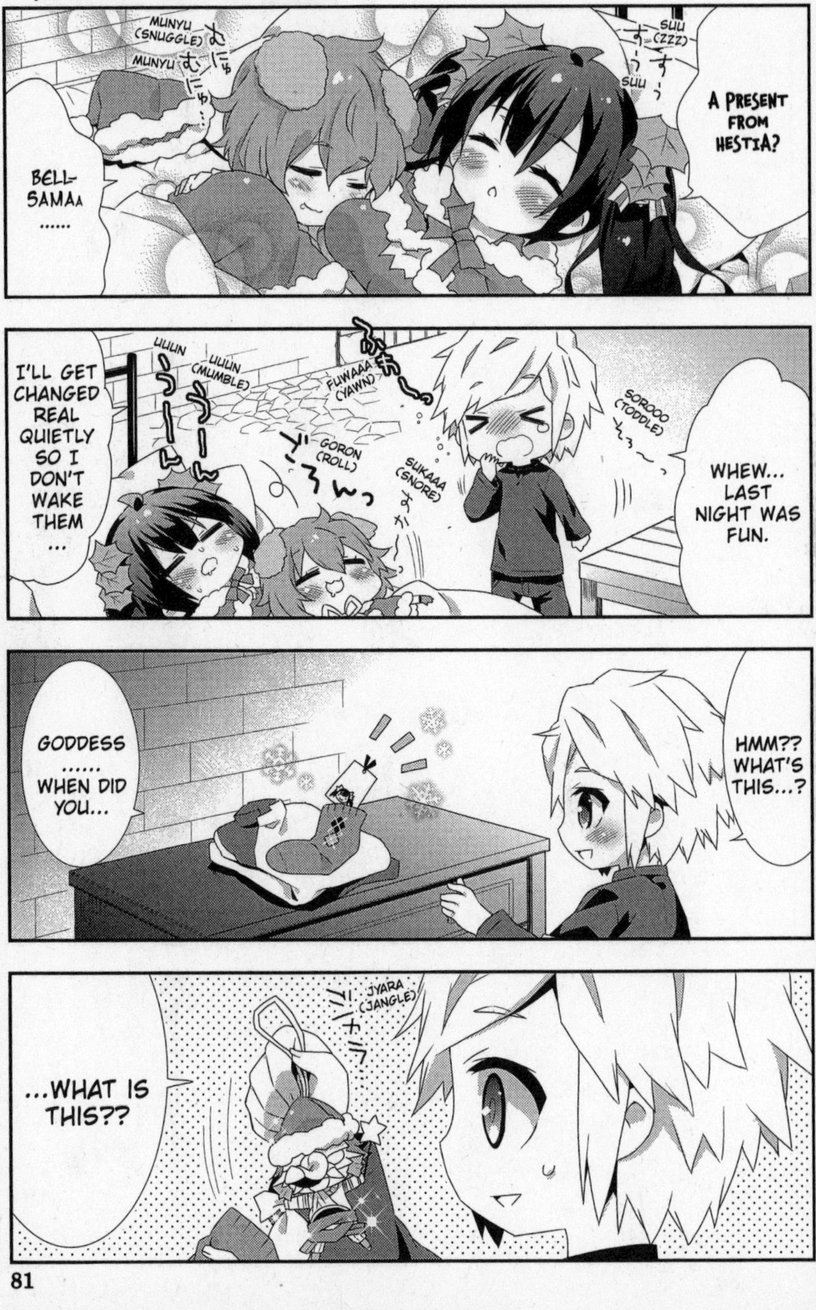
A PRESENT FROM HESTIA?
SUU (ZZZ) SUU
MUNYU (SNUGGLE) MUNYU
BELL-SAMAA ......
WHEW... LAST NIGHT WAS FUN.
SOROOO (TODDLE)
FUWAAA (YAWN)
SUKAAA (SNORE)
GORON (ROLL)
UUUN UUUN (MUMBLE)
I'LL GET CHANGED REAL QUIETLY SO I DON'T WAKE THEM ...
HMM?? WHAT'S THIS...?
GODDESS ...... WHEN DID YOU...
JYARA (JANGLE)
...WHAT IS THIS??

GANESHA FIGURES, COMING SOON TO A STORE NEAR YOU (TEMPORARILY).♡

NOT OFFICIALLY AUTHORIZED BY FUJINO OMORI-SENSEI!!

☆DEITY STATUS☆
SIXTH ENTRY

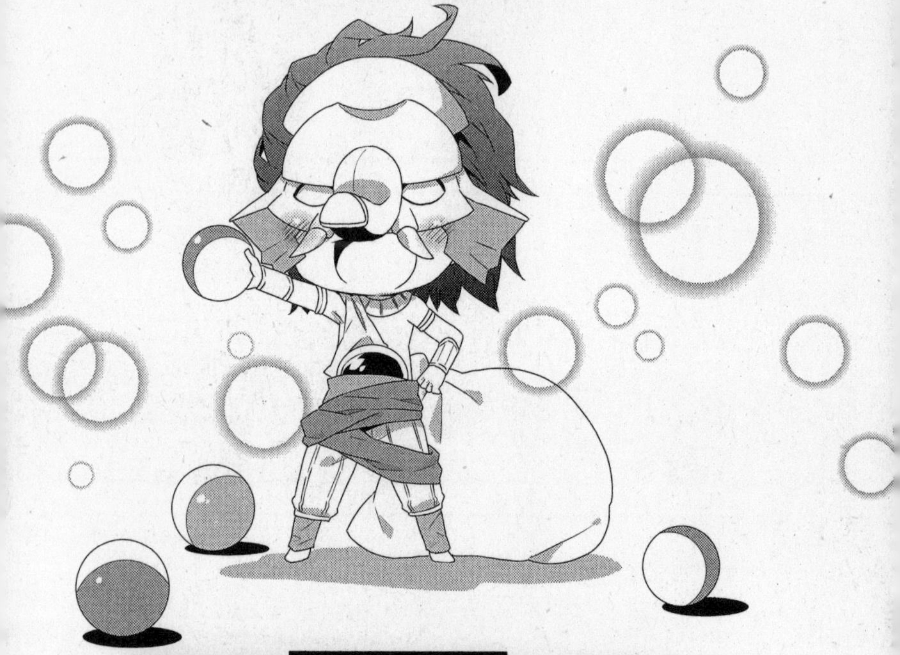

GANESHA

A FRIENDLY DEITY WHO LOVES FESTIVALS. ADORED BY PEOPLE OF ORARIO AND ADORES HIMSELF!!!

WEALTH: 999 CHARISMA: 999
Sensibility: (self-professed)
999,999,999...

※ AS THIS IS UNOFFICIAL, A FEW LIBERTIES HAVE BEEN TAKEN.

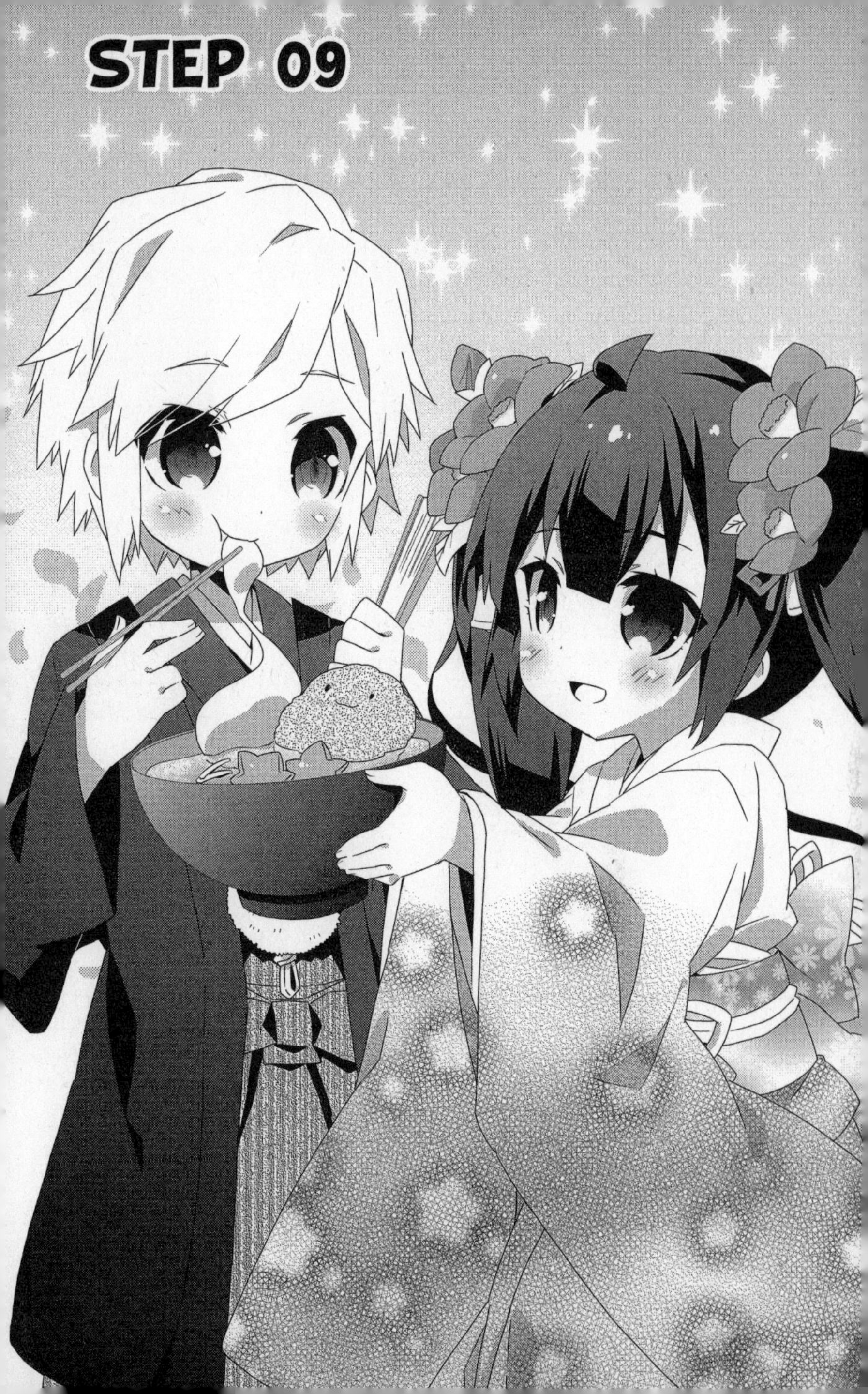
STEP 09

BENEVOLENT HEPHAISTOS ♡

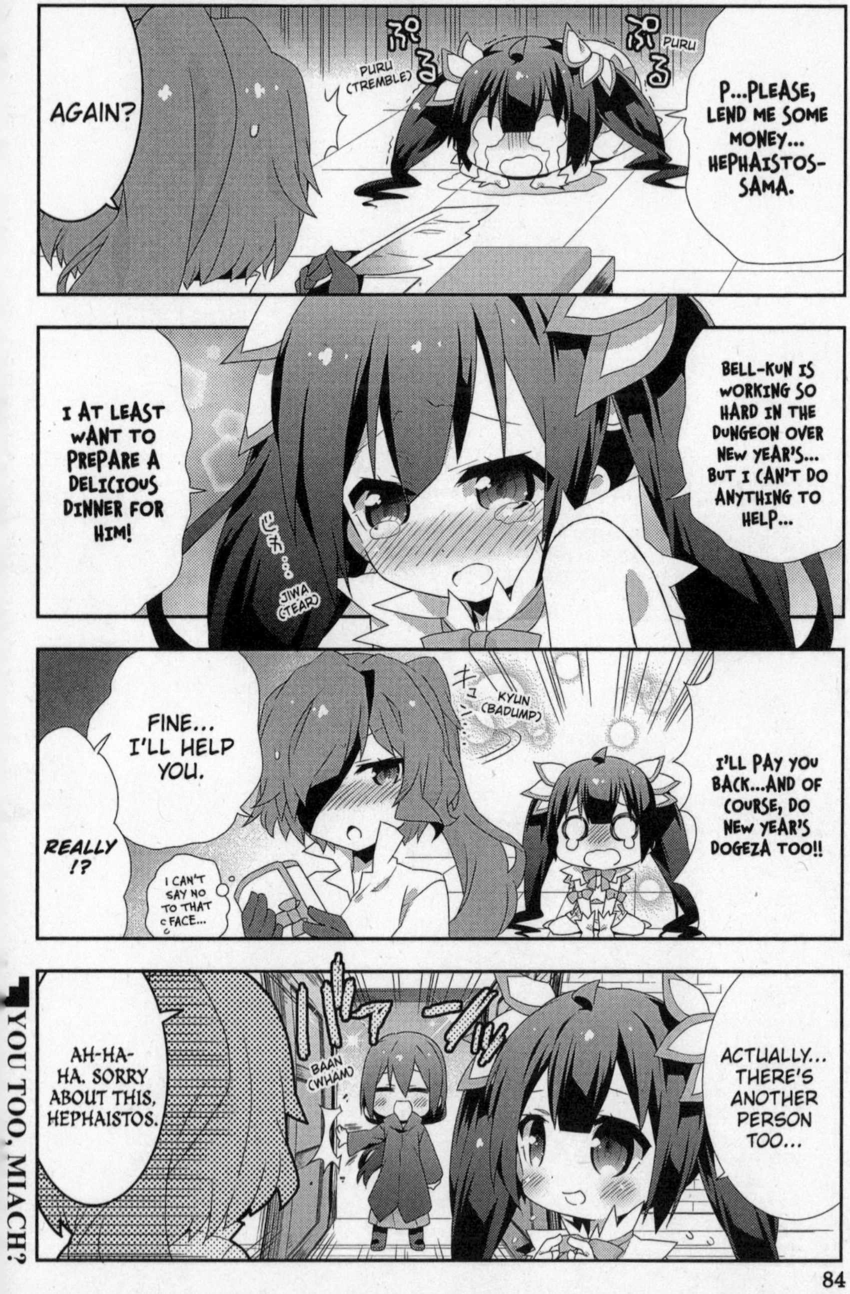
P...PLEASE, LEND ME SOME MONEY... HEPHAISTOS-SAMA.
PURU
PURU (TREMBLE)
AGAIN?
BELL-KUN IS WORKING SO HARD IN THE DUNGEON OVER NEW YEAR'S... BUT I CAN'T DO ANYTHING TO HELP...
JIWA (TEAR)
I AT LEAST WANT TO PREPARE A DELICIOUS DINNER FOR HIM!
I'LL PAY YOU BACK...AND OF COURSE, DO NEW YEAR'S DOGEZA TOO!!
KYUN (BADUMP)
FINE... I'LL HELP YOU.
I CAN'T SAY NO TO THAT FACE...
REALLY!?
ACTUALLY... THERE'S ANOTHER PERSON TOO...
BAAN (WHAM)
AH-HA-HA. SORRY ABOUT THIS, HEPHAISTOS.

YOU TOO, MIACH?

THE GREAT YEAR-END SALES

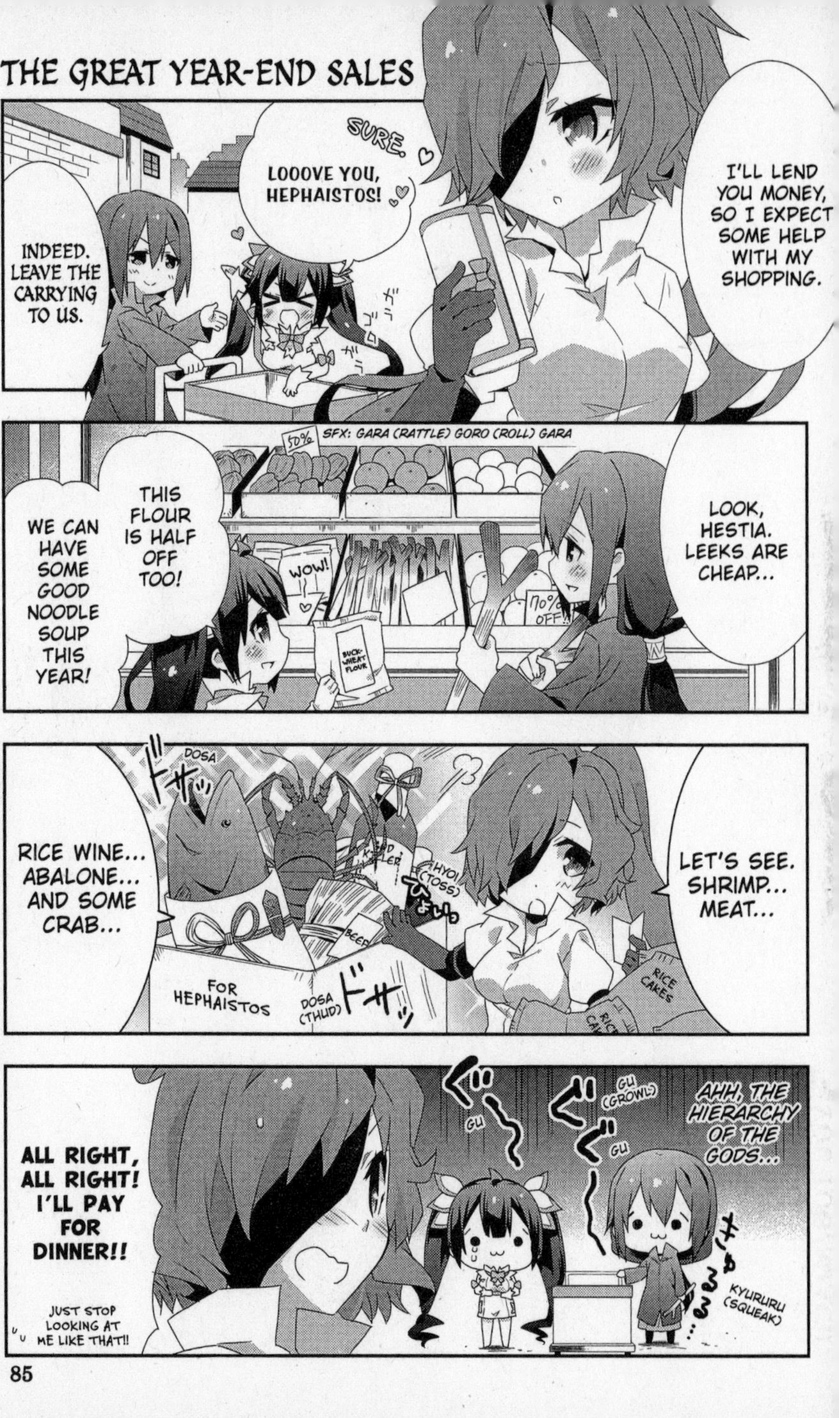

I'LL LEND YOU MONEY, SO I EXPECT SOME HELP WITH MY SHOPPING.
SURE.
LOOOVE YOU, HEPHAISTOS!
INDEED. LEAVE THE CARRYING TO US.
SFX: GARA (RATTLE) GORO (ROLL) GARA
LOOK, HESTIA. LEEKS ARE CHEAP...
70% OFF
50%
WOW!
BUCK-WHEAT FLOUR
THIS FLOUR IS HALF OFF TOO!
WE CAN HAVE SOME GOOD NOODLE SOUP THIS YEAR!
LET'S SEE. SHRIMP... MEAT...
RICE CAKES
HYO! (TOSS)
DOSA (THUD)
BEEF
FOR HEPHAISTOS
DOSA
RICE WINE... ABALONE... AND SOME CRAB...
AHH, THE HIERARCHY OF THE GODS...
KYURURU (SQUEAK)
GU (GROWL)
GU
GU
ALL RIGHT, ALL RIGHT! I'LL PAY FOR DINNER!!
JUST STOP LOOKING AT ME LIKE THAT!!

RELYING ON OTHERS FOR EVERYTHING.

NEW YEAR'S MEAL COMPLETE!!

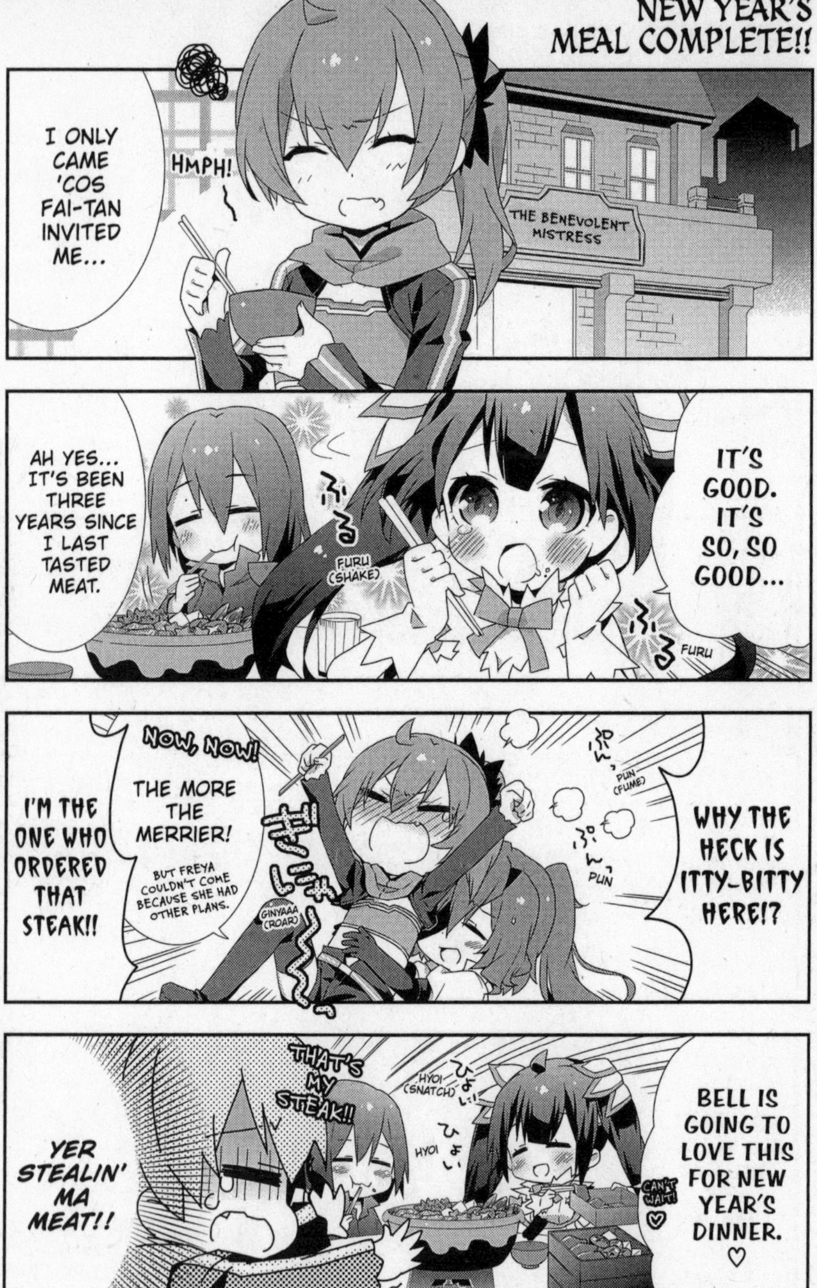
THE BENEVOLENT MISTRESS
HMPH!
I ONLY CAME 'COS FAI-TAN INVITED ME...
IT'S GOOD. IT'S SO, SO GOOD...
ふる
FURU
ふる
FURU (SHAKE)
AH YES... IT'S BEEN THREE YEARS SINCE I LAST TASTED MEAT.
WHY THE HECK IS ITTY-BITTY HERE!?
ぷん
PUN (FUME)
ぷん
PUN
NOW, NOW!
THE MORE THE MERRIER!
BUT FREYA COULDN'T COME BECAUSE SHE HAD OTHER PLANS.
GINYAAA (ROAR)
I'M THE ONE WHO ORDERED THAT STEAK!!
BELL IS GOING TO LOVE THIS FOR NEW YEAR'S DINNER. ♡
CAN'T WAIT! ♡
ひょい
HYOI (SNATCH)
ひょい
HYOI
THAT'S MY STEAK!!
YER STEALIN' MA MEAT!!

WHERE DID THOSE SPECIAL BOXES COME FROM? (PUZZLED)

FLUFFY?

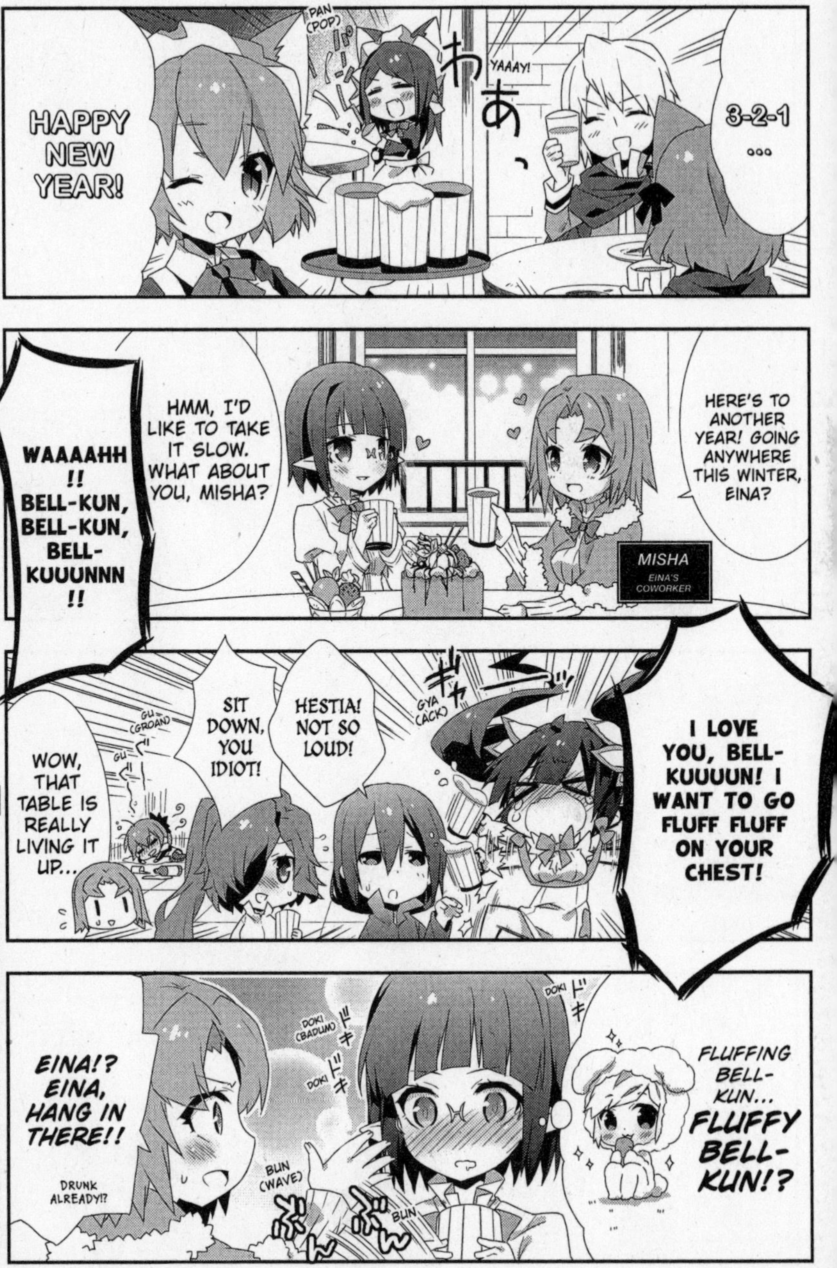

3-2-1 ...
YAAAY!
PAN (POP)
HAPPY NEW YEAR!
HERE'S TO ANOTHER YEAR! GOING ANYWHERE THIS WINTER, EINA?
MISHA
EINA'S COWORKER
HMM, I'D LIKE TO TAKE IT SLOW. WHAT ABOUT YOU, MISHA?
WAAAAHH!! BELL-KUN, BELL-KUN, BELL-KUUUNNN!!
I LOVE YOU, BELL-KUUUUN! I WANT TO GO FLUFF FLUFF ON YOUR CHEST!
GYA (ACK)
HESTIA! NOT SO LOUD!
SIT DOWN, YOU IDIOT!
GU (GROAN)
GU
WOW, THAT TABLE IS REALLY LIVING IT UP...
FLUFFING BELL-KUN... FLUFFY BELL-KUN!?
DOKI
DOKI (BADUM)
DOKI
BUN
BUN (WAVE)
EINA!? EINA, HANG IN THERE!!
DRUNK ALREADY!?

EPIC DESIRE FOR THAT FIGURE.

SYR WAS OFF TODAY.

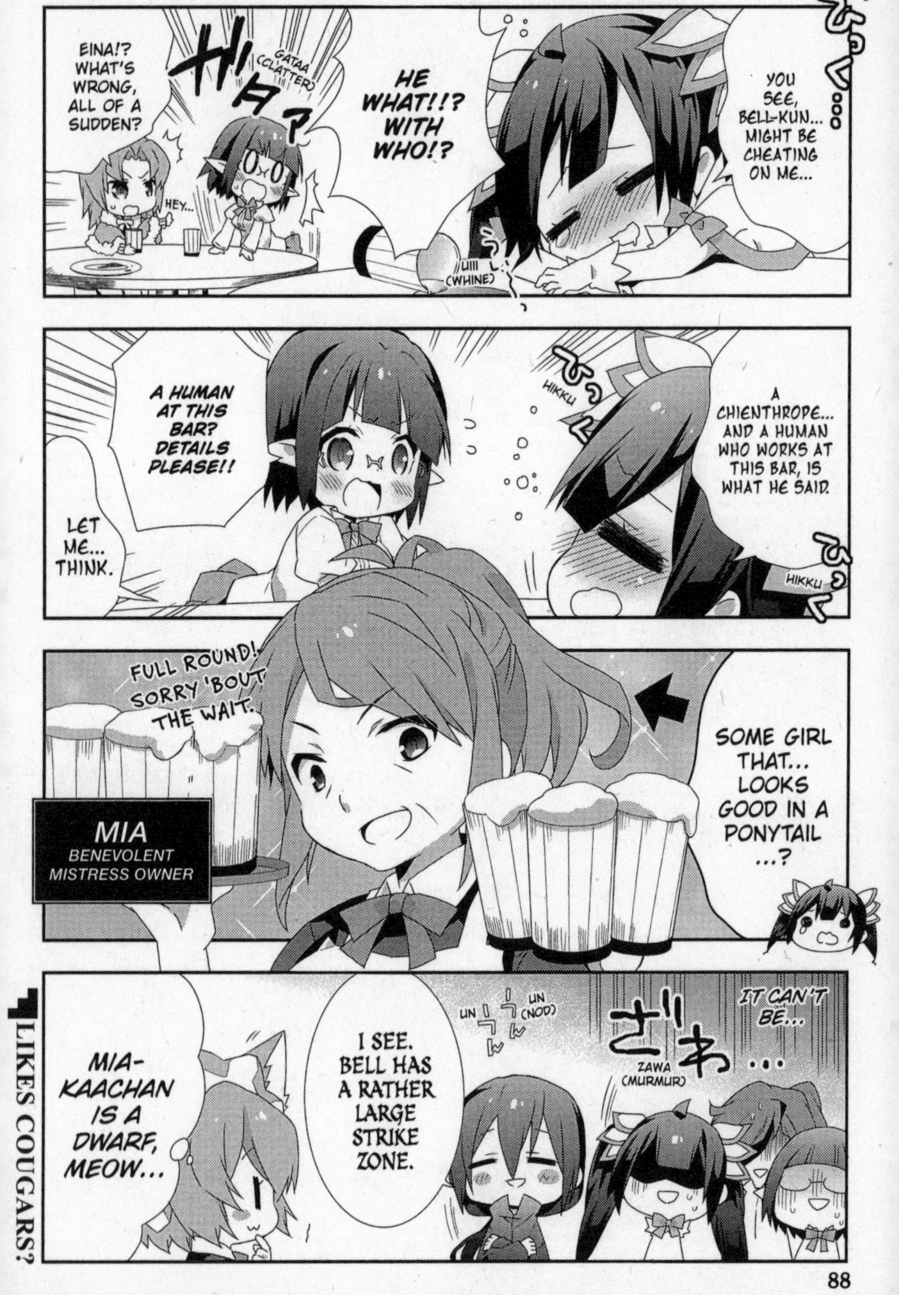
HIKKU (HICCUP)
YOU SEE, BELL-KUN... MIGHT BE CHEATING ON ME...
UIII (WHINE)
HE WHAT!!? WITH WHO!?
GATAA (CLATTER)
EINA!? WHAT'S WRONG, ALL OF A SUDDEN?
HEY...
HIKKU
A CHIENTHROPE... AND A HUMAN WHO WORKS AT THIS BAR, IS WHAT HE SAID.
A HUMAN AT THIS BAR? DETAILS PLEASE!!
LET ME... THINK.
HIKKU
SOME GIRL THAT... LOOKS GOOD IN A PONYTAIL ...?
FULL ROUND! SORRY 'BOUT THE WAIT.
MIA
BENEVOLENT MISTRESS OWNER
IT CAN'T BE...
ZAWA (MURMUR)
UN UN (NOD)
I SEE. BELL HAS A RATHER LARGE STRIKE ZONE.
MIA-KAACHAN IS A DWARF, MEOW...

LIKES COUGARS?

NEW YEAR'S DEPARTURE

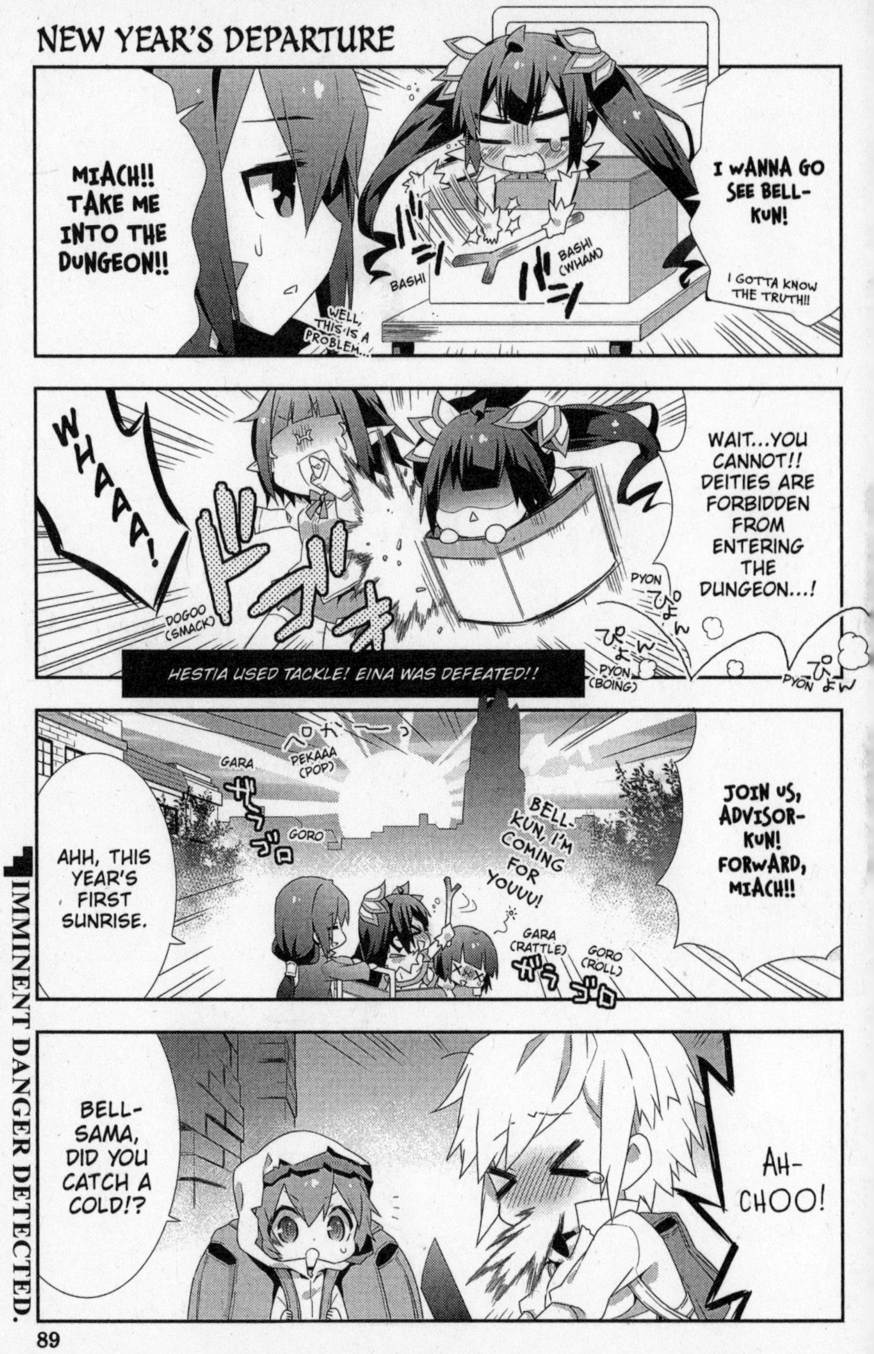
I WANNA GO SEE BELL-KUN!
I GOTTA KNOW THE TRUTH!!
BASHI (WHAM)
BASHI
MIACH!! TAKE ME INTO THE DUNGEON!!
WELL, THIS IS A PROBLEM...
WAIT...YOU CANNOT!! DEITIES ARE FORBIDDEN FROM ENTERING THE DUNGEON...!
PYON
PYON (BOING)
PYON
WHAAAA!
DOGOO (SMACK)
HESTIA USED TACKLE! EINA WAS DEFEATED!!
JOIN US, ADVISOR-KUN! FORWARD, MIACH!!
BELL-KUN, I'M COMING FOR YOUUU!
PEKAAA (POP)
GARA
GORO
GARA (RATTLE)
GORO (ROLL)
AHH, THIS YEAR'S FIRST SUNRISE.
AH-CHOO!
BELL-SAMA, DID YOU CATCH A COLD!?

IMMINENT DANGER DETECTED.

AFTER THE PARTY♡

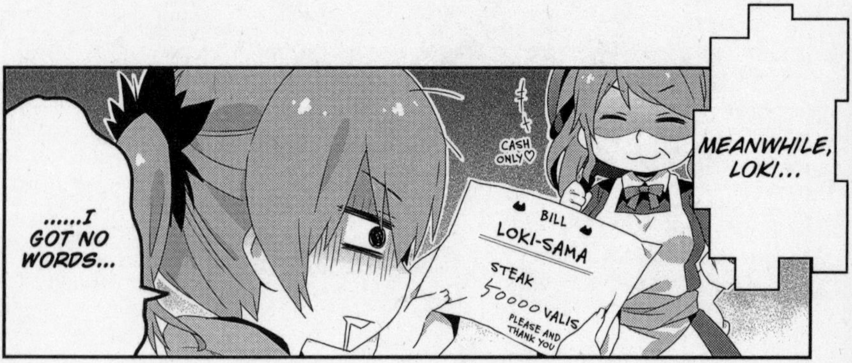
MEANWHILE, LOKI...
CASH ONLY♡
BILL
LOKI-SAMA
STEAK 50000 VALIS
PLEASE AND THANK YOU
......I GOT NO WORDS...

THANKS FOR THE FOOD.

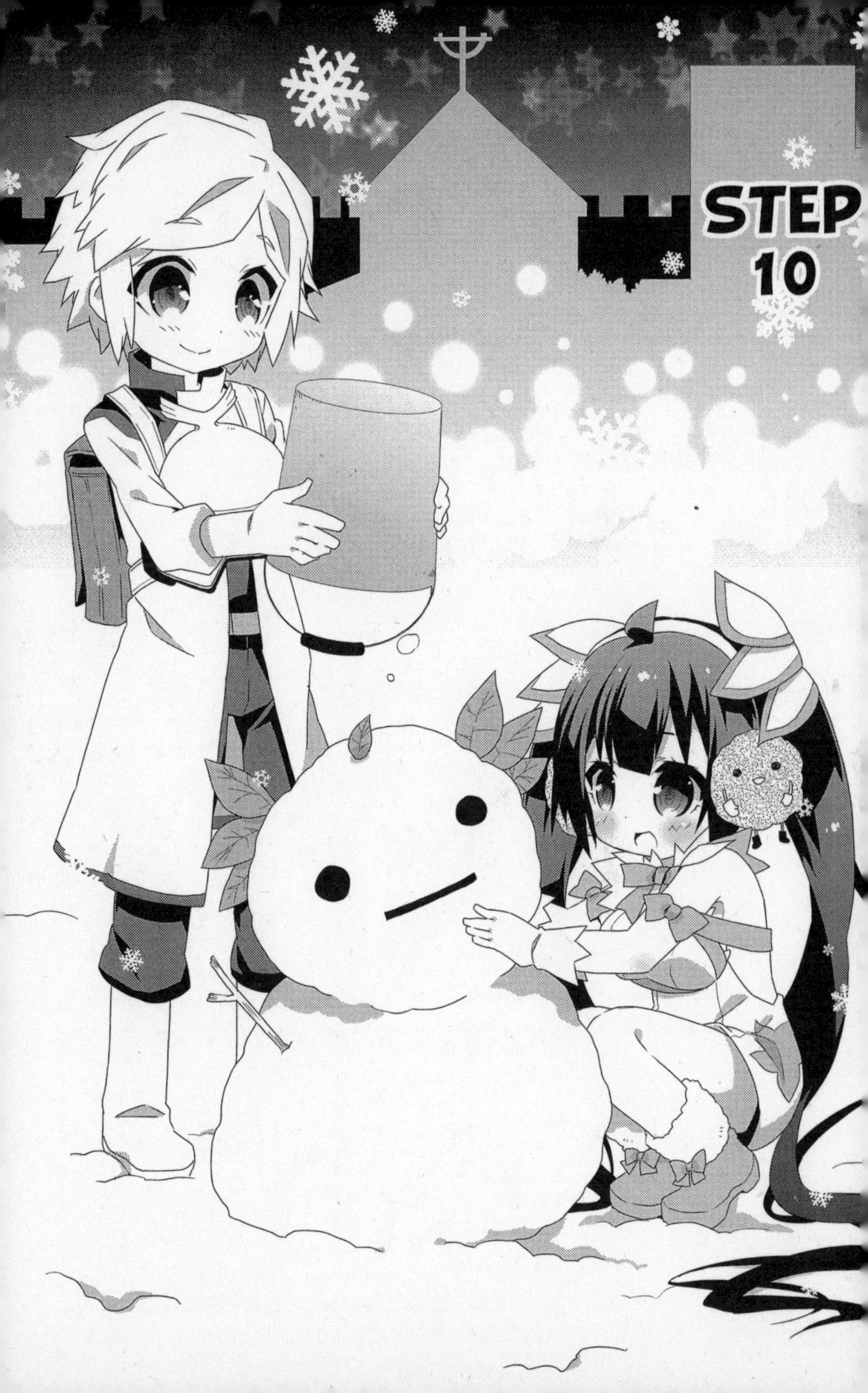
STEP 10

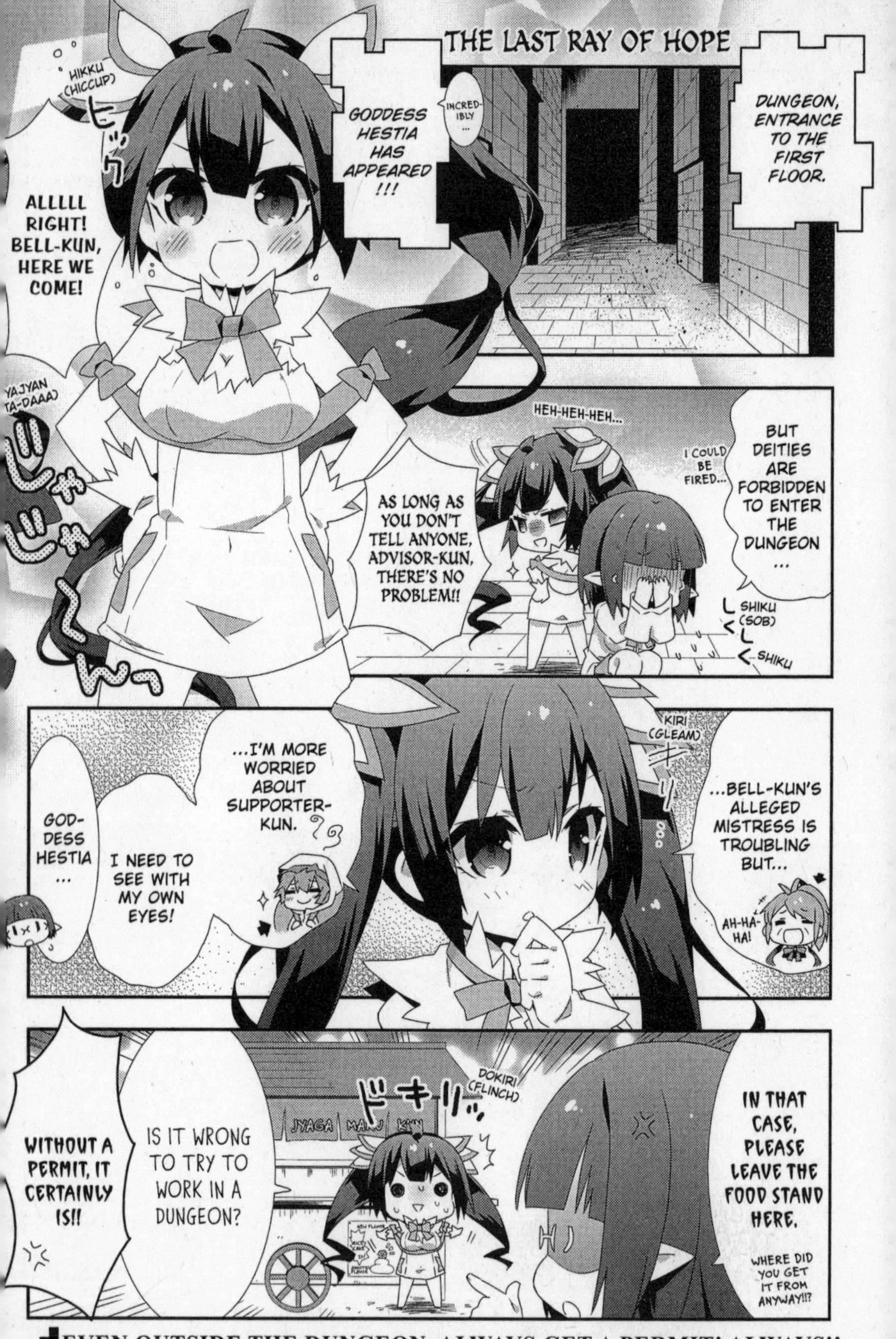
THE LAST RAY OF HOPE
DUNGEON, ENTRANCE TO THE FIRST FLOOR.
INCRED-IBLY...
GODDESS HESTIA HAS APPEARED!!!
HIKKU (HICCUP)
ALLLLL RIGHT! BELL-KUN, HERE WE COME!
JAJYAN (TA-DAAA)
BUT DEITIES ARE FORBIDDEN TO ENTER THE DUNGEON...
I COULD BE FIRED...
HEH-HEH-HEH...
AS LONG AS YOU DON'T TELL ANYONE, ADVISOR-KUN, THERE'S NO PROBLEM!!
SHIKU (SOB)
SHIKU
KIRI (GLEAM)
...BELL-KUN'S ALLEGED MISTRESS IS TROUBLING BUT...
AH-HA-HA!
...I'M MORE WORRIED ABOUT SUPPORTER-KUN.
I NEED TO SEE WITH MY OWN EYES!
GOD-DESS HESTIA...
IN THAT CASE, PLEASE LEAVE THE FOOD STAND HERE.
WHERE DID YOU GET IT FROM ANYWAY!!?
DOKIRI (FLINCH)
JYAGA MARU KUN
IS IT WRONG TO TRY TO WORK IN A DUNGEON?
WITHOUT A PERMIT, IT CERTAINLY IS!!

EVEN OUTSIDE THE DUNGEON, ALWAYS GET A PERMIT! ALWAYS!!

WHO'S THE GUARD?

WOULDN'T IT BE BETTER TO RETURN TO THE SURFACE...?

THE DUNGEON SURE IS A DARK AND GLOOMY PLACE.

ヒタ HITA

ヒタ HITA (STEP)

ヒタ HITA

ヒタ HITA

I'M ALL SOBERED UP...

...INDEED.

コクリ KOKURI (NOD)

MIACH! WE'RE COUNTING ON YOU IF SOMETHING HAPPENS!

OH, GOD MIACH.

I FORGOT YOU WERE WITH US...

IF SOMETHING HAPPENS TO YOU TWO, IT'LL ALSO HAPPEN TO ME, I THINK.

NIKO (SMILE)

HOP TO IT, ADVISOR-KUN.

NOOOOOO!

NOW, LET'S HURRY UP AND FIND BELL!

ザ ZA (RUN)

ザ ZA

ザ ZA

ブル BURU (TREMBLE)

ブル BURU

テ TE (TROT)

テ TE

テ TE

HESTIA	EINA	MIACH
H:15	H:20	H:30
M:15	M:90	M:80
DEITY: LV 1	GUIDE: LV 2	DEITY: LV 1

MIACH'S WEAPON (LEEK): 98 YEN.

PARTY UNITY

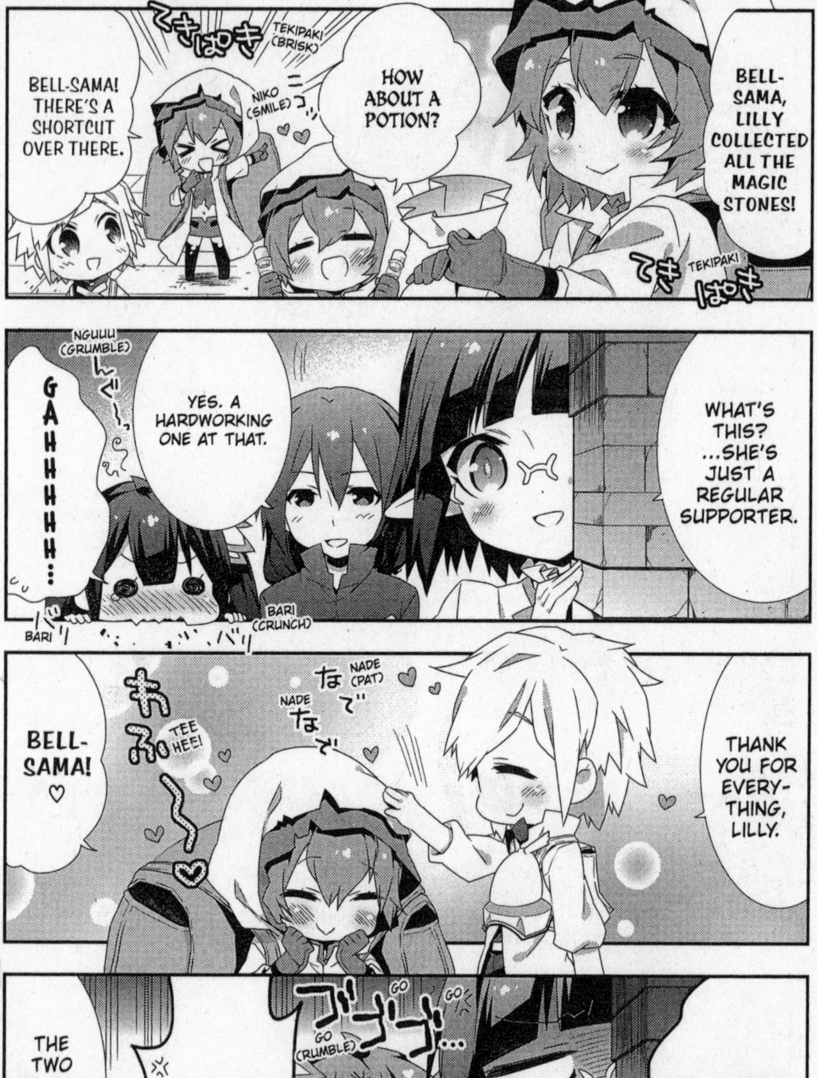
BELL-SAMA, LILLY COLLECTED ALL THE MAGIC STONES!
てきぱき
TEKIPAKI
HOW ABOUT A POTION?
ニコッ
NIKO (SMILE)
てきぱき
TEKIPAKI (BRISK)
BELL-SAMA! THERE'S A SHORTCUT OVER THERE.
WHAT'S THIS? ...SHE'S JUST A REGULAR SUPPORTER.
YES. A HARDWORKING ONE AT THAT.
BARI (CRUNCH)
NGUUU (GRUMBLE)
GAHHHHHH...
BARI
THANK YOU FOR EVERYTHING, LILLY.
なで
NADE (PAT)
なで
NADE
TEE HEE!
BELL-SAMA! ♡
YES, THERE IS SOMETHING STRANGE HERE, GODDESS HESTIA!!
ビキッ
BIKI (CRACK)
ゴゴゴ...
GO
GO
GO (RUMBLE)
SO, YOU SEE IT TOO, ADVISOR-KUN!!
HA HA HA.
THE TWO OF YOU ARE FAR STRANGER.

FIERY SOLIDARITY.

FIRST BATTLE?

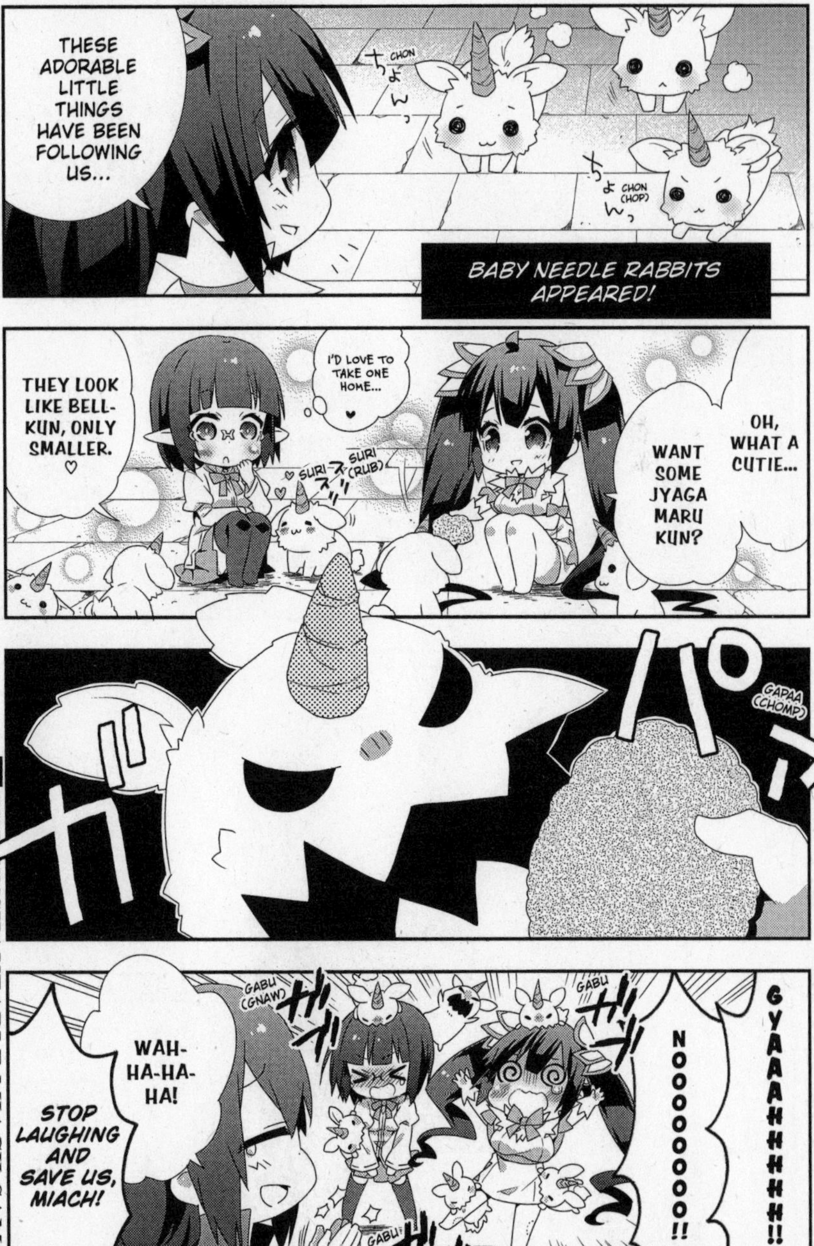

ちょんっ CHON (HOP)
ちょんっ CHON
THESE ADORABLE LITTLE THINGS HAVE BEEN FOLLOWING US...
BABY NEEDLE RABBITS APPEARED!
OH, WHAT A CUTIE...
WANT SOME JYAGA MARU KUN?
I'D LOVE TO TAKE ONE HOME... ♥
SURI SURI (RUB)
THEY LOOK LIKE BELL-KUN, ONLY SMALLER. ♡
GAPAA (CHOMP)
GYAAAHHHHH!!
NOOOOOOOO!!
GABU
GABU (GNAW)
WAH-HA-HA-HA!
STOP LAUGHING AND SAVE US, MIACH!
GABU

SUGGESTED JOB CHANGE?

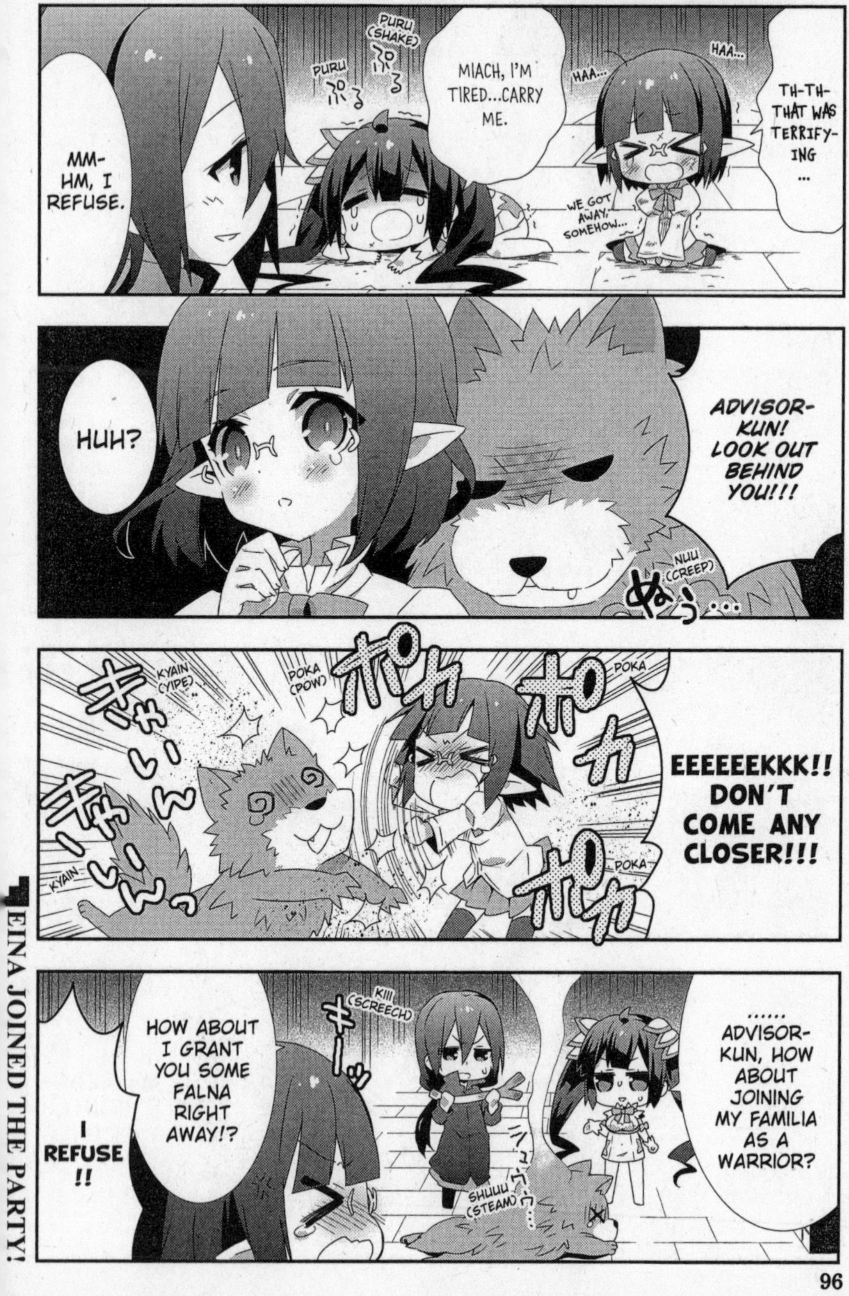
HAA...
HAA...
TH-TH-THAT WAS TERRIFYING...
WE GOT AWAY, SOMEHOW...
MIACH, I'M TIRED...CARRY ME.
PURU (SHAKE)
PURU
MM-HM, I REFUSE.
ADVISOR-KUN! LOOK OUT BEHIND YOU!!!
HUH?
NUU (CREEP)
EEEEEEKKK!! DON'T COME ANY CLOSER!!!
POKA
POKA
POKA (POW)
KYAIN (YIPE)
KYAIN
......ADVISOR-KUN, HOW ABOUT JOINING MY FAMILIA AS A WARRIOR?
SHUUU (STEAM)
KIII (SCREECH)
HOW ABOUT I GRANT YOU SOME FALNA RIGHT AWAY!?
I REFUSE!!

EINA JOINED THE PARTY!

DISPLAYING HER TRUE POWER

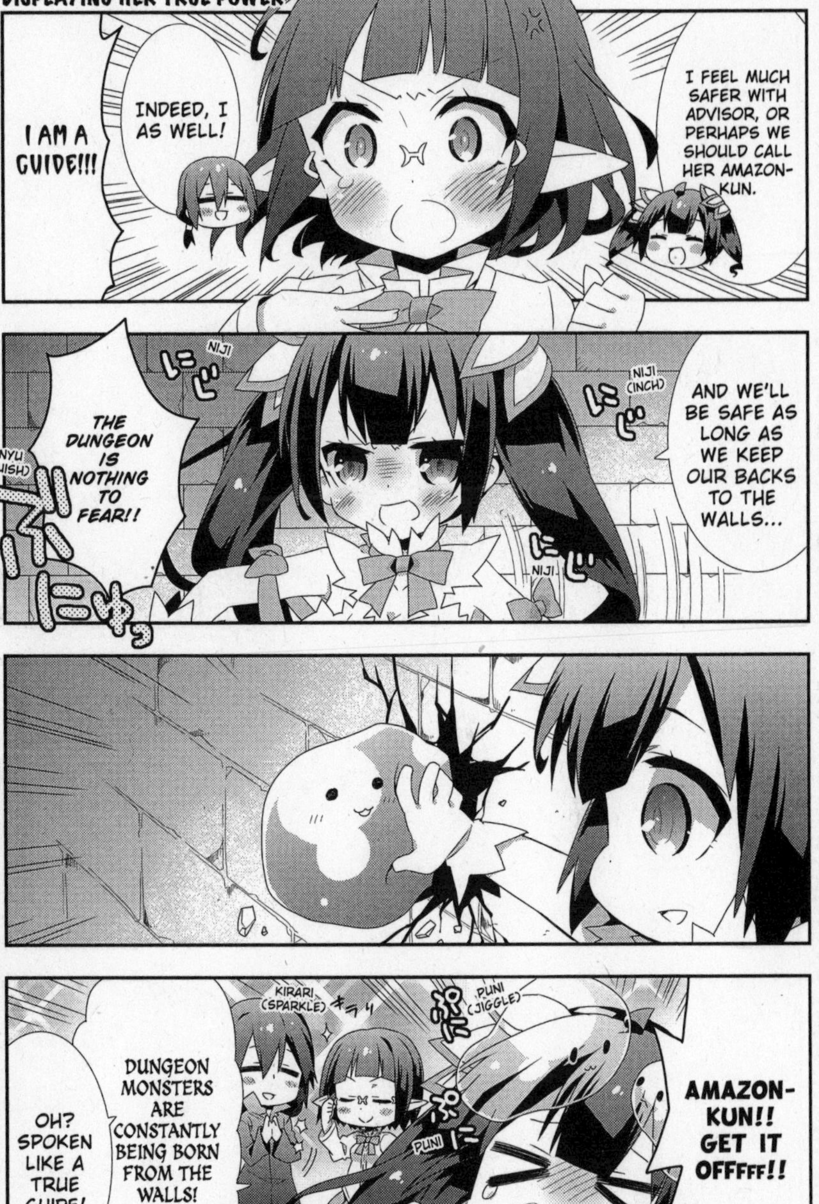
I FEEL MUCH SAFER WITH ADVISOR, OR PERHAPS WE SHOULD CALL HER AMAZON-KUN.
INDEED, I AS WELL!
I AM A GUIDE!!!
にじ NIJI
AND WE'LL BE SAFE AS LONG AS WE KEEP OUR BACKS TO THE WALLS...
にじ NIJI (INCH)
にじ NIJI
THE DUNGEON IS NOTHING TO FEAR!!
ぶにゅっ BUNYU (SQUISH)
AMAZON-KUN!! GET IT OFFFFFF!!
ぷに PUNI (JIGGLE)
ぷに PUNI
キラリ KIRARI (SPARKLE)
DUNGEON MONSTERS ARE CONSTANTLY BEING BORN FROM THE WALLS!
OH? SPOKEN LIKE A TRUE GUIDE!

THIS CREATURE IS QUITE STICKY.

THE LAST RAY OF HOPE

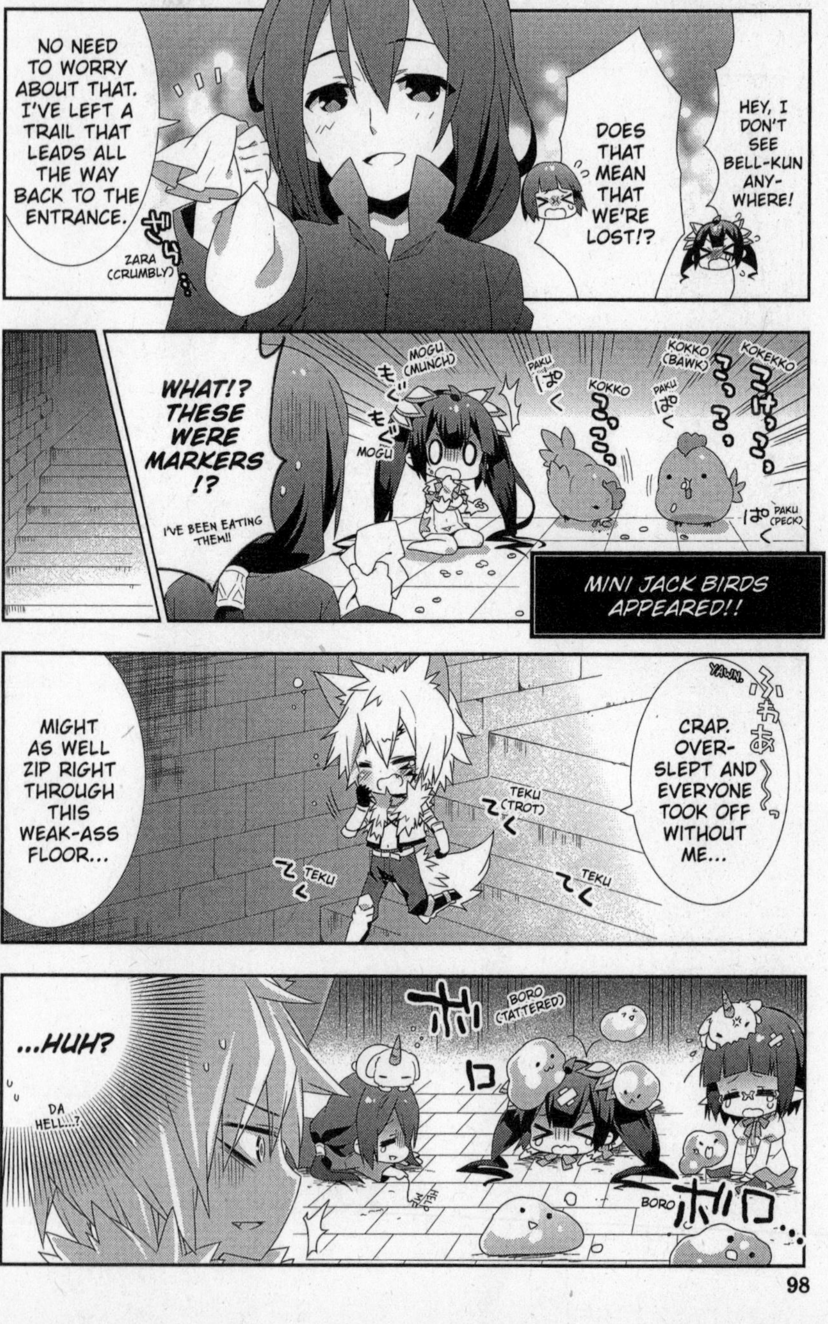
HEY, I DON'T SEE BELL-KUN ANYWHERE!
DOES THAT MEAN THAT WE'RE LOST!?
NO NEED TO WORRY ABOUT THAT. I'VE LEFT A TRAIL THAT LEADS ALL THE WAY BACK TO THE ENTRANCE.
ZARA (CRUMBLY)
KOKEKKO
KOKKO (BAWK)
PAKU (PECK)
PAKU
KOKKO
PAKU
MOGU (MUNCH)
MOGU
WHAT!? THESE WERE MARKERS!?
I'VE BEEN EATING THEM!!
MINI JACK BIRDS APPEARED!!
YAWN.
CRAP. OVER-SLEPT AND EVERYONE TOOK OFF WITHOUT ME...
TEKU (TROT)
TEKU
TEKU
MIGHT AS WELL ZIP RIGHT THROUGH THIS WEAK-ASS FLOOR...
BORO (TATTERED)
BORO
HELP ME
...HUH?
DA HELL...?

DOWN THE STAIRS AND STRAIGHT INTO A CATASTROPHE.

CANINE SAVIOR

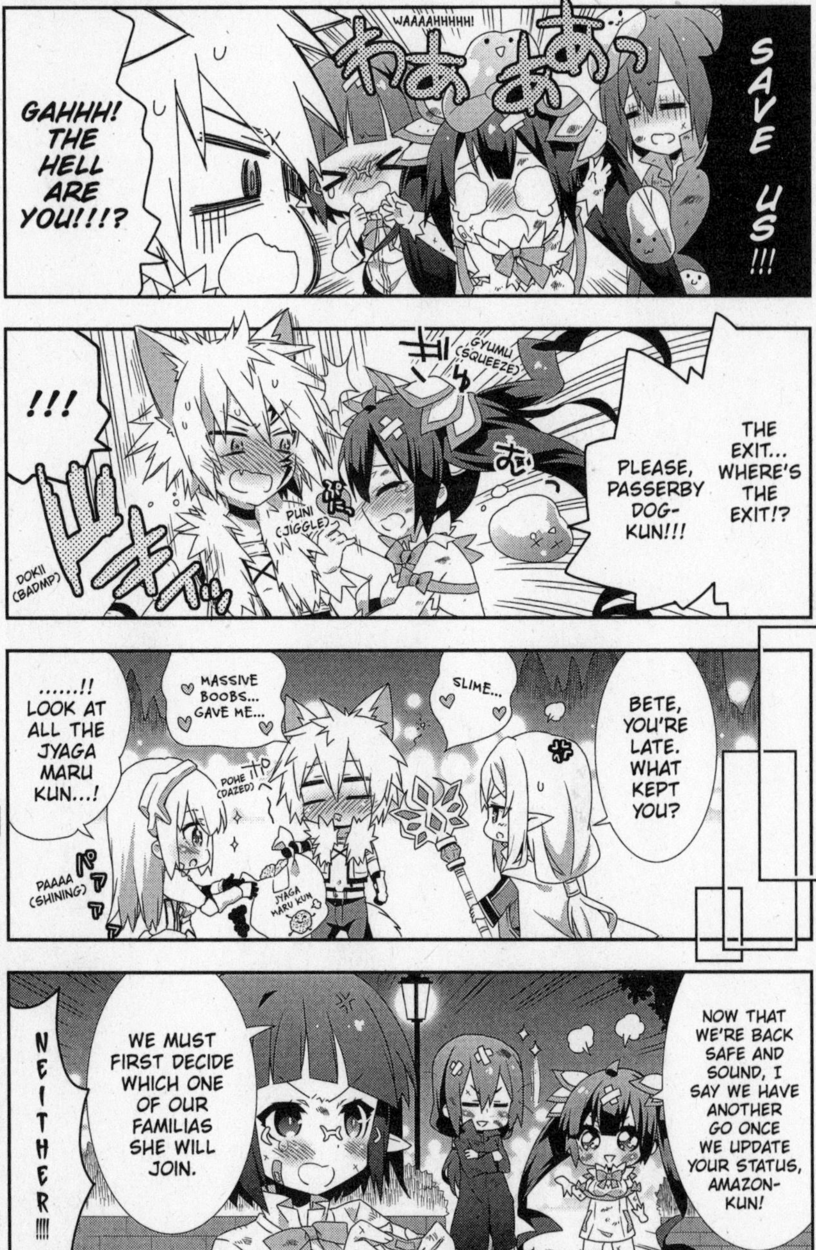
SAVE US!!!
わあああっ
WAAAAHHHHH!
GAHHH! THE HELL ARE YOU!!!?
THE EXIT... WHERE'S THE EXIT!?
PLEASE, PASSERBY DOG-KUN!!!
GYUMU (SQUEEZE)
PUNI (JIGGLE)
!!!
DOKII (BADMP)
BETE, YOU'RE LATE. WHAT KEPT YOU?
SLIME...
MASSIVE BOOBS... GAVE ME...
POHE (DAZED)
......!! LOOK AT ALL THE JYAGA MARU KUN...!
PAAAA (SHINING)
JYAGA MARU KUN
NOW THAT WE'RE BACK SAFE AND SOUND, I SAY WE HAVE ANOTHER GO ONCE WE UPDATE YOUR STATUS, AMAZON-KUN!
WE MUST FIRST DECIDE WHICH ONE OF OUR FAMILIAS SHE WILL JOIN.
NEITHER!!!!

WHY DO THEY NEVER LEARN?

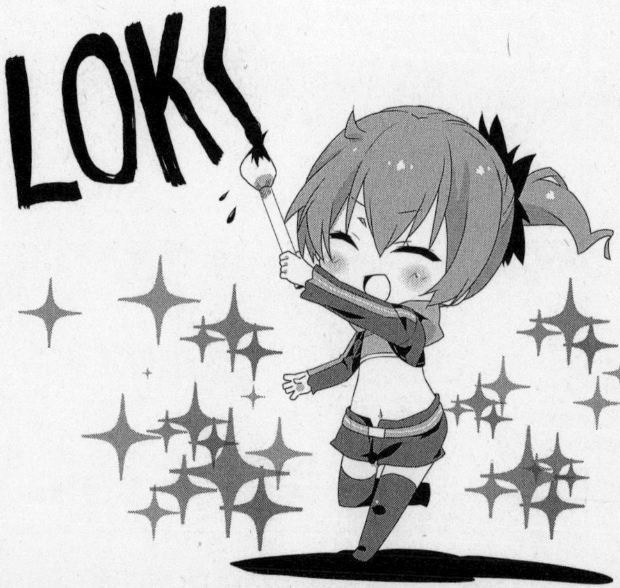
LOKI

SPECIAL STEP
<LOKI'S DAYS>

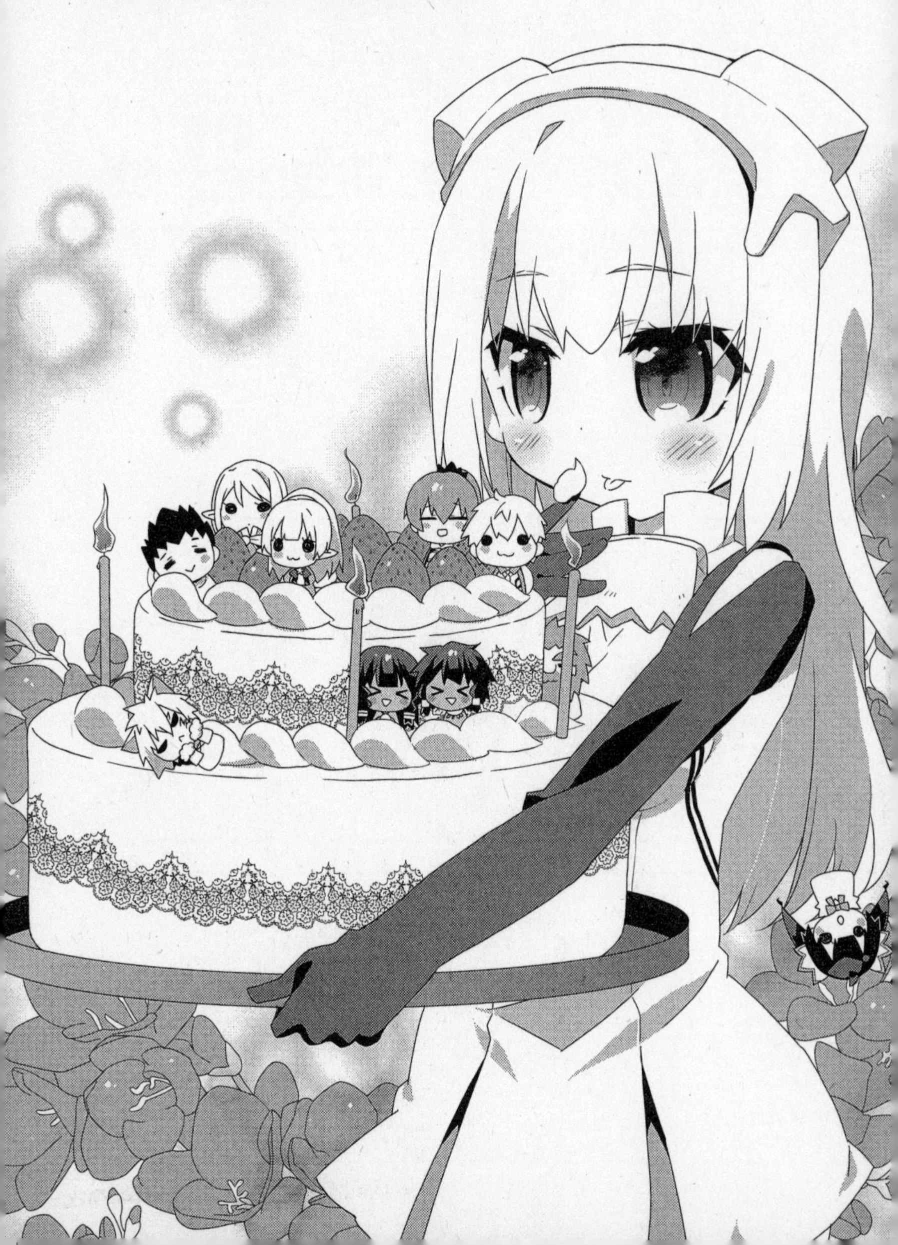

LOKI'S AMBITION

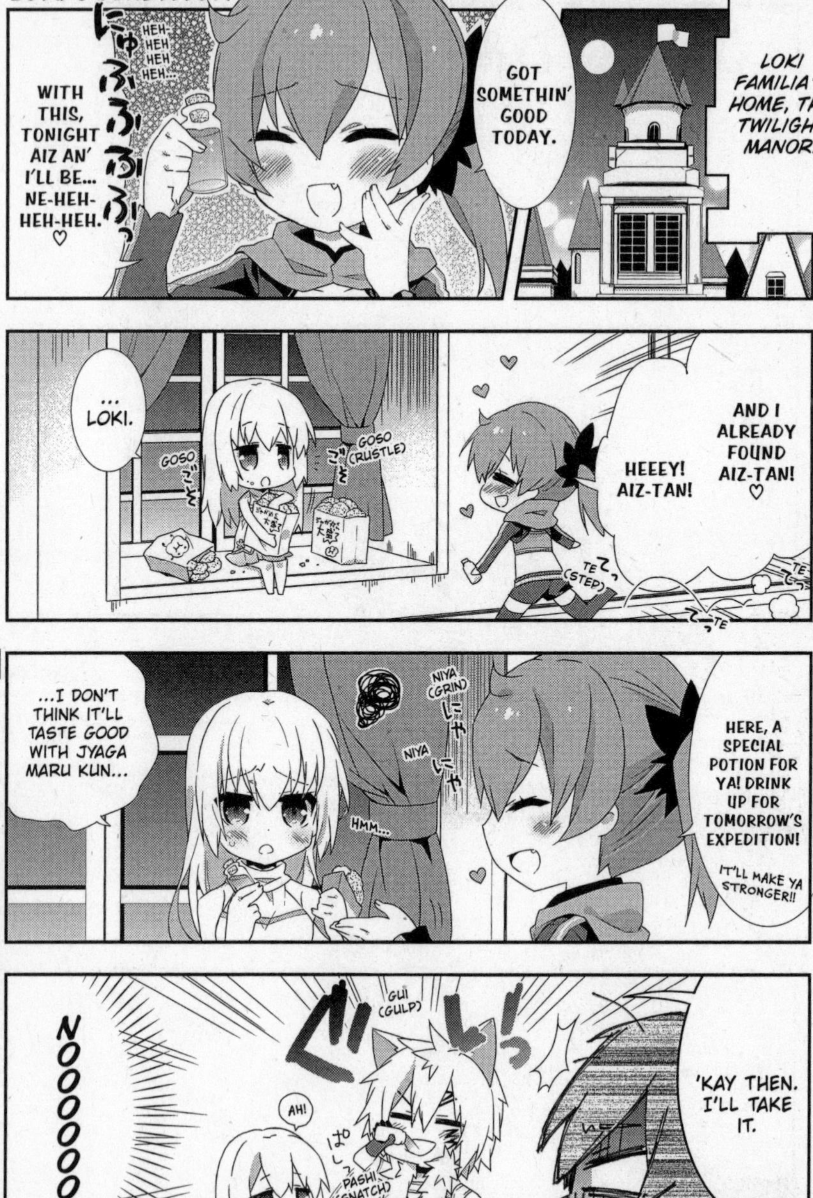

LOKI FAMILIA'S HOME, THE TWILIGHT MANOR.
GOT SOMETHIN' GOOD TODAY.
HEH-HEH HEH HEH...
WITH THIS, TONIGHT AIZ AN' I'LL BE... NE-HEH-HEH-HEH. ♡
AND I ALREADY FOUND AIZ-TAN! ♡
HEEEY! AIZ-TAN!
TE
TE (STEP)
TE
GOSO (CRUSTLE)
GOSO
... LOKI.
HERE, A SPECIAL POTION FOR YA! DRINK UP FOR TOMORROW'S EXPEDITION!
IT'LL MAKE YA STRONGER!!
NIYA (GRIN)
NIYA
HMM...
...I DON'T THINK IT'LL TASTE GOOD WITH JYAGA MARU KUN...
'KAY THEN. I'LL TAKE IT.
GUI (GULP)
AH!
PASHI (SNATCH)
NOOOOOOO!

AMBITION, CRUSHED IN THREE SECONDS.

IT STARTS KICKING IN ♡

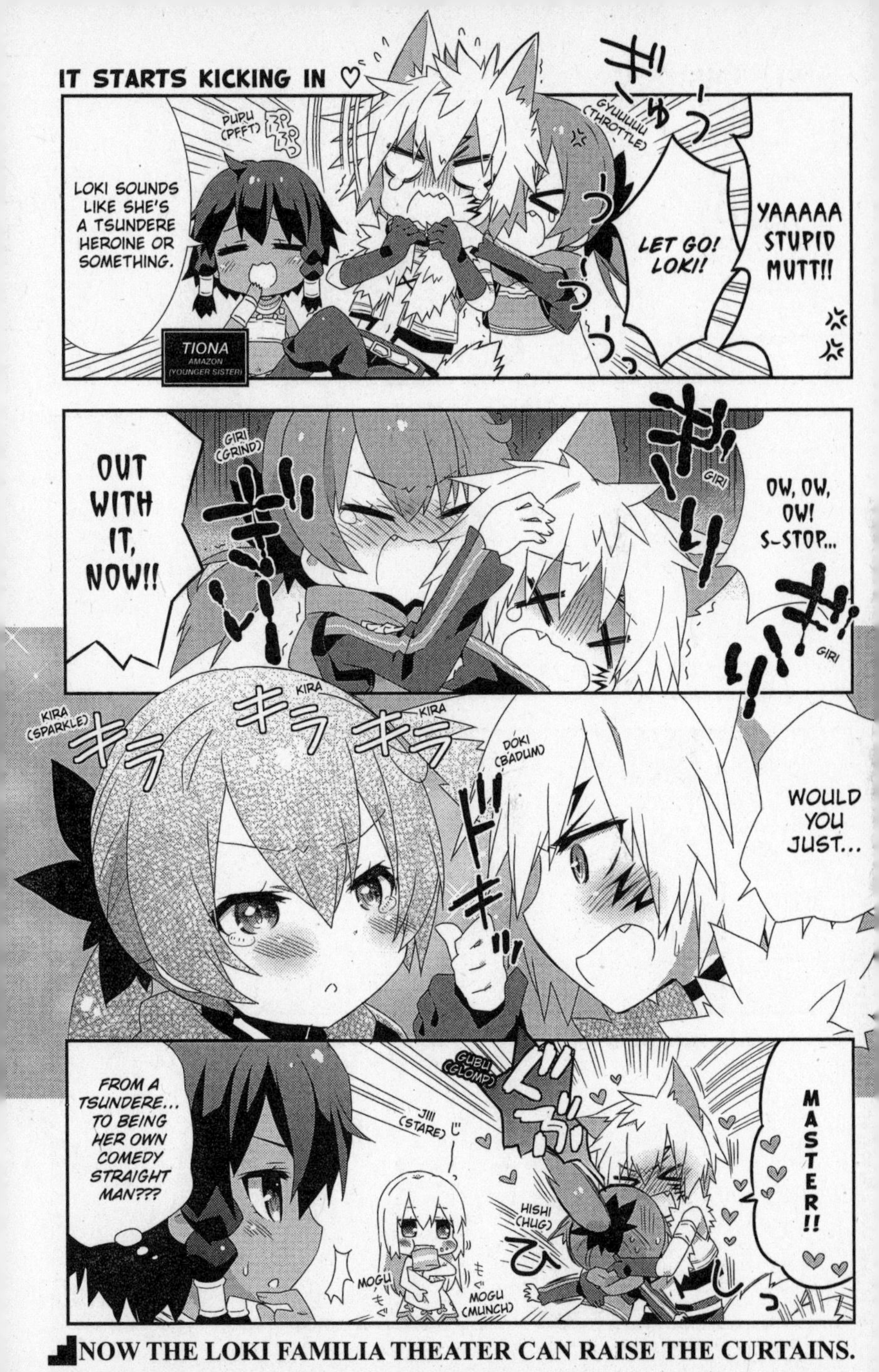
GYUUUUU (THROTTLE)
YAAAAA STUPID MUTT!!
LET GO! LOKI!
PUPU (PFFT)
LOKI SOUNDS LIKE SHE'S A TSUNDERE HEROINE OR SOMETHING.
TIONA
AMAZON
(YOUNGER SISTER)
GIRI
OW, OW, OW! S-STOP...
GIRI
GIRI (GRIND)
OUT WITH IT, NOW!!
WOULD YOU JUST...
DOKI (BADUM)
KIRA
KIRA
KIRA (SPARKLE)
キラ キラ キラ
MASTER!!
GUBU (GLOMP)
HISHI (HUG)
JIII (STARE)
FROM A TSUNDERE... TO BEING HER OWN COMEDY STRAIGHT MAN???
MOGU
MOGU (MUNCH)

NOW THE LOKI FAMILIA THEATER CAN RAISE THE CURTAINS.

LOKI'S PREDICAMENT

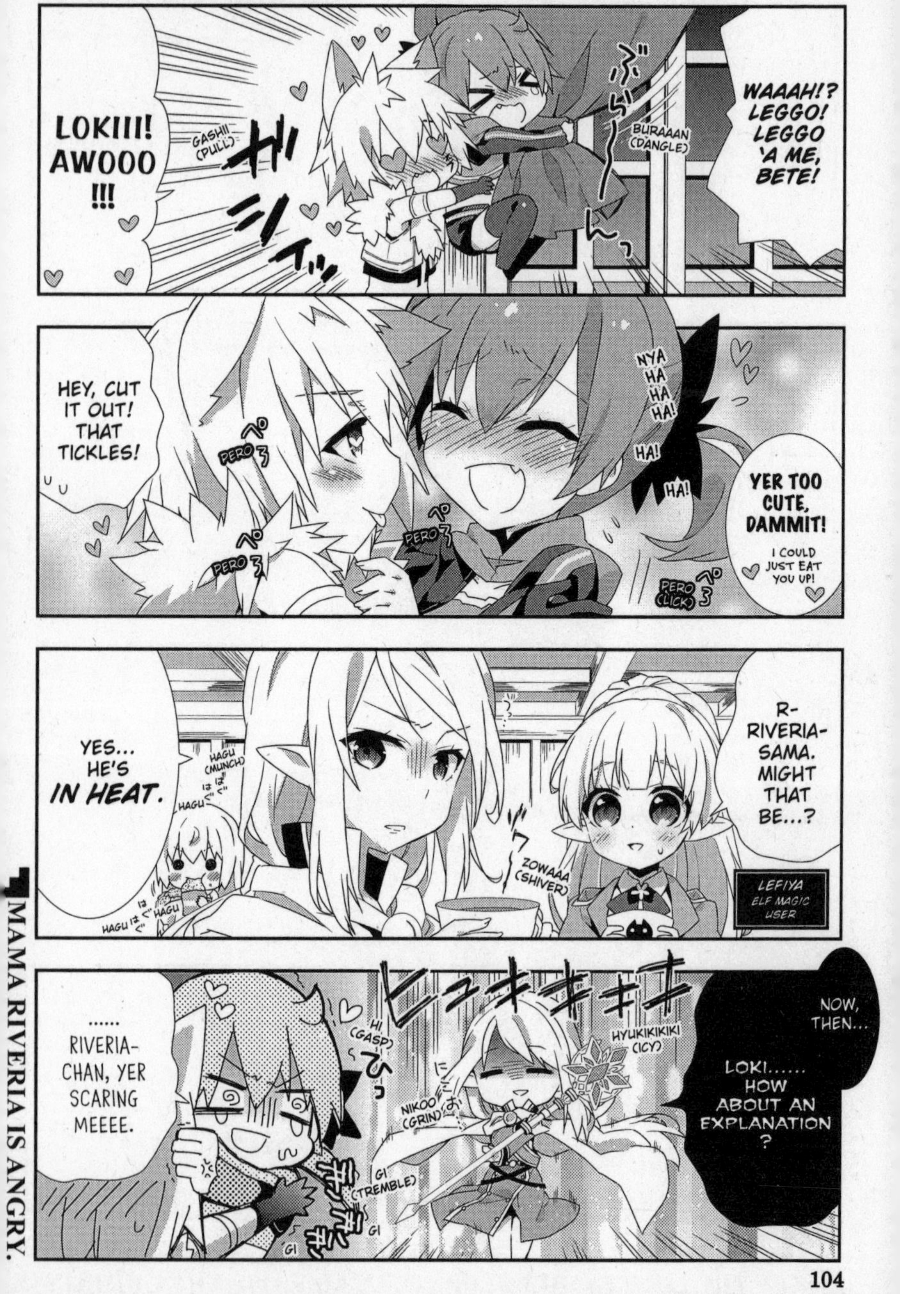

WAAAH!? LEGGO! LEGGO 'A ME, BETE!
BURAAAN (DANGLE)
GASHI!! (PULL)
LOKIII! AWOOO !!!
YER TOO CUTE, DAMMIT!
I COULD JUST EAT YOU UP!
PERO (LICK)
NYA HA HA HA! HA! HA!
PERO
PERO
PERO
HEY, CUT IT OUT! THAT TICKLES!
R-RIVERIA-SAMA. MIGHT THAT BE...?
LEFIYA ELF MAGIC USER
ZOWAAA (SHIVER)
YES... HE'S *IN HEAT*.
HAGU (MUNCH)
HAGU
HAGU
HAGU
NOW, THEN...
LOKI...... HOW ABOUT AN EXPLANATION?
HYUKIKIKIKI (ICY)
NIKOO (GRIN)
HI (GASP)
GI (TREMBLE)
GI
GI
...... RIVERIA-CHAN, YER SCARING MEEEE.

MAMA RIVERIA IS ANGRY.

FLIRTING?

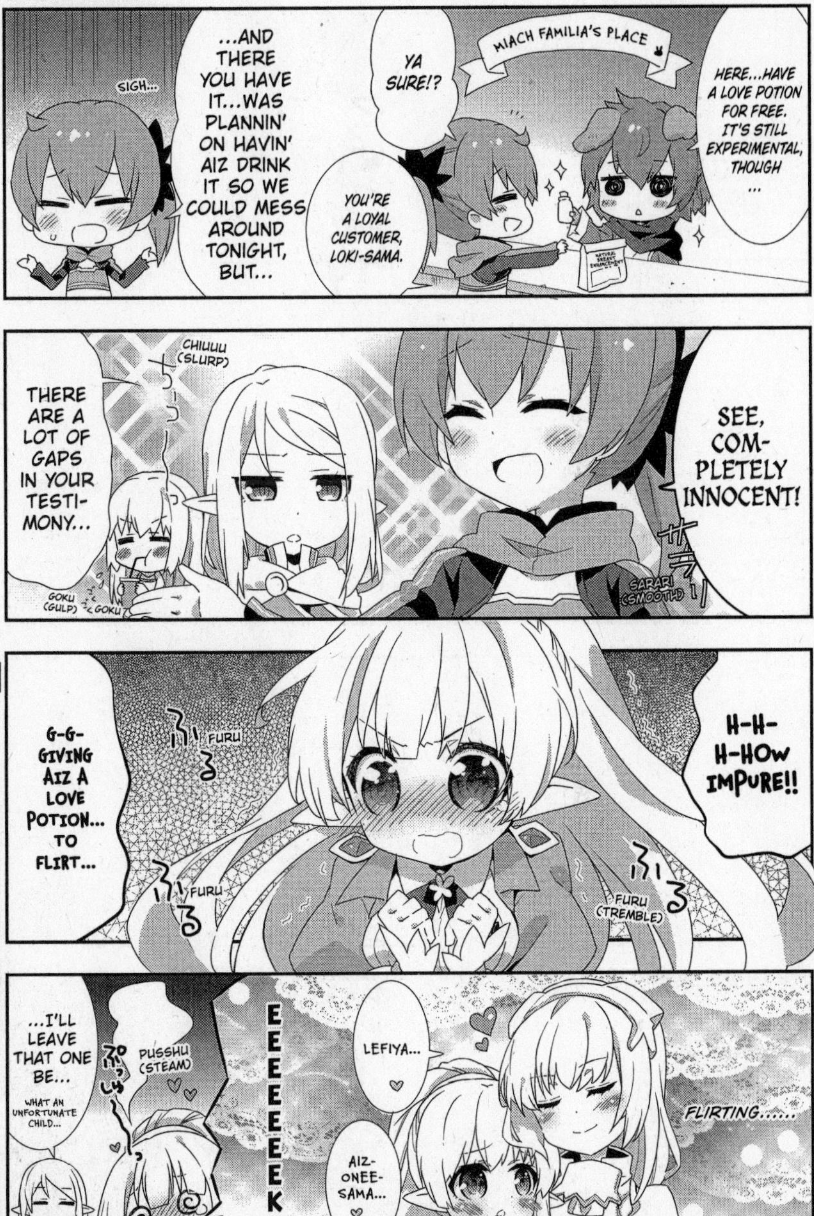

HERE...HAVE A LOVE POTION FOR FREE. IT'S STILL EXPERIMENTAL, THOUGH ...
MIACH FAMILIA'S PLACE
YA SURE!?
YOU'RE A LOYAL CUSTOMER, LOKI-SAMA.
NATURAL BREAST ENHANCEMENT
...AND THERE YOU HAVE IT...WAS PLANNIN' ON HAVIN' AIZ DRINK IT SO WE COULD MESS AROUND TONIGHT, BUT...
SIGH...
SEE, COMPLETELY INNOCENT!
SARARI (SMOOTH)
CHIUUU (SLURP)
THERE ARE A LOT OF GAPS IN YOUR TESTIMONY...
GOKU (GULP) GOKU
H-H-H-HOW IMPURE!!
FURU (TREMBLE)
FURU
G-G-GIVING AIZ A LOVE POTION... TO FLIRT...
FURU
FLIRTING......
LEFIYA...
AIZ-ONEE-SAMA...
EEEEEEEEEK!
PUSSHU (STEAM)
...I'LL LEAVE THAT ONE BE...
WHAT AN UNFORTUNATE CHILD...

OLDER SISTER SUSPICIONS, ON THE RISE.

THE KABE-DON EFFECT

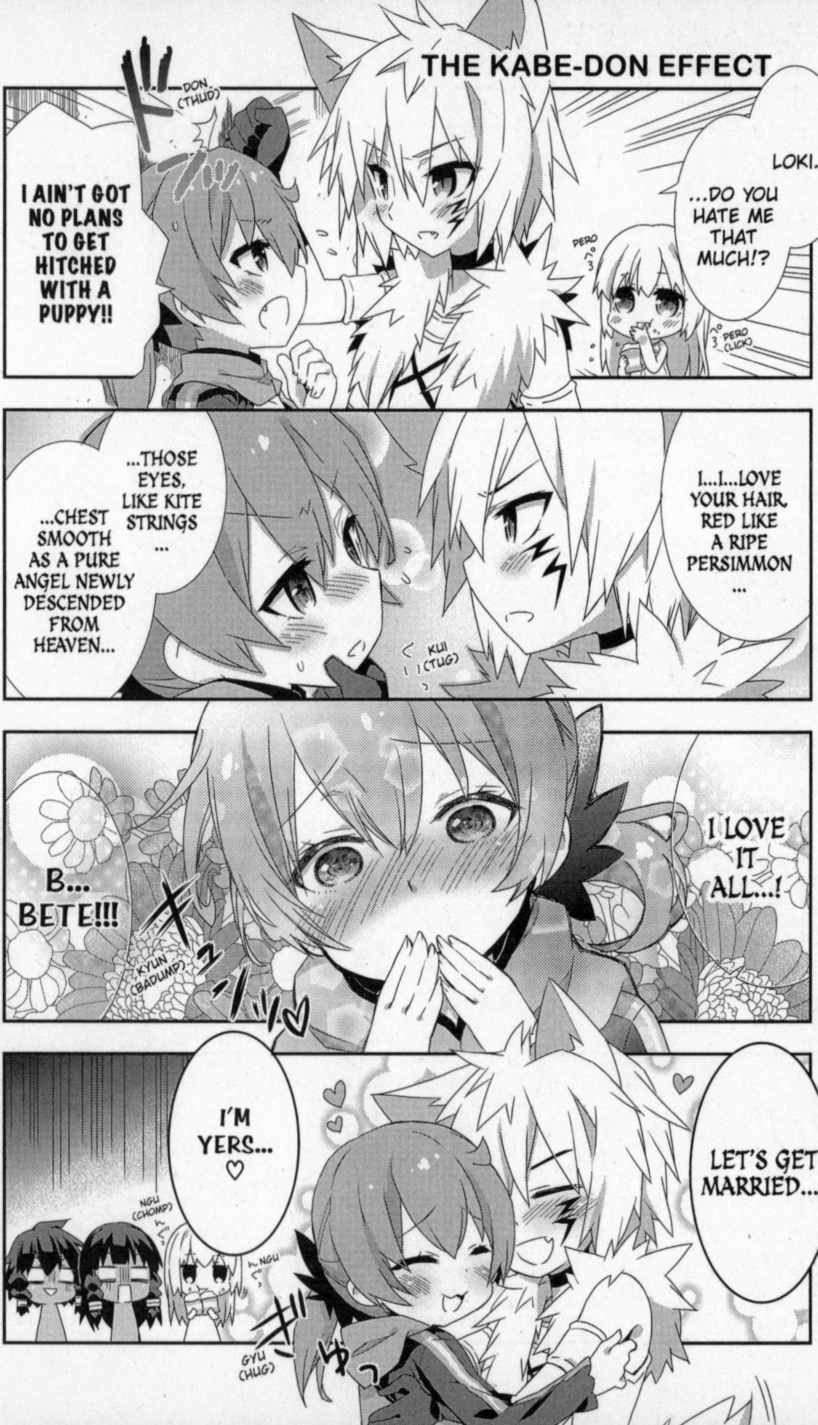
LOKI...
...DO YOU HATE ME THAT MUCH!?
PERO
PERO (CLICK)
DON (THUD)
I AIN'T GOT NO PLANS TO GET HITCHED WITH A PUPPY!!
I...I...LOVE YOUR HAIR, RED LIKE A RIPE PERSIMMON ...
KUI (TUG)
...THOSE EYES, LIKE KITE STRINGS ...
...CHEST SMOOTH AS A PURE ANGEL NEWLY DESCENDED FROM HEAVEN...
I LOVE IT ALL...!
B... BETE!!!
KYUN (BADUMP)
LET'S GET MARRIED...
I'M YERS... ♡
NGU
NGU (CHOMP)
GYU (HUG)

THE PICKUP LINE SOUNDED MEAN.

BECAUSE HE'S A WEREWOLF

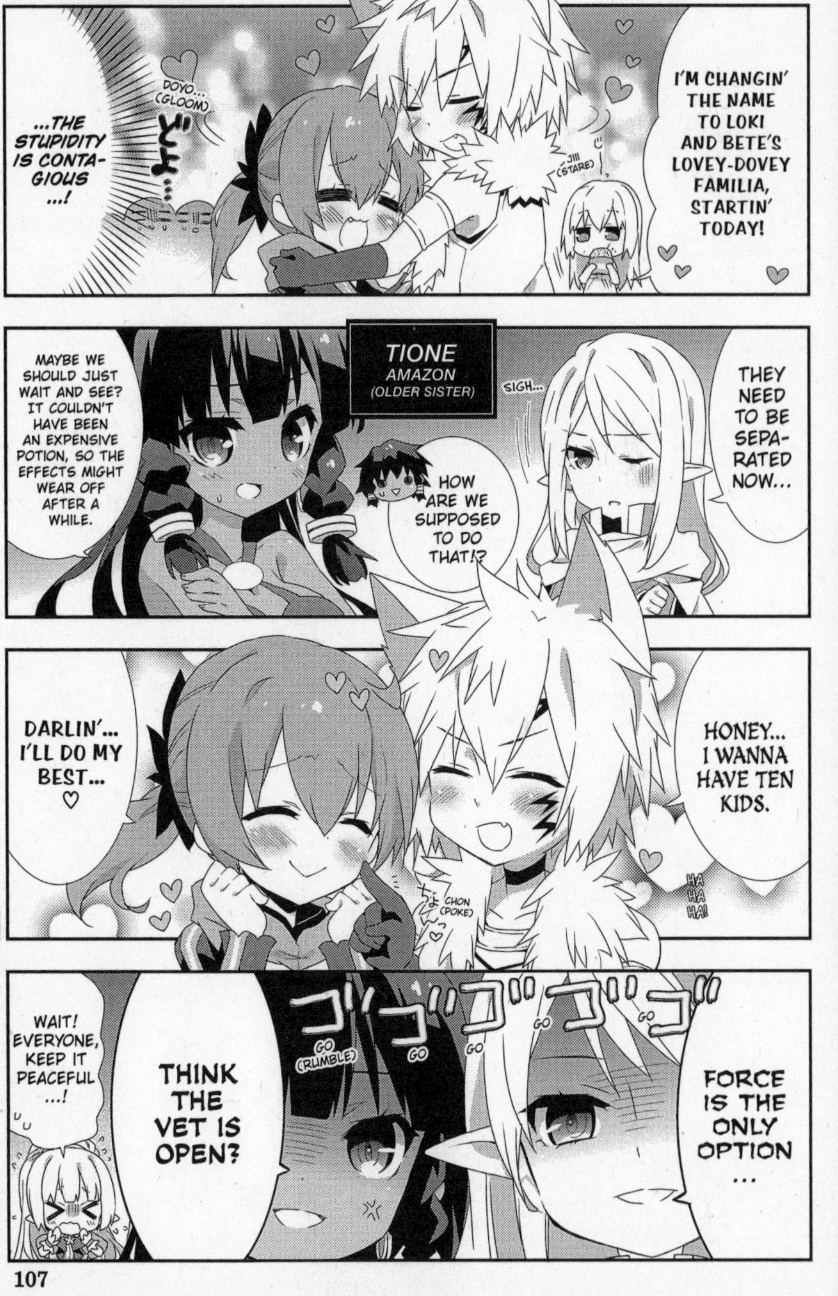
I'M CHANGIN' THE NAME TO LOKI AND BETE'S LOVEY-DOVEY FAMILIA, STARTIN' TODAY!
JIII (STARE)
DOYO... (GLOOM)
...THE STUPIDITY IS CONTAGIOUS ...!
THEY NEED TO BE SEPARATED NOW...
SIGH...
TIONE
AMAZON
(OLDER SISTER)
HOW ARE WE SUPPOSED TO DO THAT!?
MAYBE WE SHOULD JUST WAIT AND SEE? IT COULDN'T HAVE BEEN AN EXPENSIVE POTION, SO THE EFFECTS MIGHT WEAR OFF AFTER A WHILE.
HONEY... I WANNA HAVE TEN KIDS.
HA HA HA!
CHON (POKE)
DARLIN'... I'LL DO MY BEST... ♡
FORCE IS THE ONLY OPTION...
GO GO GO GO (RUMBLE)
THINK THE VET IS OPEN?
WAIT! EVERYONE, KEEP IT PEACEFUL ...!

BY FORCE! BY FORCE!!

BETE, THE VIRTUOUS...

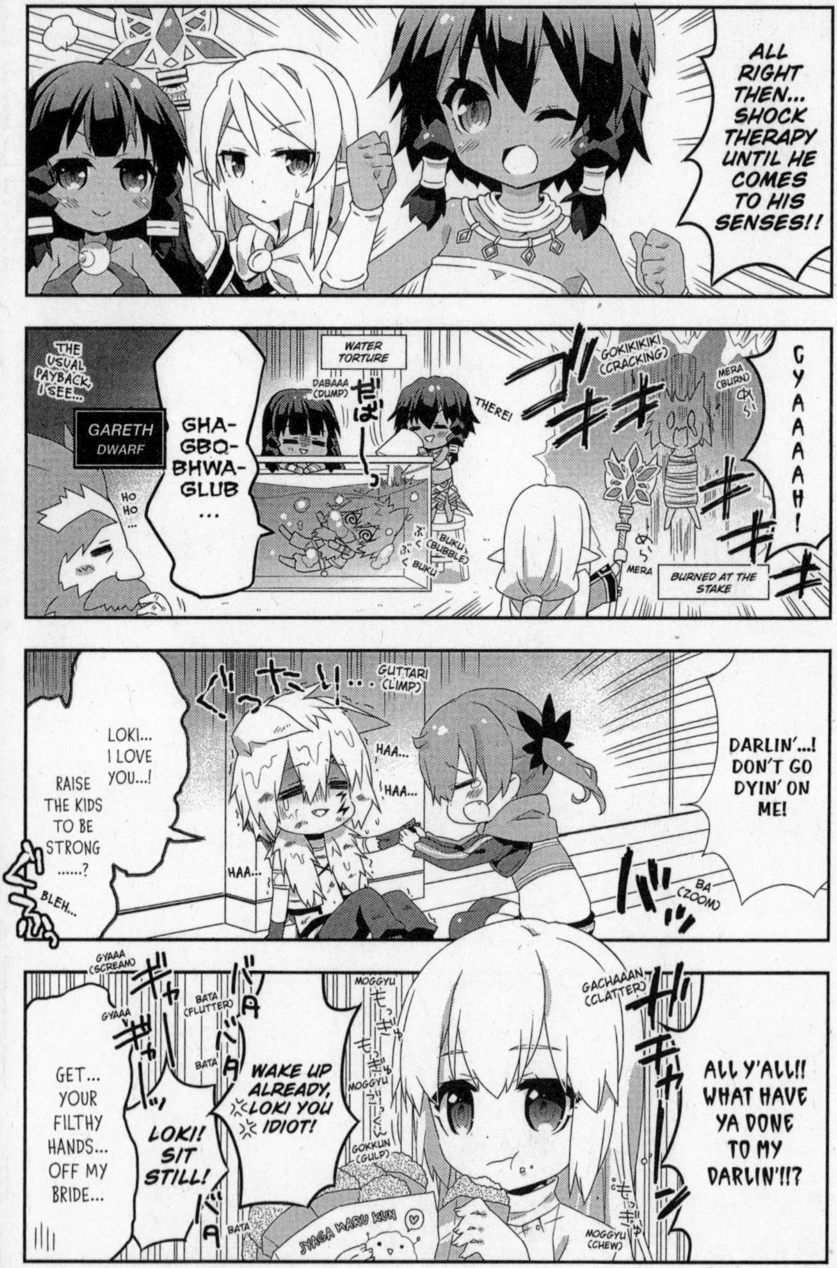
ALL RIGHT THEN... SHOCK THERAPY UNTIL HE COMES TO HIS SENSES!!
GYAAAAAH!
MERA (BURN)
GOKIKIKIKI (CRACKING)
BURNED AT THE STAKE
MERA
THERE!
WATER TORTURE
DABAAA (DUMP)
BUKU (BUBBLE) BUKU
GHA-GBO-BHWA-GLUB...
HO HO...
GARETH DWARF
THE USUAL PAYBACK, I SEE...
DARLIN'...! DON'T GO DYIN' ON ME!
BA (ZOOM)
GUTTARI (LIMP)
HAA... HAA...
HAA...
LOKI... I LOVE YOU...!
RAISE THE KIDS TO BE STRONG ......?
BLEH...
ALL Y'ALL!! WHAT HAVE YA DONE TO MY DARLIN'!!?
GACHAAAN (CLATTER)
MOGGYU (CHEW)
MOGGYU
MOGGYU
GOKKUN (GULP)
JYAGA MARU KUN
WAKE UP ALREADY, LOKI YOU IDIOT!
BATA (FLUTTER)
BATA
BATA
LOKI! SIT STILL!
GYAAA (SCREAM)
GYAAA
GET... YOUR FILTHY HANDS... OFF MY BRIDE...

WHAT IS THIS? (LOST FOR WORDS)

MAJESTIC LEADER

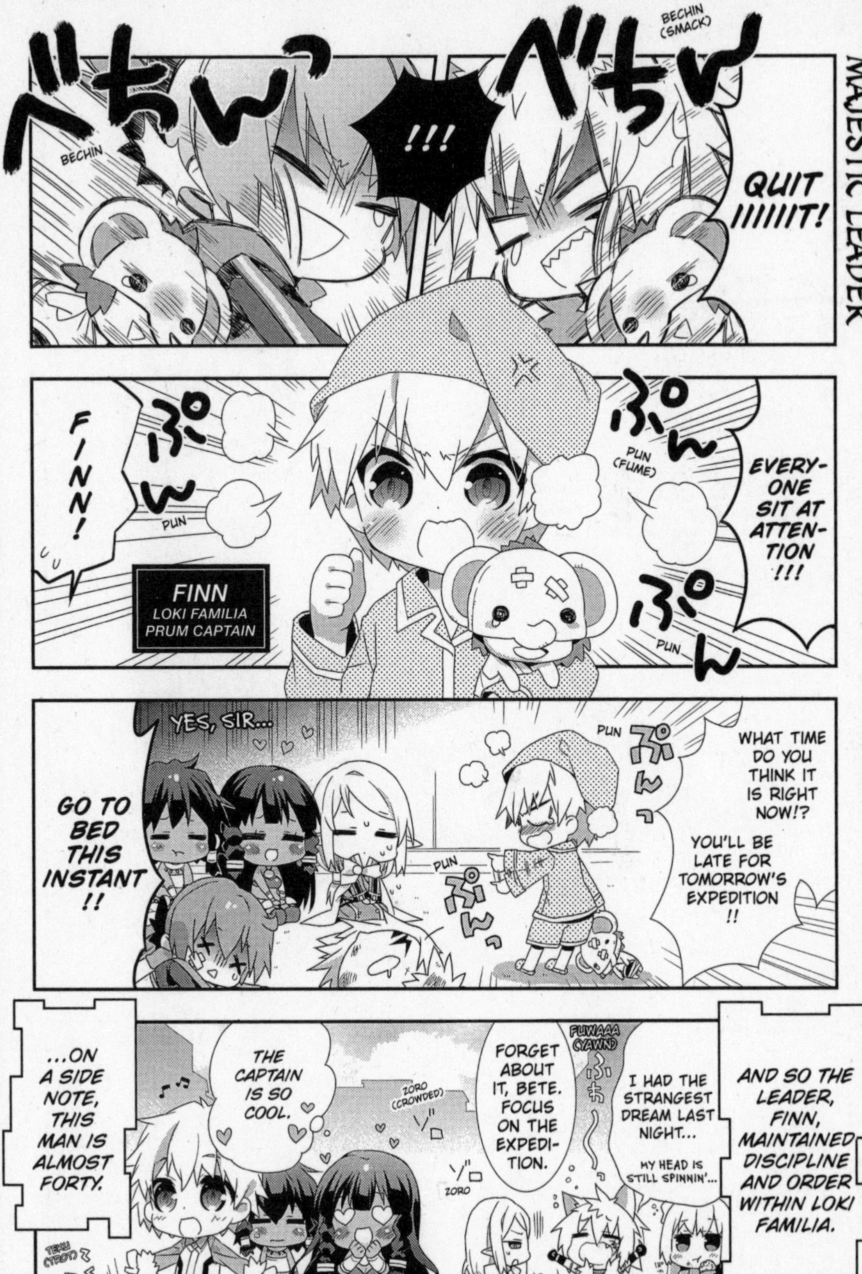

べちん
BECHIN (SMACK)
QUIT IIIIIIIT!
!!!
べちん
BECHIN
ぷん
PUN (FUME)
EVERY-ONE SIT AT ATTEN-TION!!!
ぷん
PUN
ぷん
PUN
FINN!
FINN
LOKI FAMILIA
PRUM CAPTAIN
WHAT TIME DO YOU THINK IT IS RIGHT NOW!?
PUN
ぷんっ
YOU'LL BE LATE FOR TOMORROW'S EXPEDITION!!
PUN
ぷんっ
YES, SIR...
GO TO BED THIS INSTANT!!
AND SO THE LEADER, FINN, MAINTAINED DISCIPLINE AND ORDER WITHIN LOKI FAMILIA.
I HAD THE STRANGEST DREAM LAST NIGHT...
FUWAAA (YAWN)
ふわ〜
MY HEAD IS STILL SPINNIN'...
POKAAA (CHEW)
FORGET ABOUT IT, BETE. FOCUS ON THE EXPEDI-TION.
ZORO (CROWDED)
ゾロ
ZORO
ゾロ
THE CAPTAIN IS SO COOL.
...ON A SIDE NOTE, THIS MAN IS ALMOST FORTY.
TEKU (TROT)
TEKU

BEWARE AIZ'S APPETITE (FOR JYAGA MARU KUN).

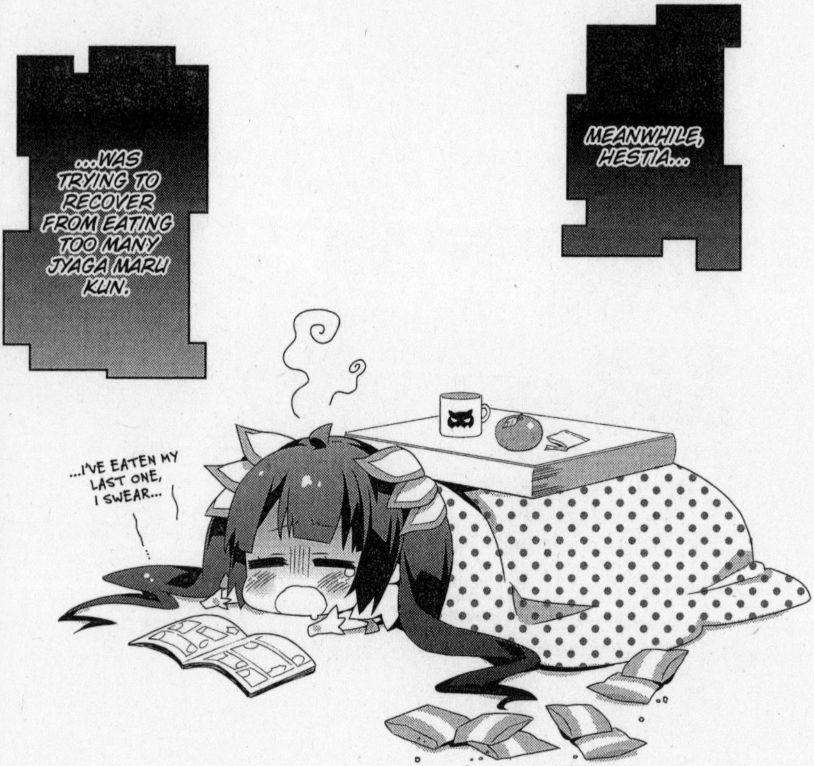
MEANWHILE, HESTIA...
...WAS TRYING TO RECOVER FROM EATING TOO MANY JYAGA MARU KUN.
...I'VE EATEN MY LAST ONE, I SWEAR...

STEP 11

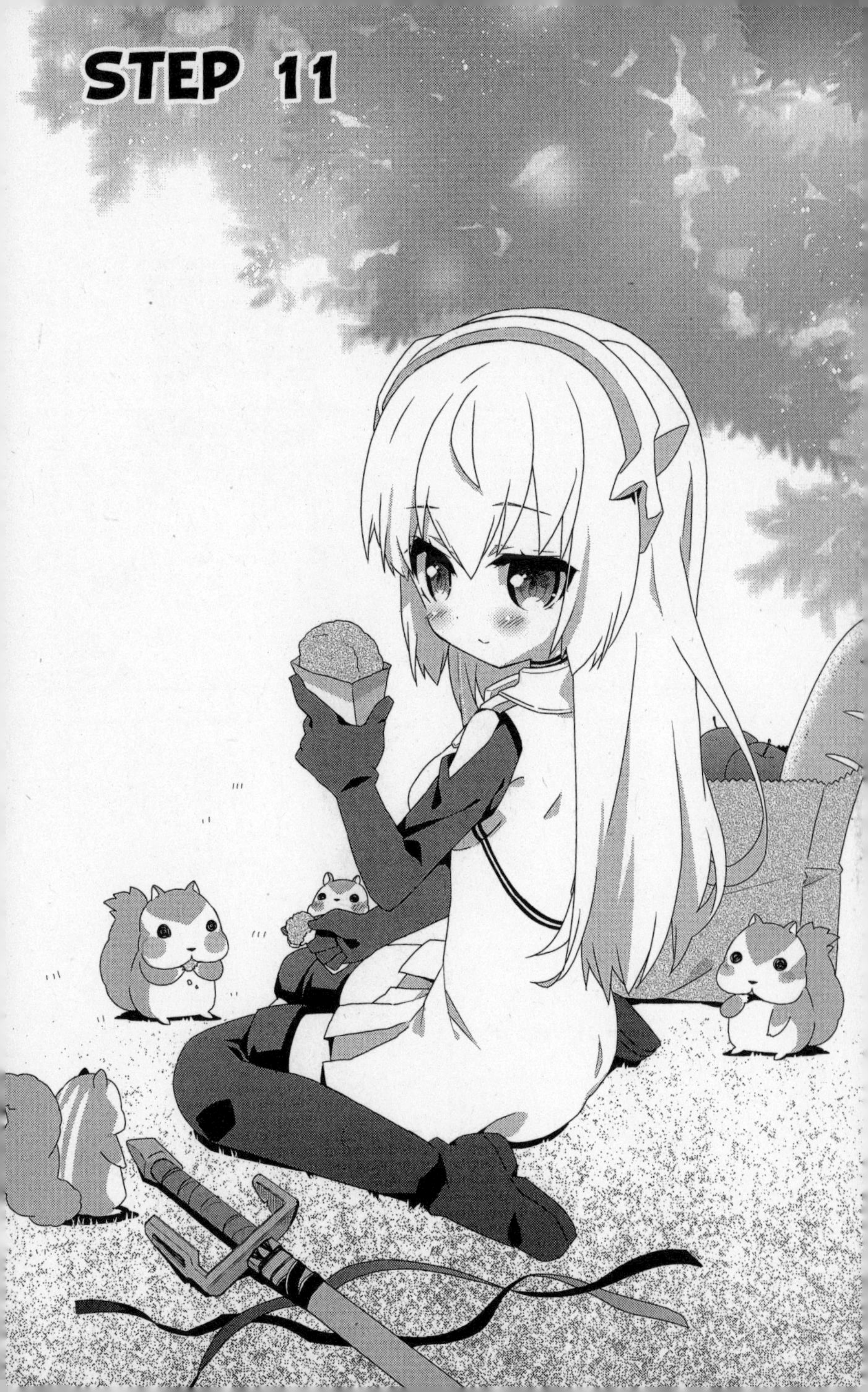

TRIED TOO HARD TO LOOK COOL.

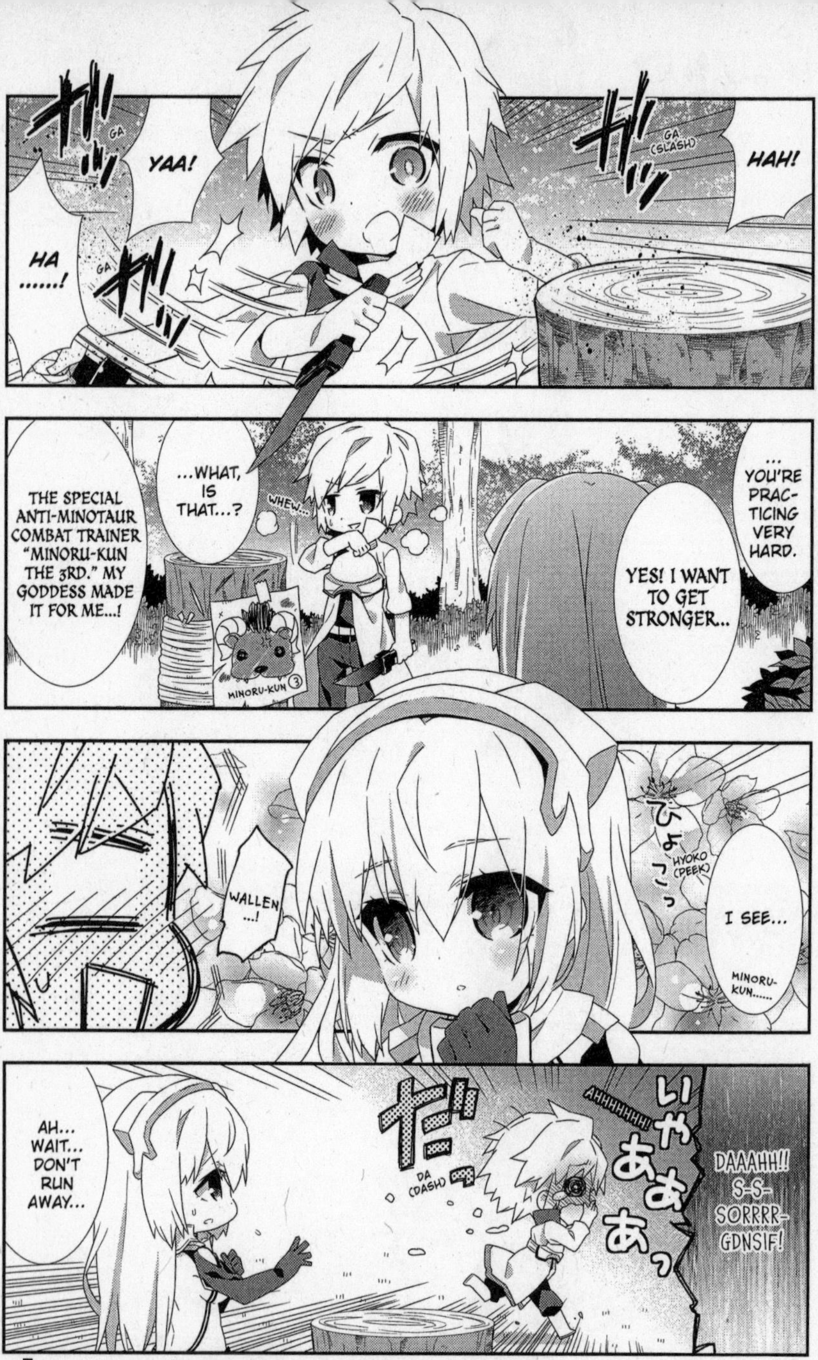

HAH!
GA (SLASH)
GA
YAA!
HA ......!
GA
... YOU'RE PRAC-TICING VERY HARD.
YES! I WANT TO GET STRONGER..
WHEW...
...WHAT, IS THAT...?
THE SPECIAL ANTI-MINOTAUR COMBAT TRAINER "MINORU-KUN THE 3RD." MY GODDESS MADE IT FOR ME...!
MINORU-KUN ③
ひょこっ
HYOKO (PEEK)
I SEE...
MINORU-KUN......
WALLEN ...!
DAAAHH!! S-S-SORRRR-GDNSIF!
いやあああっ
AHHHHHHH!
だっ
DA (DASH)
AH... WAIT... DON'T RUN AWAY...

...AND IT WAS GOING SO WELL TOO.

IN HEAVEN

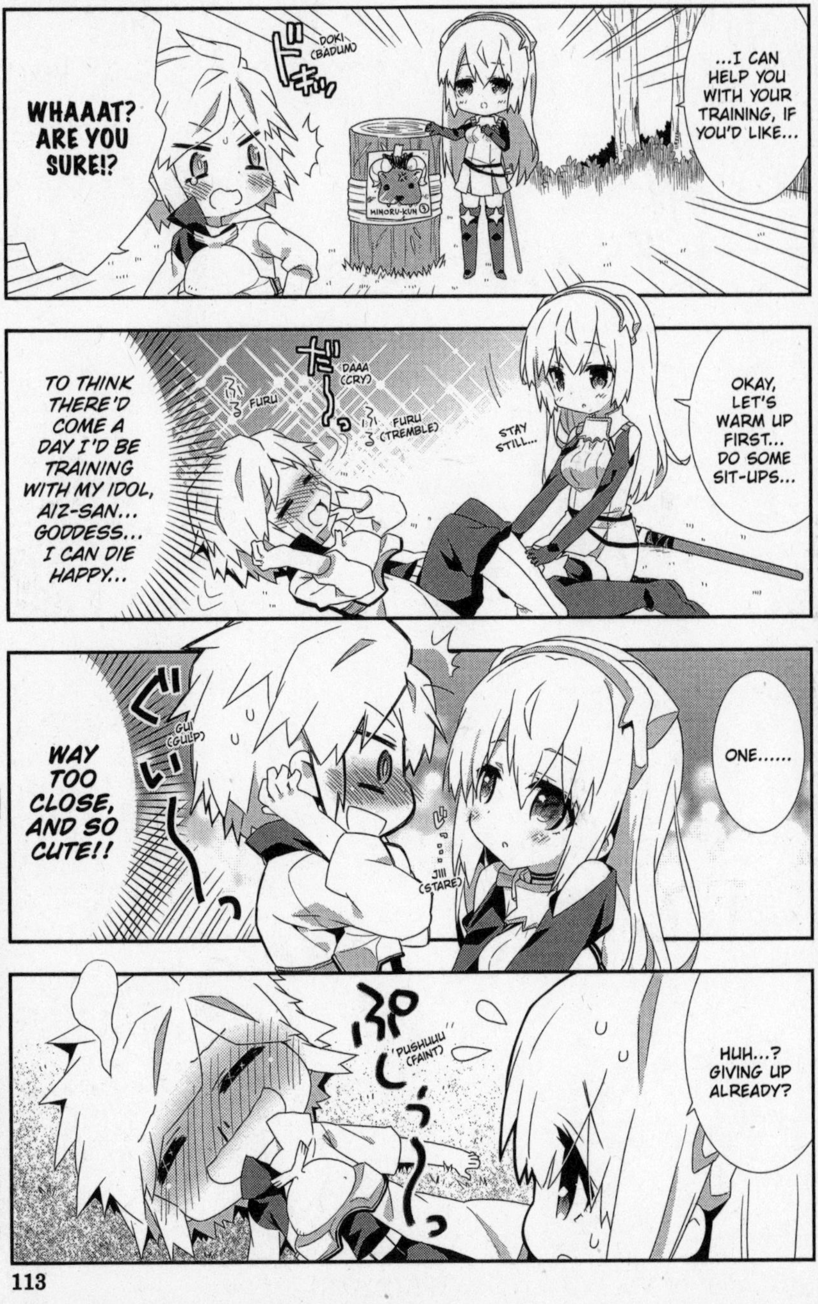
...I CAN HELP YOU WITH YOUR TRAINING, IF YOU'D LIKE...
MINORU-KUN
ドキッ
DOKI (BADUM)
WHAAAT? ARE YOU SURE!?
OKAY, LET'S WARM UP FIRST... DO SOME SIT-UPS...
STAY STILL...
ふる
FURU (TREMBLE)
だ~っ
DAAA (CRY)
ふる
FURU
TO THINK THERE'D COME A DAY I'D BE TRAINING WITH MY IDOL, AIZ-SAN... GODDESS... I CAN DIE HAPPY...
ONE......
じー
JIII (STARE)
ぐい
GUI (GULP)
WAY TOO CLOSE, AND SO CUTE!!
HUH...? GIVING UP ALREADY?
ぷしゅう
PUSHUUU (FAINT)

ALL BOYS HAVE DIRTY MINDS...

LILLY FORGES AHEAD REGARDLESS

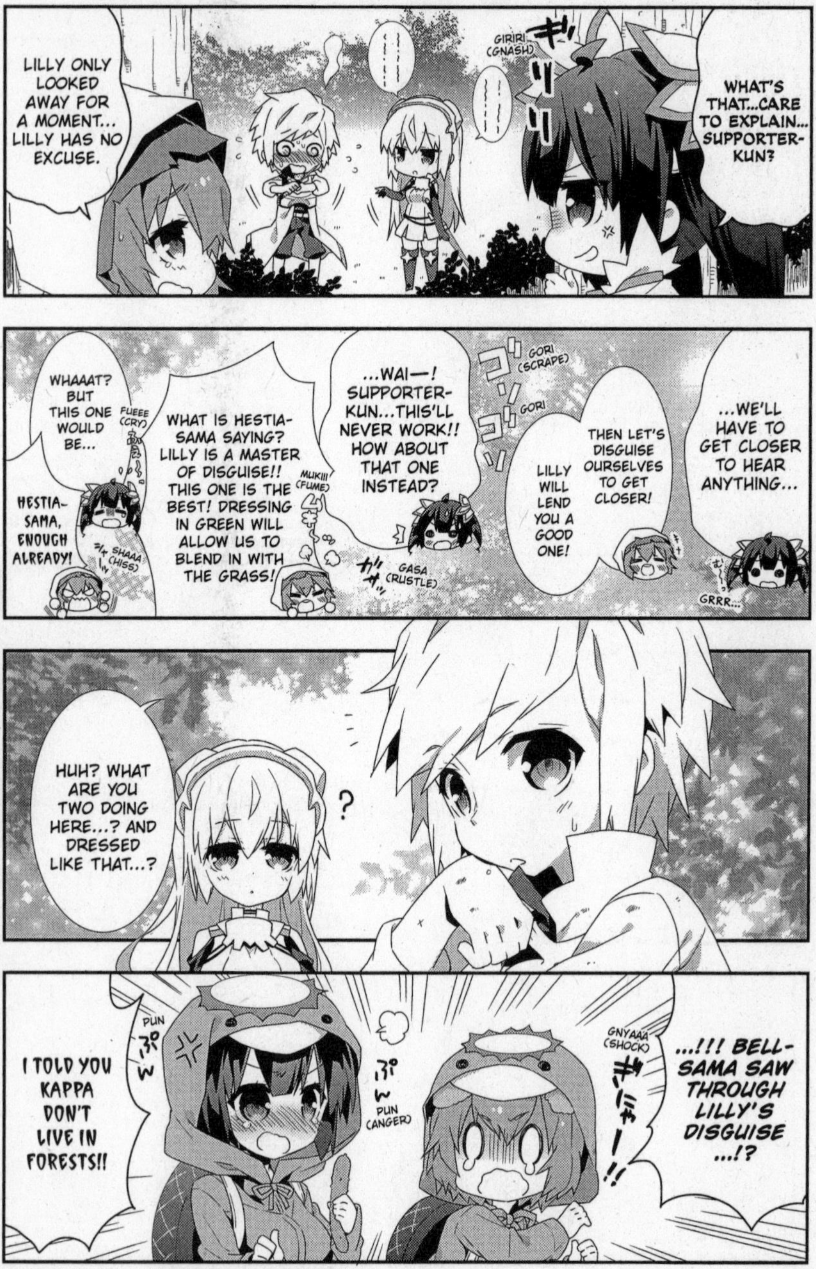
WHAT'S THAT...CARE TO EXPLAIN... SUPPORTER-KUN?
GIRIRI (GNASH)
......
......
LILLY ONLY LOOKED AWAY FOR A MOMENT... LILLY HAS NO EXCUSE.
...WE'LL HAVE TO GET CLOSER TO HEAR ANYTHING...
GRRR...
THEN LET'S DISGUISE OURSELVES TO GET CLOSER!
LILLY WILL LEND YOU A GOOD ONE!
GORI (SCRAPE)
GORI
...WAI—! SUPPORTER-KUN...THIS'LL NEVER WORK!! HOW ABOUT THAT ONE INSTEAD?
MUKIII (FUME)
GASA (RUSTLE)
WHAT IS HESTIA-SAMA SAYING? LILLY IS A MASTER OF DISGUISE!! THIS ONE IS THE BEST! DRESSING IN GREEN WILL ALLOW US TO BLEND IN WITH THE GRASS!
FUEEE (CRY)
WHAAAT? BUT THIS ONE WOULD BE...
SHAAA (HISS)
HESTIA-SAMA, ENOUGH ALREADY!
?
HUH? WHAT ARE YOU TWO DOING HERE...? AND DRESSED LIKE THAT...?
...!!! BELL-SAMA SAW THROUGH LILLY'S DISGUISE ...!?
GNYAAA (SHOCK)
PUN (ANGER)
PUN
I TOLD YOU KAPPA DON'T LIVE IN FORESTS!!

I, THE AUTHOR, AM A FAN OF SHIGERU MIZUKI.

※ KAPPA ARE ONLY IN JAPAN AND DON'T EXIST IN ORARIO.

HOW TO USE A KNIFE

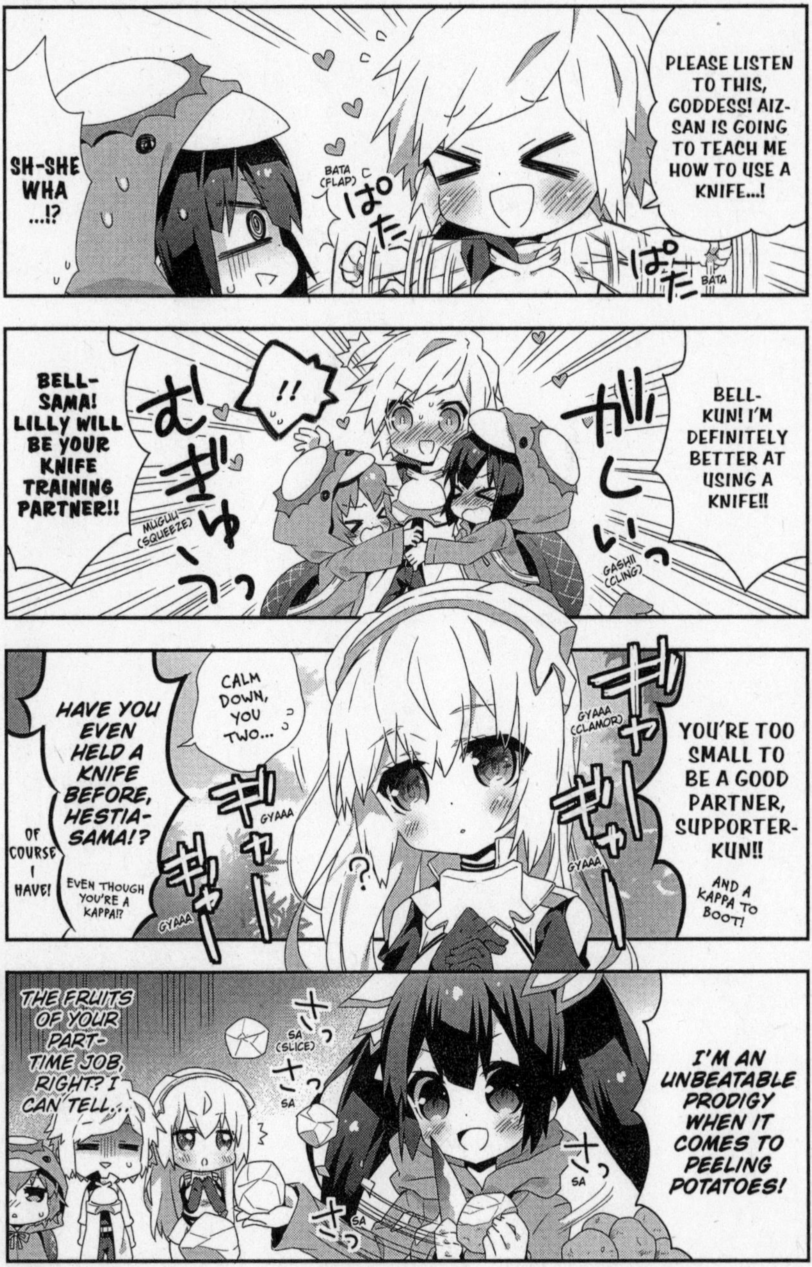
PLEASE LISTEN TO THIS, GODDESS! AIZ-SAN IS GOING TO TEACH ME HOW TO USE A KNIFE...!
ぱた
BATA (FLAP)
ぱた
BATA
SH-SHE WHA ...!?
BELL-KUN! I'M DEFINITELY BETTER AT USING A KNIFE!!
がしぃっ
GASHII (CLING)
!!
むぎゅうっ
MUGUU (SQUEEZE)
BELL-SAMA! LILLY WILL BE YOUR KNIFE TRAINING PARTNER!!
YOU'RE TOO SMALL TO BE A GOOD PARTNER, SUPPORTER-KUN!!
AND A KAPPA TO BOOT!
ギャーギャー
GYAAA (CLAMOR)
GYAAA
CALM DOWN, YOU TWO...
HAVE YOU EVEN HELD A KNIFE BEFORE, HESTIA-SAMA!?
OF COURSE I HAVE!
EVEN THOUGH YOU'RE A KAPPA!?
ギャーギャー
GYAAA
GYAAA
I'M AN UNBEATABLE PRODIGY WHEN IT COMES TO PEELING POTATOES!
さっ
SA (SLICE)
さっ
SA
さっ
SA
さっ
SA
THE FRUITS OF YOUR PART-TIME JOB, RIGHT? I CAN TELL...

THE DIVINE DEED.

POTATO >>> AN INSURMOUNTABLE WALL > BELL-KUN

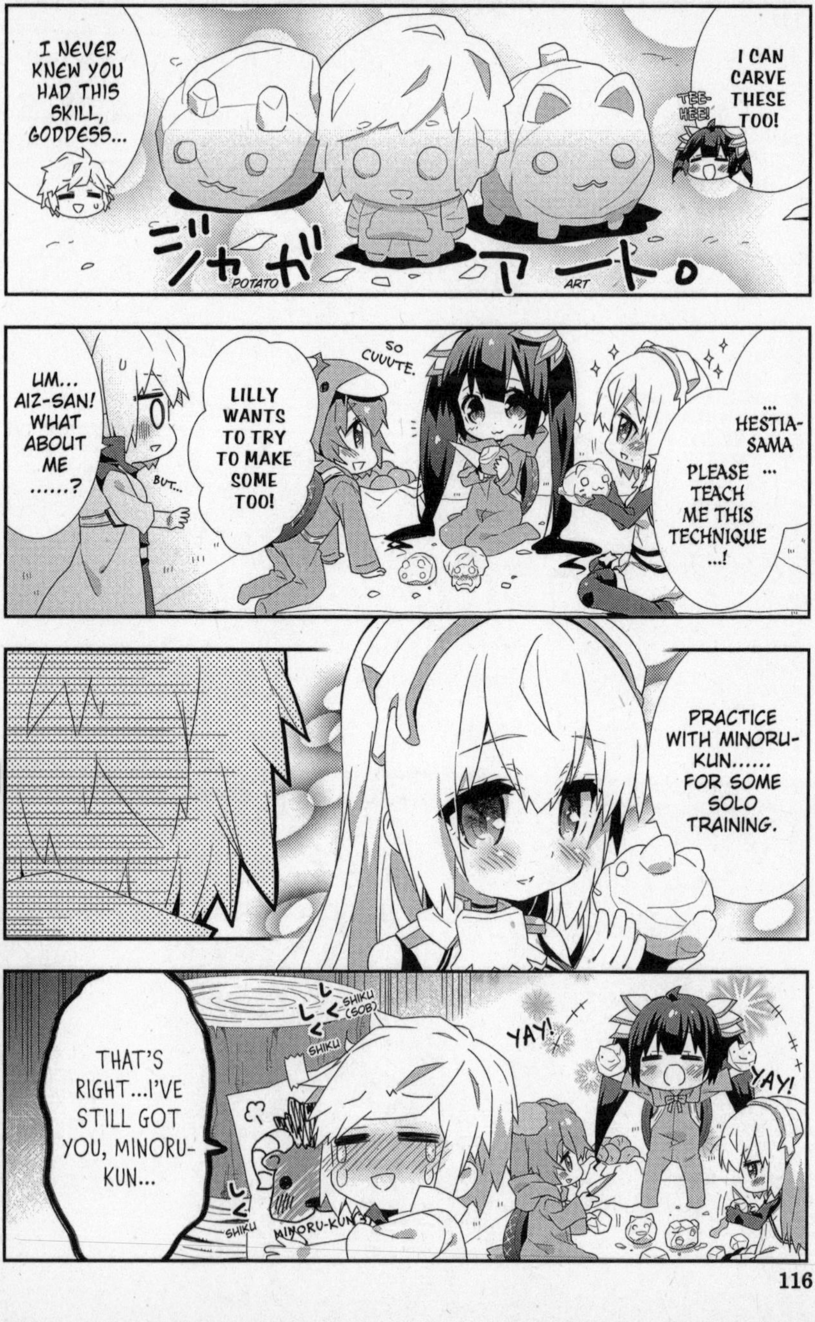

I CAN CARVE THESE TOO!
TEE-HEE!
I NEVER KNEW YOU HAD THIS SKILL, GODDESS...
ジャガアート
POTATO
ART
... HESTIA-SAMA ... PLEASE TEACH ME THIS TECHNIQUE ...!
SO CUUUTE.
LILLY WANTS TO TRY TO MAKE SOME TOO!
BUT...
UM... AIZ-SAN! WHAT ABOUT ME ......?
PRACTICE WITH MINORU-KUN...... FOR SOME SOLO TRAINING.
YAY!
YAY!
しく SHIKU (SOB)
しく SHIKU
しく SHIKU
MINORU-KUN
THAT'S RIGHT...I'VE STILL GOT YOU, MINORU-KUN...

WHY IS MINORU-KUN BLUSHING?

Is it **WRONG** ⅜ to try to **PiCK UP** GiRLS iN A **DUNGEON?**

☞ **FOUR-PANEL COMIC**

[**DAYS OF GODDESS**]

STEP 12

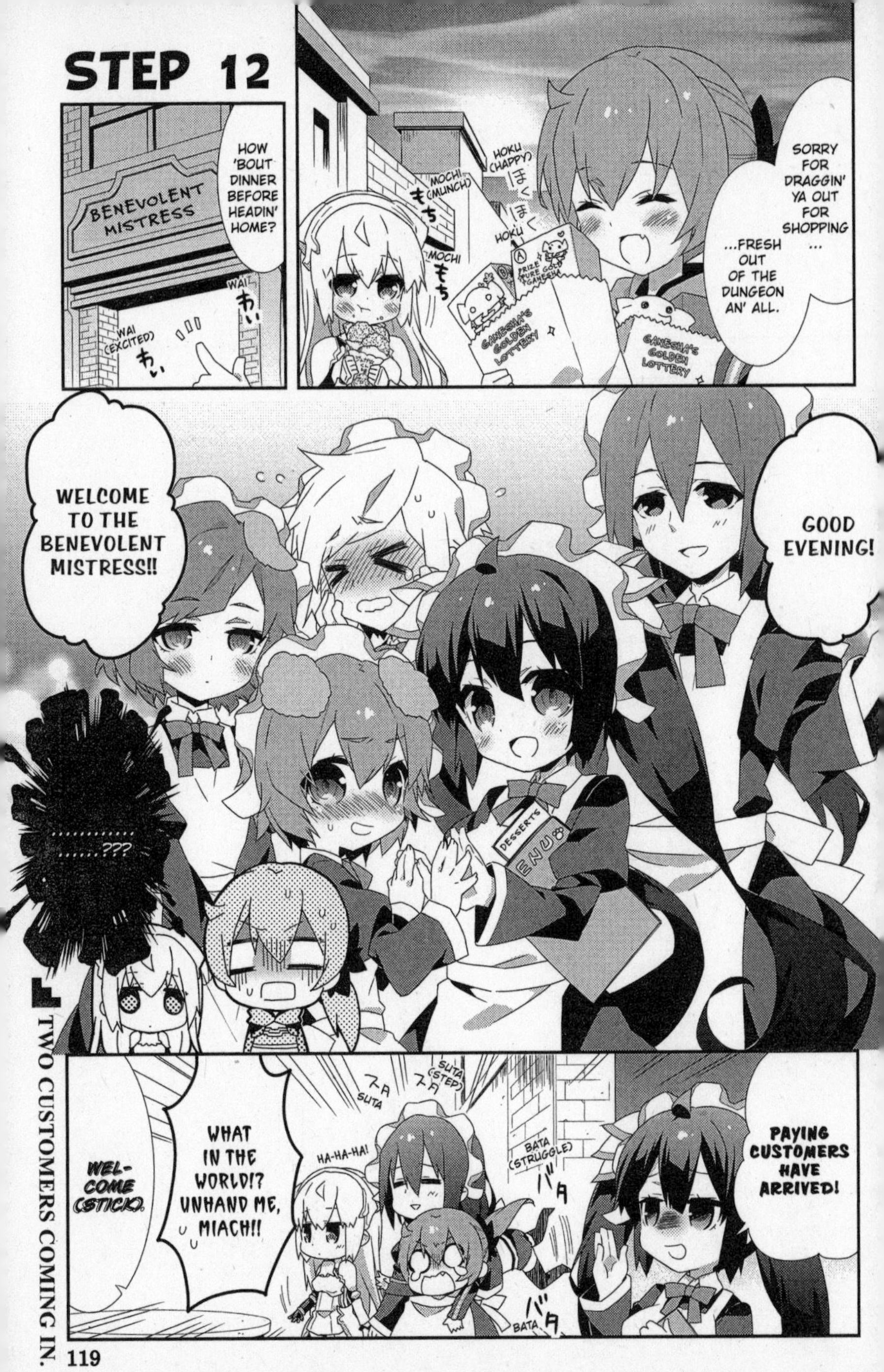

SORRY FOR DRAGGIN' YA OUT FOR SHOPPING ...
...FRESH OUT OF THE DUNGEON AN' ALL.
HOKU (HAPPY) ほく
ほく HOKU
MOCHI (MUNCH) もち
MOCHI もち
PRIZE PURE GOLD GANESHA
GANESHA'S GOLDEN LOTTERY
GANESHA'S GOLDEN LOTTERY
HOW 'BOUT DINNER BEFORE HEADIN' HOME?
BENEVOLENT MISTRESS
WAI わい
WAI (EXCITED) わい
GOOD EVENING!
WELCOME TO THE BENEVOLENT MISTRESS!!
DESSERTS
ENU
....???
PAYING CUSTOMERS HAVE ARRIVED!
BATA (STRUGGLE) バタ
BATA バタ
SUTA (STEP) スタ
SUTA スタ
HA-HA-HA!
WHAT IN THE WORLD!? UNHAND ME, MIACH!!
WEL-COME (STICK).

TWO CUSTOMERS COMING IN.

TARGETED BELL-KUN!?

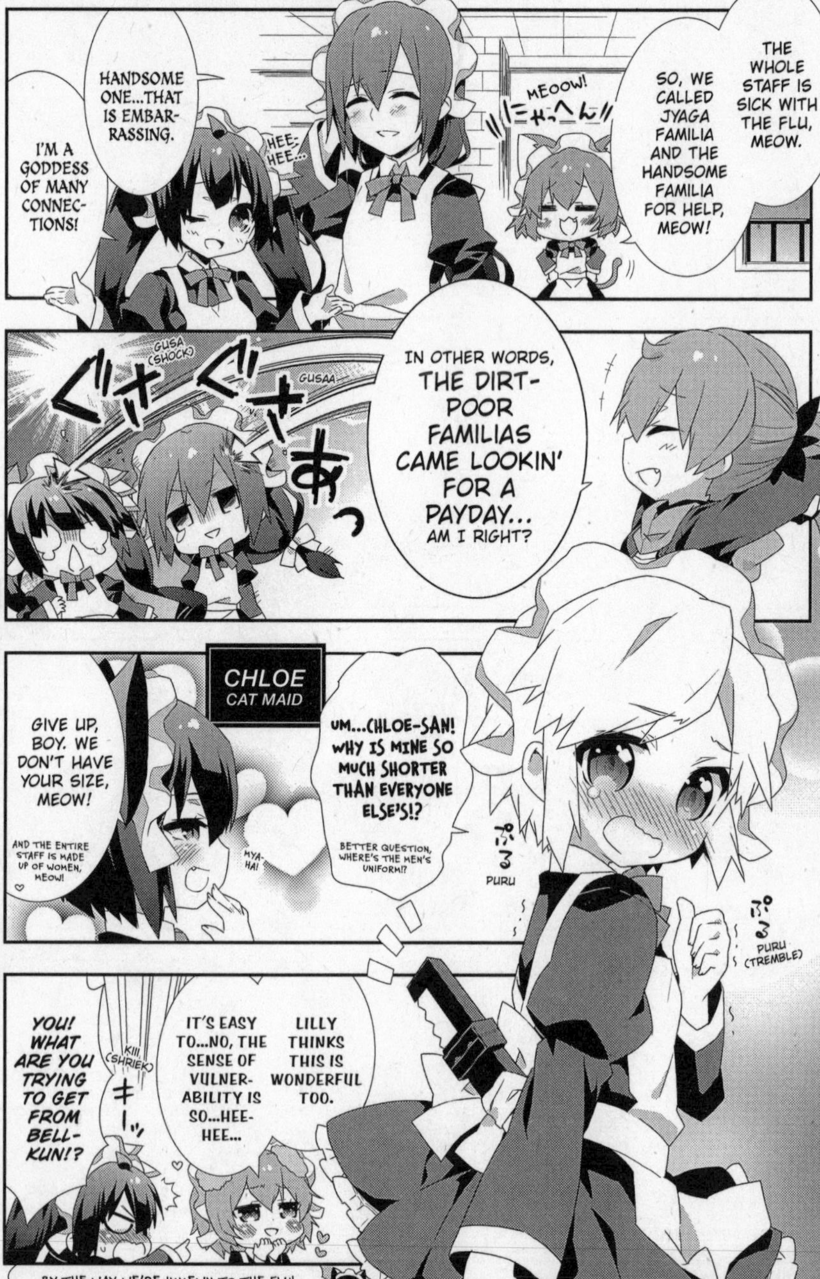
THE WHOLE STAFF IS SICK WITH THE FLU, MEOW.
SO, WE CALLED JYAGA FAMILIA AND THE HANDSOME FAMILIA FOR HELP, MEOW!
MEOOW!
HEE-HEE...
HANDSOME ONE...THAT IS EMBARRASSING.
I'M A GODDESS OF MANY CONNECTIONS!
IN OTHER WORDS, THE DIRT-POOR FAMILIAS CAME LOOKIN' FOR A PAYDAY... AM I RIGHT?
GUSAA
GUSA (SHOCK)
PURU (TREMBLE)
PURU
UM...CHLOE-SAN! WHY IS MINE SO MUCH SHORTER THAN EVERYONE ELSE'S!?
BETTER QUESTION, WHERE'S THE MEN'S UNIFORM!?
CHLOE CAT MAID
MYA-HA!
GIVE UP, BOY. WE DON'T HAVE YOUR SIZE, MEOW!
AND THE ENTIRE STAFF IS MADE UP OF WOMEN, MEOW!
LILLY THINKS THIS IS WONDERFUL TOO.
IT'S EASY TO...NO, THE SENSE OF VULNERABILITY IS SO...HEE-HEE...
KIII (SHRIEK)
YOU! WHAT ARE YOU TRYING TO GET FROM BELL-KUN!?
BY THE WAY, WE'RE IMMEWN TO THE FLU!

THE MAIN HEROINE BURSTS ONTO THE SCENE.

WHICH WOULD YOU LIKE?

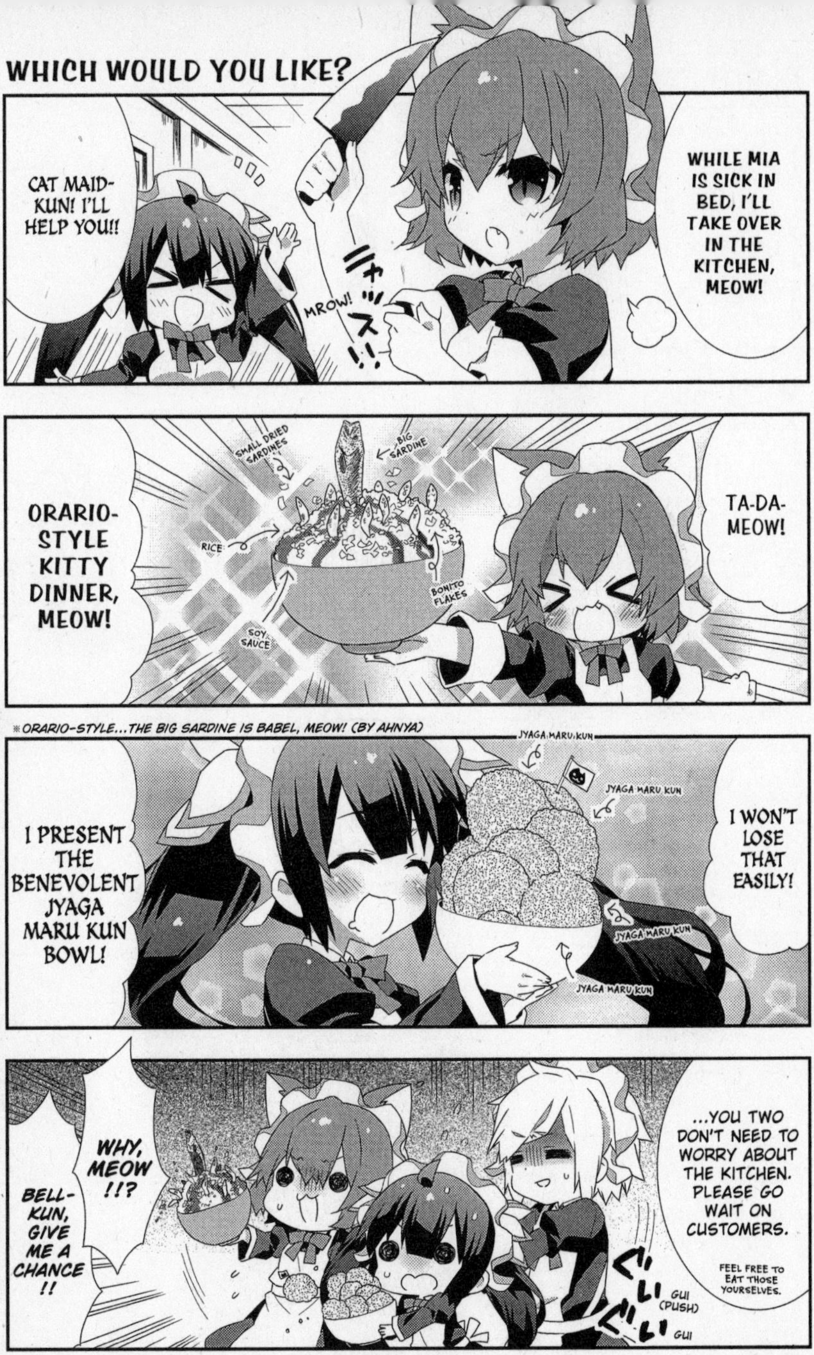
WHILE MIA IS SICK IN BED, I'LL TAKE OVER IN THE KITCHEN, MEOW!
ニャッス!!
MROW!
CAT MAID-KUN! I'LL HELP YOU!!
TA-DA-MEOW!
BIG SARDINE
SMALL DRIED SARDINES
RICE
BONITO FLAKES
SOY SAUCE
ORARIO-STYLE KITTY DINNER, MEOW!
※ORARIO-STYLE...THE BIG SARDINE IS BABEL, MEOW! (BY AHNYA)
I WON'T LOSE THAT EASILY!
JYAGA MARU KUN
JYAGA MARU KUN
JYAGA MARU KUN
JYAGA MARU KUN
I PRESENT THE BENEVOLENT JYAGA MARU KUN BOWL!
...YOU TWO DON'T NEED TO WORRY ABOUT THE KITCHEN. PLEASE GO WAIT ON CUSTOMERS.
FEEL FREE TO EAT THOSE YOURSELVES.
GUI (PUSH)
GUI
WHY, MEOW!!?
BELL-KUN, GIVE ME A CHANCE!!

CAT AHNYA + GODDESS HESTIA= DISASTER.

A GIRL'S HEART AND AN OMELETTE

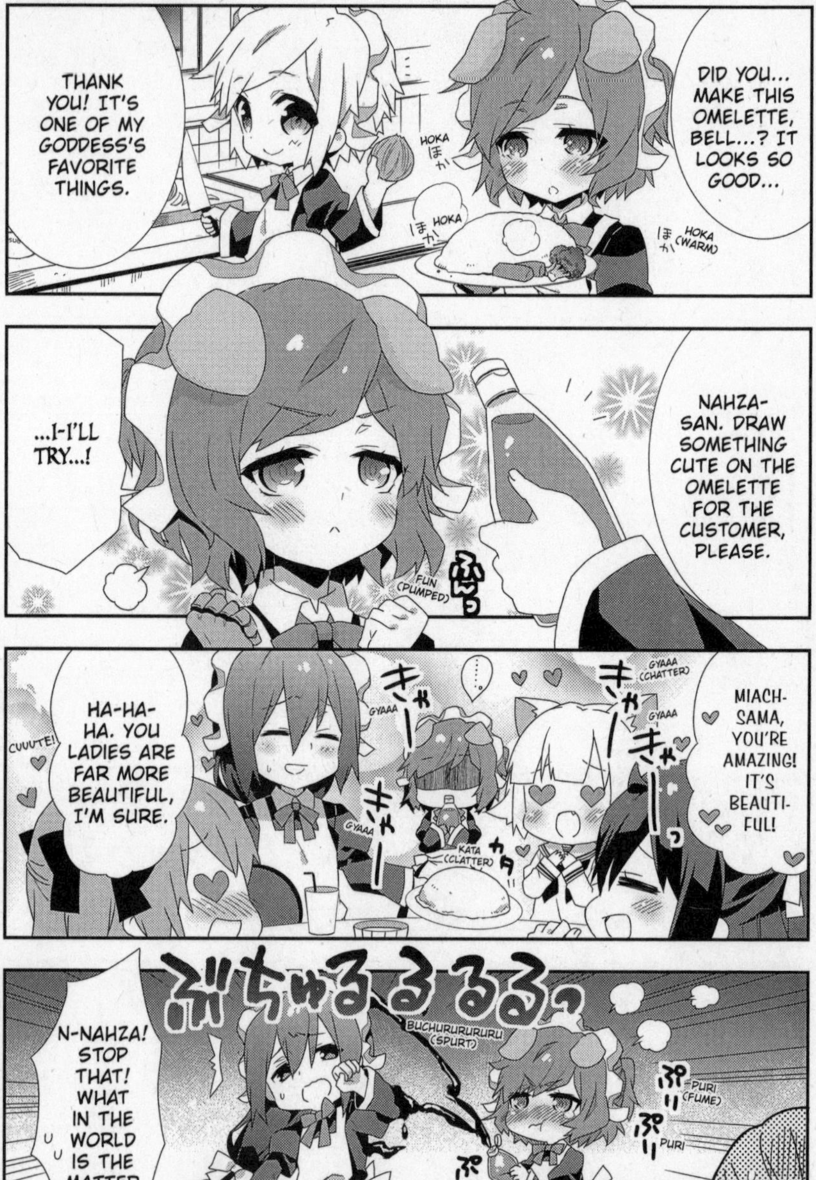
DID YOU... MAKE THIS OMELETTE, BELL...? IT LOOKS SO GOOD...
HOKA (WARM)
HOKA
HOKA
THANK YOU! IT'S ONE OF MY GODDESS'S FAVORITE THINGS.
NAHZA-SAN. DRAW SOMETHING CUTE ON THE OMELETTE FOR THE CUSTOMER, PLEASE.
FUN (PUMPED)
...I-I'LL TRY...!
MIACH-SAMA, YOU'RE AMAZING! IT'S BEAUTIFUL!
GYAAA (CHATTER)
GYAAA
.....
GYAAA
GYAAA
KATA (CLATTER)
HA-HA-HA. YOU LADIES ARE FAR MORE BEAUTIFUL, I'M SURE.
CUUUTE!
PURI (FUME)
PURI
BUCHURURURURU (SPURT)
PURI
N-NAHZA! STOP THAT! WHAT IN THE WORLD IS THE MATTER!?

I'LL PAINT THAT MAID UNIFORM RED!!

GODDESS'S KNIFE—!!

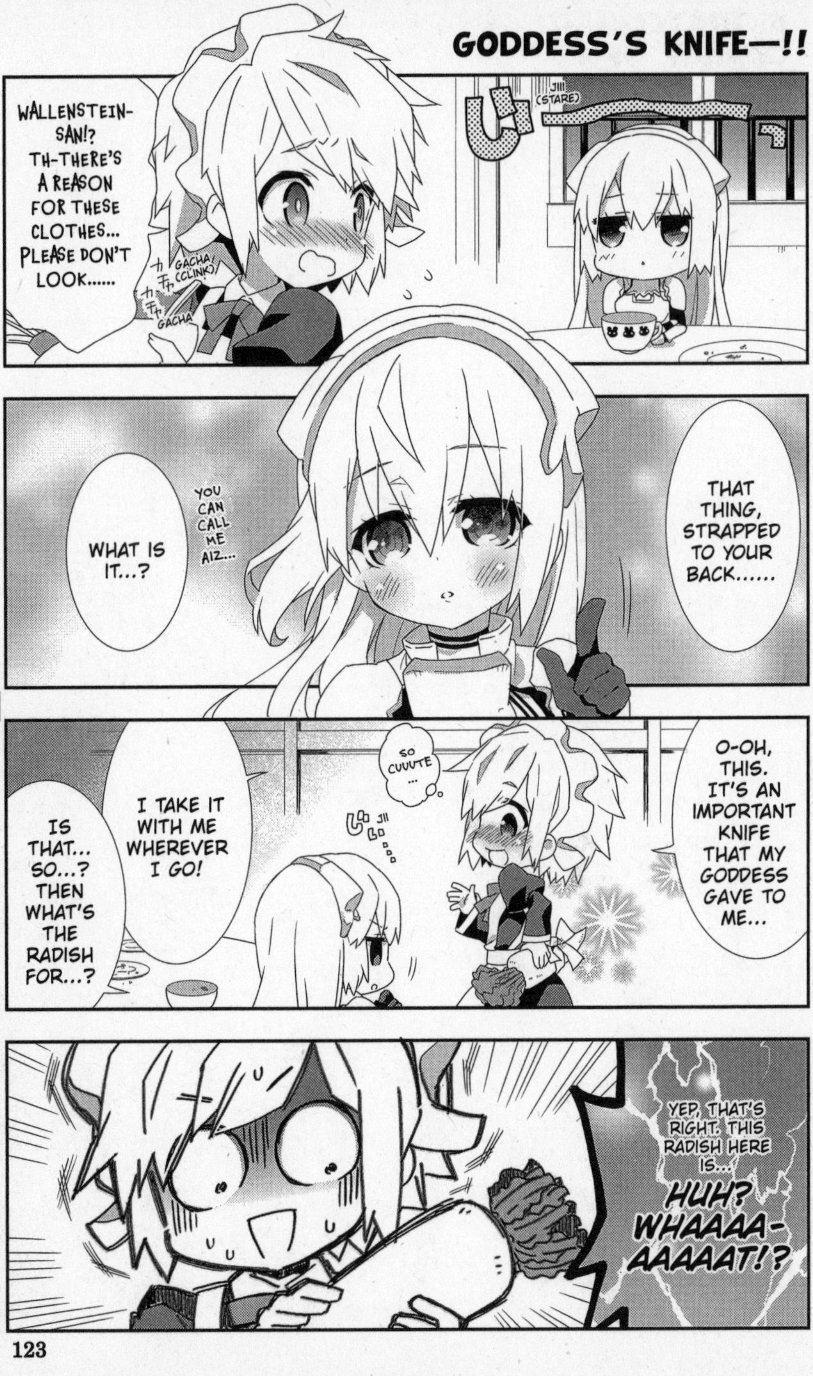
JIII (STARE)
WALLENSTEIN-SAN!? TH-THERE'S A REASON FOR THESE CLOTHES... PLEASE DON'T LOOK......
GACHA (CLINK)
GACHA
THAT THING, STRAPPED TO YOUR BACK......
YOU CAN CALL ME AIZ...
WHAT IS IT...?
O-OH, THIS. IT'S AN IMPORTANT KNIFE THAT MY GODDESS GAVE TO ME...
SO CUUUTE...
I TAKE IT WITH ME WHEREVER I GO!
JII
IS THAT... SO...? THEN WHAT'S THE RADISH FOR...?
YEP, THAT'S RIGHT. THIS RADISH HERE IS...
HUH? WHAAAAA-AAAAAT!?

THEY HAVE THE SAME WEIGHT... (EXCUSES)

BETRAYAL AND CHANGE OF HEART

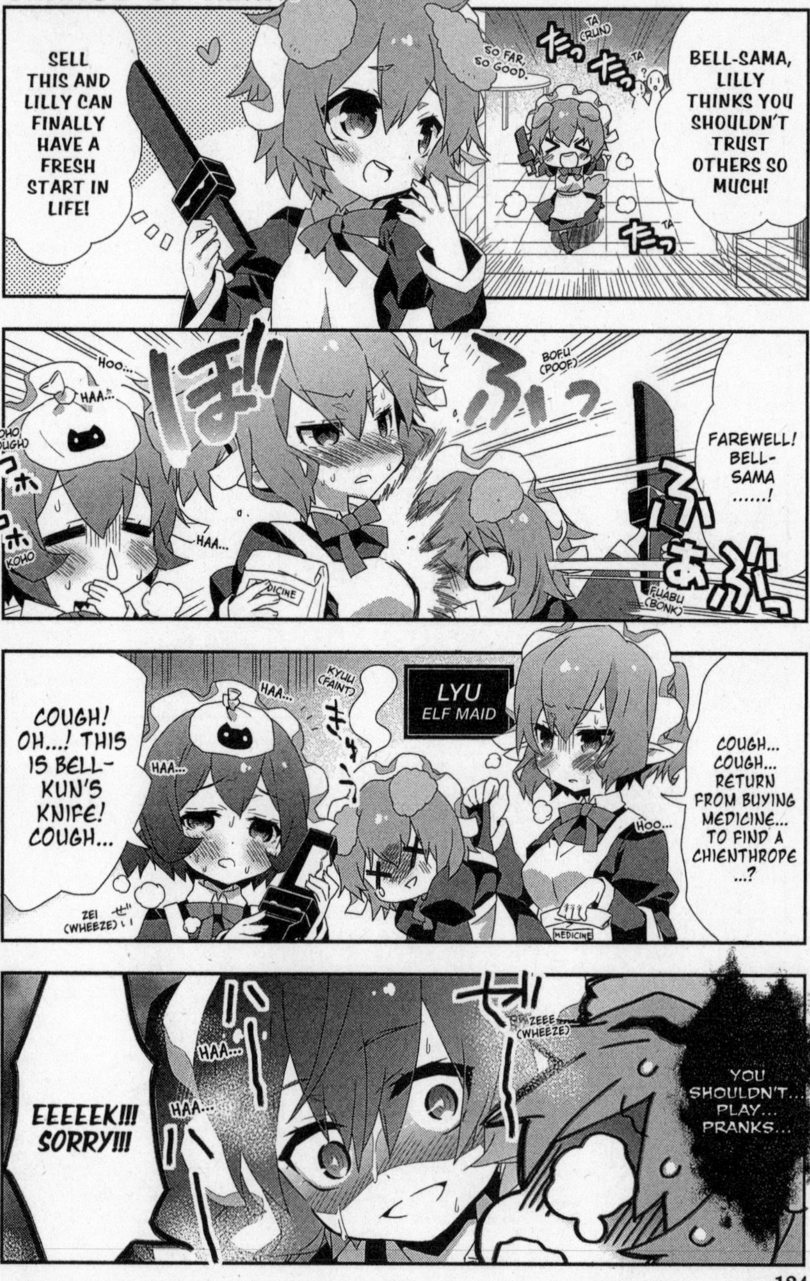

BELL-SAMA, LILLY THINKS YOU SHOULDN'T TRUST OTHERS SO MUCH!
TA (RUN)
TA
SO FAR, SO GOOD.
TA
SELL THIS AND LILLY CAN FINALLY HAVE A FRESH START IN LIFE!
FAREWELL! BELL-SAMA ......!
FUABU (BONK)
BOFU (POOF)
HAA...
HOO...
HAA...
KOHO (COUGH)
KOHO
COUGH... COUGH... RETURN FROM BUYING MEDICINE... TO FIND A CHIENTHROPE ...?
HOO...
MEDICINE
LYU ELF MAID
KYUU (FAINT)
HAA...
HAA...
COUGH! OH...! THIS IS BELL-KUN'S KNIFE! COUGH...
ZEI (WHEEZE)
YOU SHOULDN'T... PLAY... PRANKS...
ZEEE... (WHEEZE)
HAA...
HAA...
EEEEEK!!! SORRY!!!

A SIGNATURE SCENE FROM THE MAIN SERIES DOWN THE DRAIN.

A LITTLE ADVICE LEADS TO?

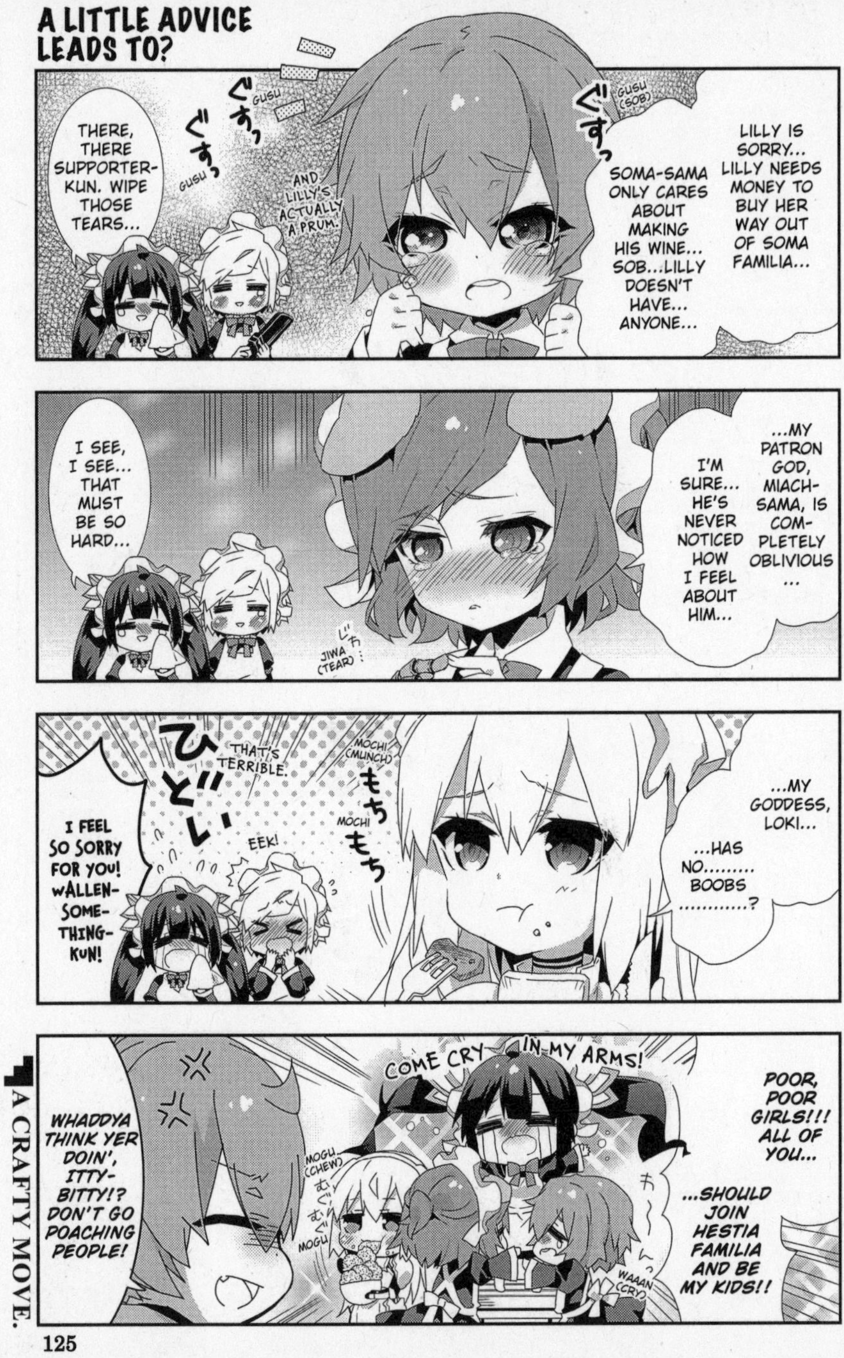
ぐすっ
GUSU (SOB)
LILLY IS SORRY... LILLY NEEDS MONEY TO BUY HER WAY OUT OF SOMA FAMILIA...
SOMA-SAMA ONLY CARES ABOUT MAKING HIS WINE... SOB...LILLY DOESN'T HAVE... ANYONE...
AND LILLY'S ACTUALLY A PRUM.
ぐすっ
GUSU
ぐすっ
GUSU
THERE, THERE SUPPORTER-KUN. WIPE THOSE TEARS...
...MY PATRON GOD, MIACH-SAMA, IS COM-PLETELY OBLIVIOUS...
I'M SURE... HE'S NEVER NOTICED HOW I FEEL ABOUT HIM...
じわ…
JIWA (TEAR)
I SEE, I SEE... THAT MUST BE SO HARD...
...MY GODDESS, LOKI...
...HAS NO......... BOOBS ....?
もち
MOCHI (MUNCH)
もち
MOCHI
EEK!
ひどい
THAT'S TERRIBLE.
I FEEL SO SORRY FOR YOU! WALLEN-SOME-THING-KUN!
POOR, POOR GIRLS!!! ALL OF YOU...
...SHOULD JOIN HESTIA FAMILIA AND BE MY KIDS!!
お～ん
WAAAN (CRY)
COME CRY IN MY ARMS!
むぐ
MOGU (CHEW)
むぐ
MOGU
WHADDYA THINK YER DOIN', ITTY-BITTY!? DON'T GO POACHING PEOPLE!

A CRAFTY MOVE.

IT'S BEEN A WHILE.

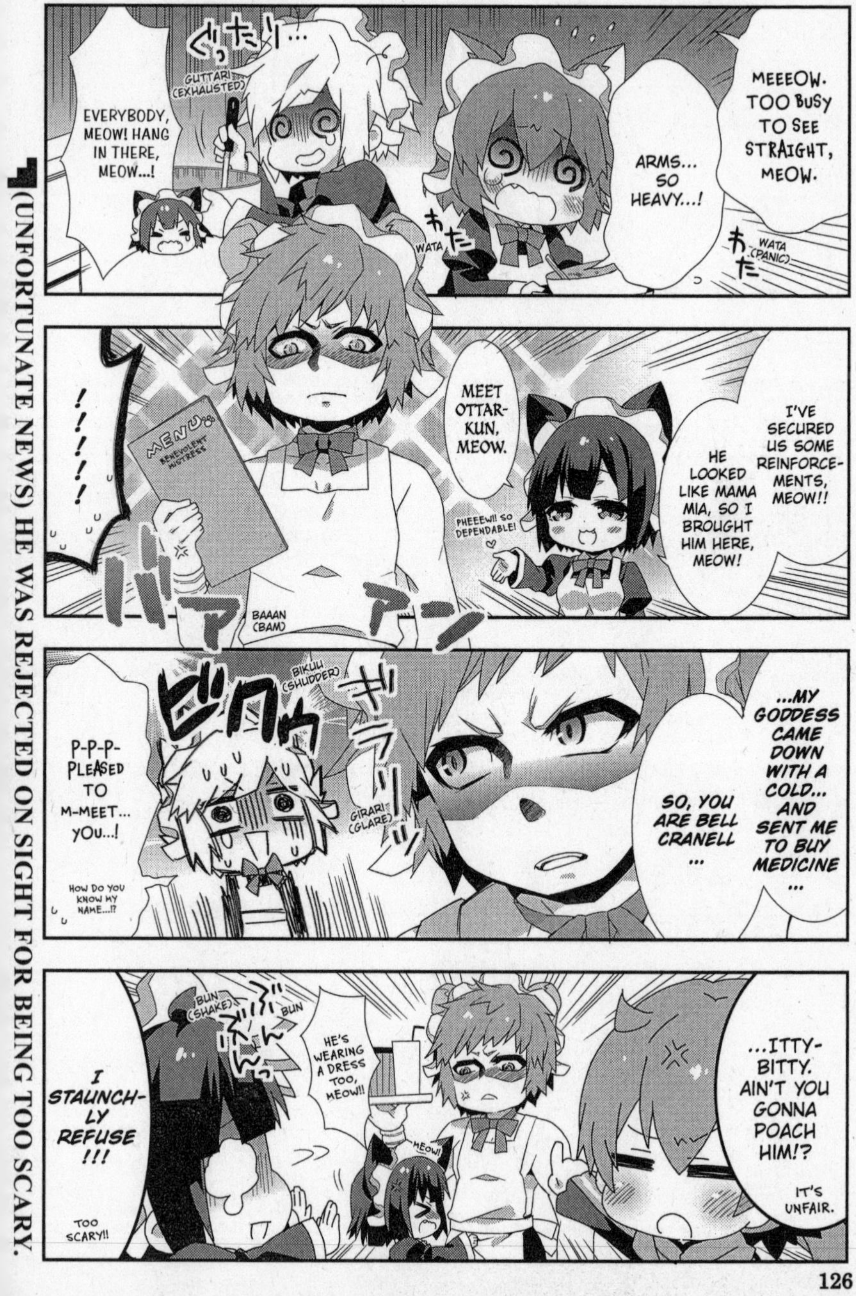
MEEEOW. TOO BUSY TO SEE STRAIGHT, MEOW.
ARMS... SO HEAVY...!
WATA (PANIC)
WATA
GUTTARI (EXHAUSTED)
EVERYBODY, MEOW! HANG IN THERE, MEOW...!
I'VE SECURED US SOME REINFORCEMENTS, MEOW!!
HE LOOKED LIKE MAMA MIA, SO I BROUGHT HIM HERE, MEOW!
MEET OTTAR-KUN, MEOW.
PHEEEW!! SO DEPENDABLE!
MENU
BENEVOLENT MISTRESS
!!!!!
BAAAN (BAM)
...MY GODDESS CAME DOWN WITH A COLD... AND SENT ME TO BUY MEDICINE...
SO, YOU ARE BELL CRANELL...
GIRARI (GLARE)
BIKUU (SHUDDER)
P-P-P-PLEASED TO M-MEET... YOU...!
HOW DO YOU KNOW MY NAME...!?
...ITTY-BITTY. AIN'T YOU GONNA POACH HIM!?
IT'S UNFAIR.
MEOW!
HE'S WEARING A DRESS TOO, MEOW!!
BUN (SHAKE)
BUN
I STAUNCHLY REFUSE!!!
TOO SCARY!!

(UNFORTUNATE NEWS) HE WAS REJECTED ON SIGHT FOR BEING TOO SCARY.

STEP 13

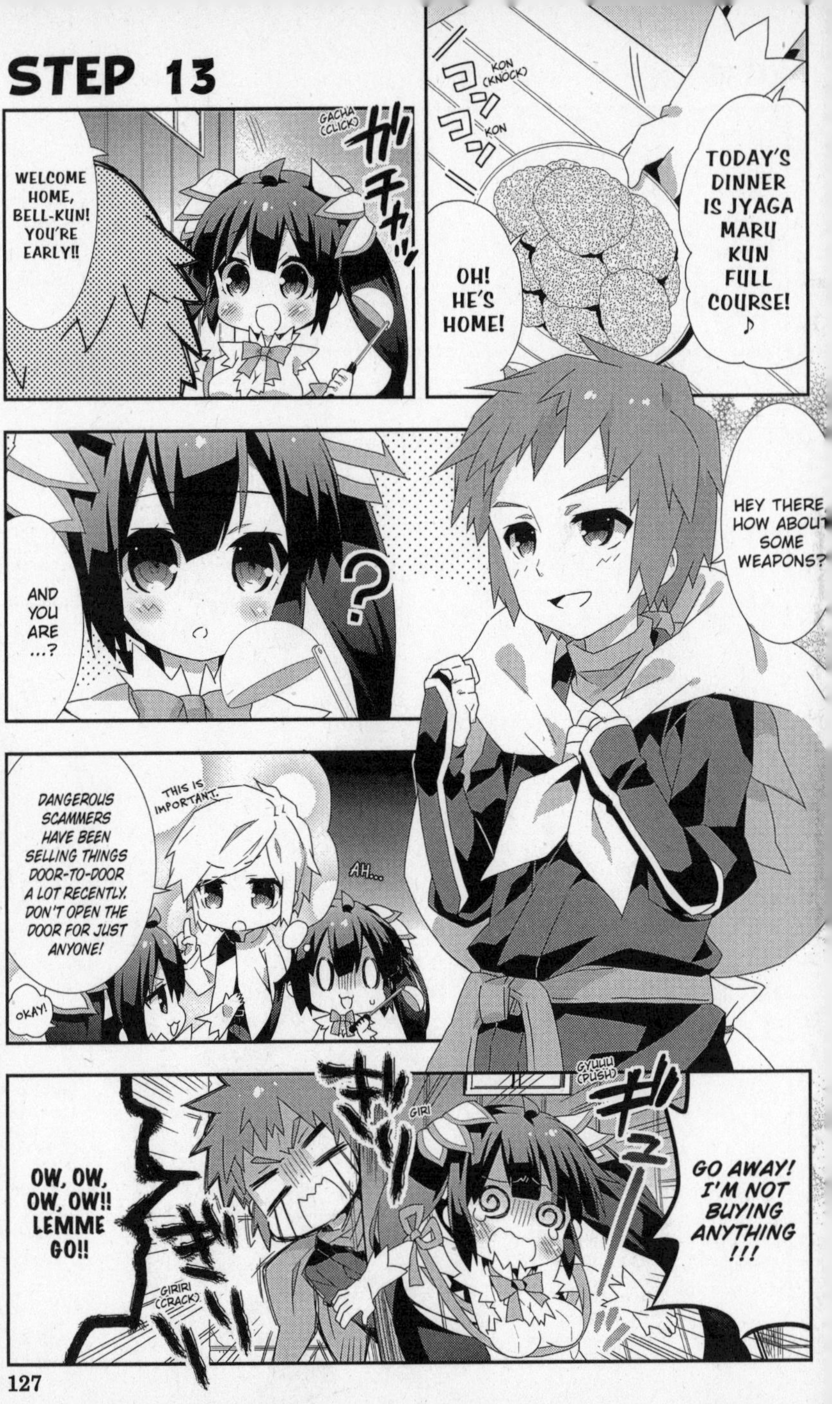

KON (KNOCK)
KON
TODAY'S DINNER IS JYAGA MARU KUN FULL COURSE! ♪
OH! HE'S HOME!
GACHA (CLICK)
WELCOME HOME, BELL-KUN! YOU'RE EARLY!!
HEY THERE, HOW ABOUT SOME WEAPONS?
AND YOU ARE ...?
THIS IS IMPORTANT.
DANGEROUS SCAMMERS HAVE BEEN SELLING THINGS DOOR-TO-DOOR A LOT RECENTLY. DON'T OPEN THE DOOR FOR JUST ANYONE!
AH...
OKAY!
GYUUU (PUSH)
GO AWAY! I'M NOT BUYING ANYTHING !!!
GIRI
OW, OW, OW, OW!! LEMME GO!!
GIRIRI (CRACK)

A SUSPICIOUS SALESMAN HAS APPEARED.

NO DEAL?

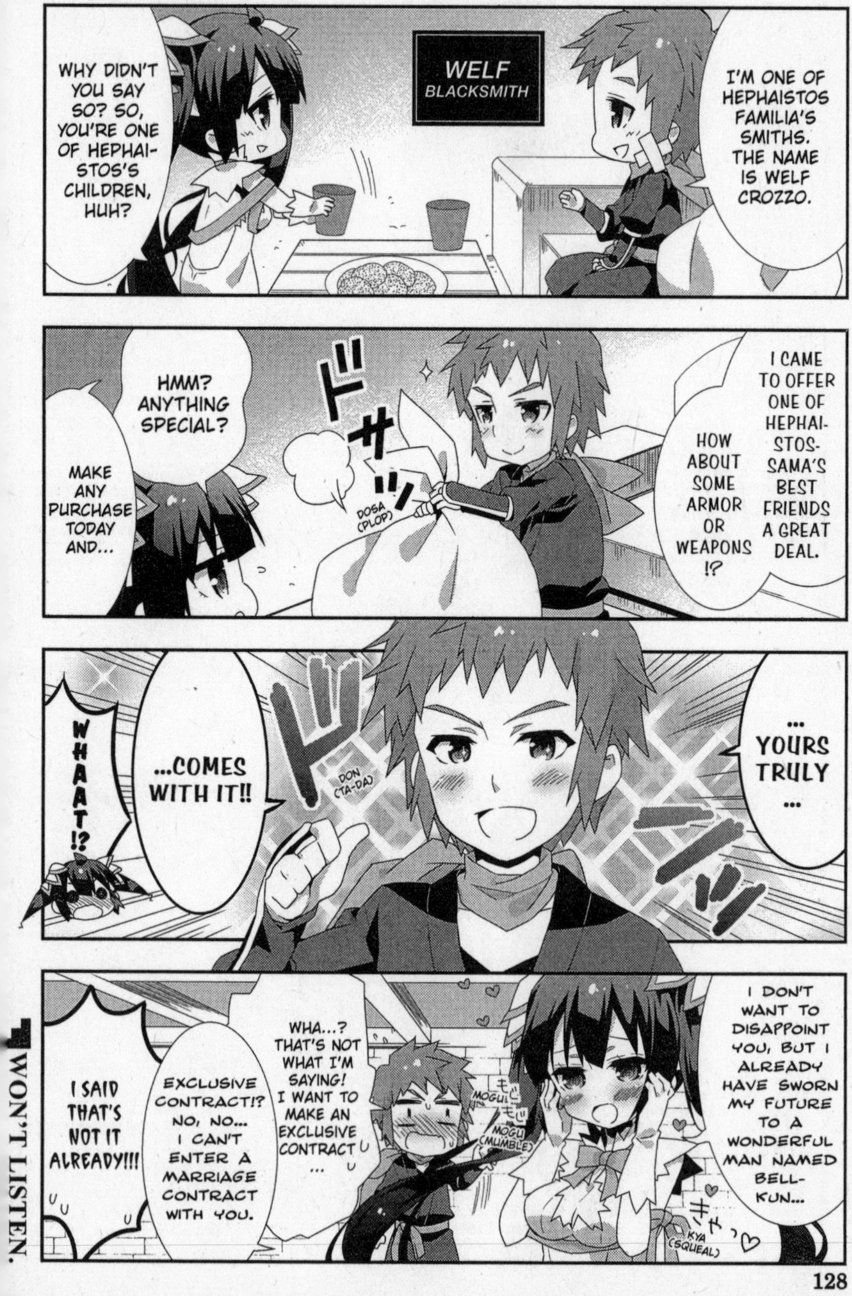
I'M ONE OF HEPHAISTOS FAMILIA'S SMITHS. THE NAME IS WELF CROZZO.
WELF
BLACKSMITH
WHY DIDN'T YOU SAY SO? SO, YOU'RE ONE OF HEPHAI-STOS'S CHILDREN, HUH?
I CAME TO OFFER ONE OF HEPHAI-STOS-SAMA'S BEST FRIENDS A GREAT DEAL.
HOW ABOUT SOME ARMOR OR WEAPONS !?
DOSA (PLOP)
HMM? ANYTHING SPECIAL?
MAKE ANY PURCHASE TODAY AND...
... YOURS TRULY ...
DON (TA-DA)
...COMES WITH IT!!
WHAAAT!?
I DON'T WANT TO DISAPPOINT YOU, BUT I ALREADY HAVE SWORN MY FUTURE TO A WONDERFUL MAN NAMED BELL-KUN...
KYA (SQUEAL)
MOGU MOGU (MUMBLE)
WHA...? THAT'S NOT WHAT I'M SAYING! I WANT TO MAKE AN EXCLUSIVE CONTRACT ...
EXCLUSIVE CONTRACT!? NO, NO... I CAN'T ENTER A MARRIAGE CONTRACT WITH YOU.
I SAID THAT'S NOT IT ALREADY!!!

WON'T LISTEN.

WHILE WE WERE OUT...!!

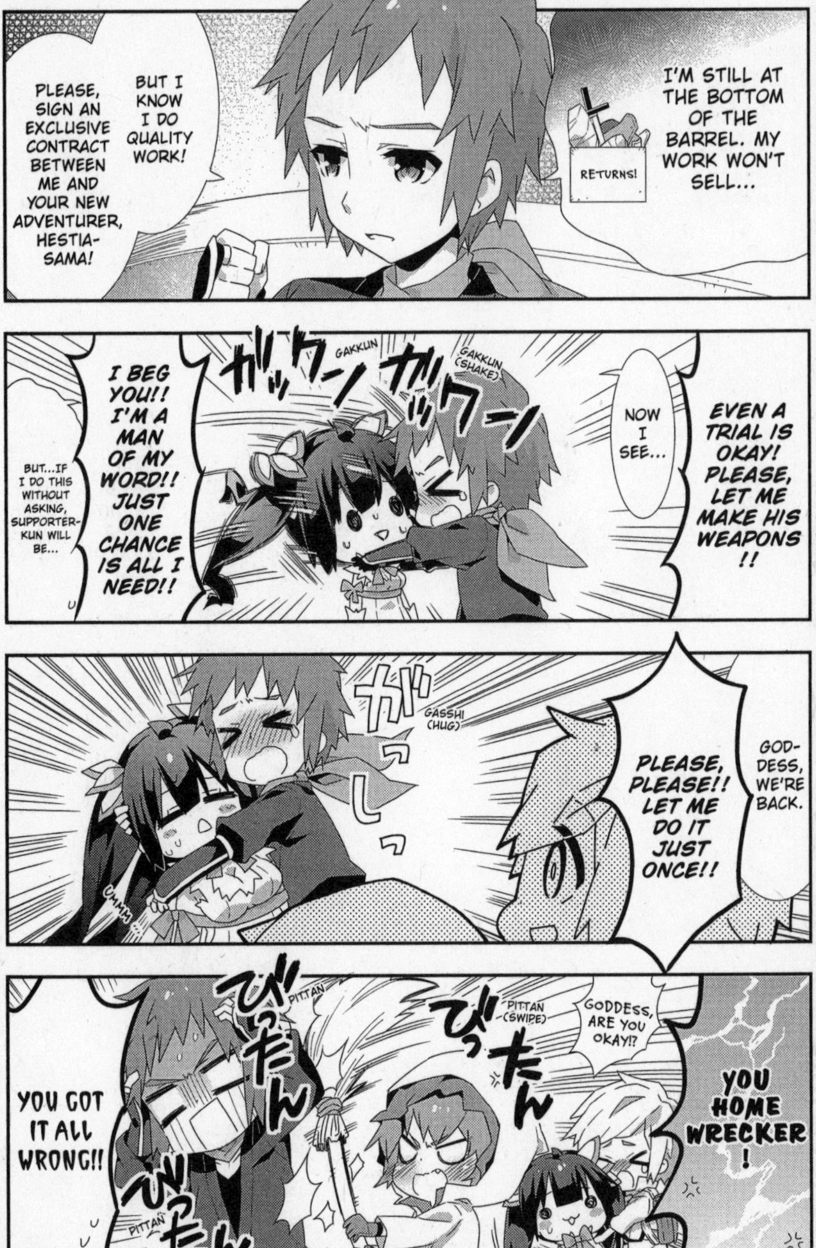

I'M STILL AT THE BOTTOM OF THE BARREL. MY WORK WON'T SELL...
RETURNS!
BUT I KNOW I DO QUALITY WORK!
PLEASE, SIGN AN EXCLUSIVE CONTRACT BETWEEN ME AND YOUR NEW ADVENTURER, HESTIA-SAMA!
EVEN A TRIAL IS OKAY! PLEASE, LET ME MAKE HIS WEAPONS!!
NOW I SEE...
GAKKUN (SHAKE)
GAKKUN
I BEG YOU!! I'M A MAN OF MY WORD!! JUST ONE CHANCE IS ALL I NEED!!
BUT...IF I DO THIS WITHOUT ASKING, SUPPORTER-KUN WILL BE...
GOD-DESS, WE'RE BACK.
PLEASE, PLEASE!! LET ME DO IT JUST ONCE!!
GASSHI (HUG)
UMMM
YOU HOME WRECKER!
GODDESS, ARE YOU OKAY!?
PITTAN (SWIPE)
PITTAN
YOU GOT IT ALL WRONG!!
PITTAN

WON'T LISTEN (AGAIN).

WELF'S NAMING SENSE

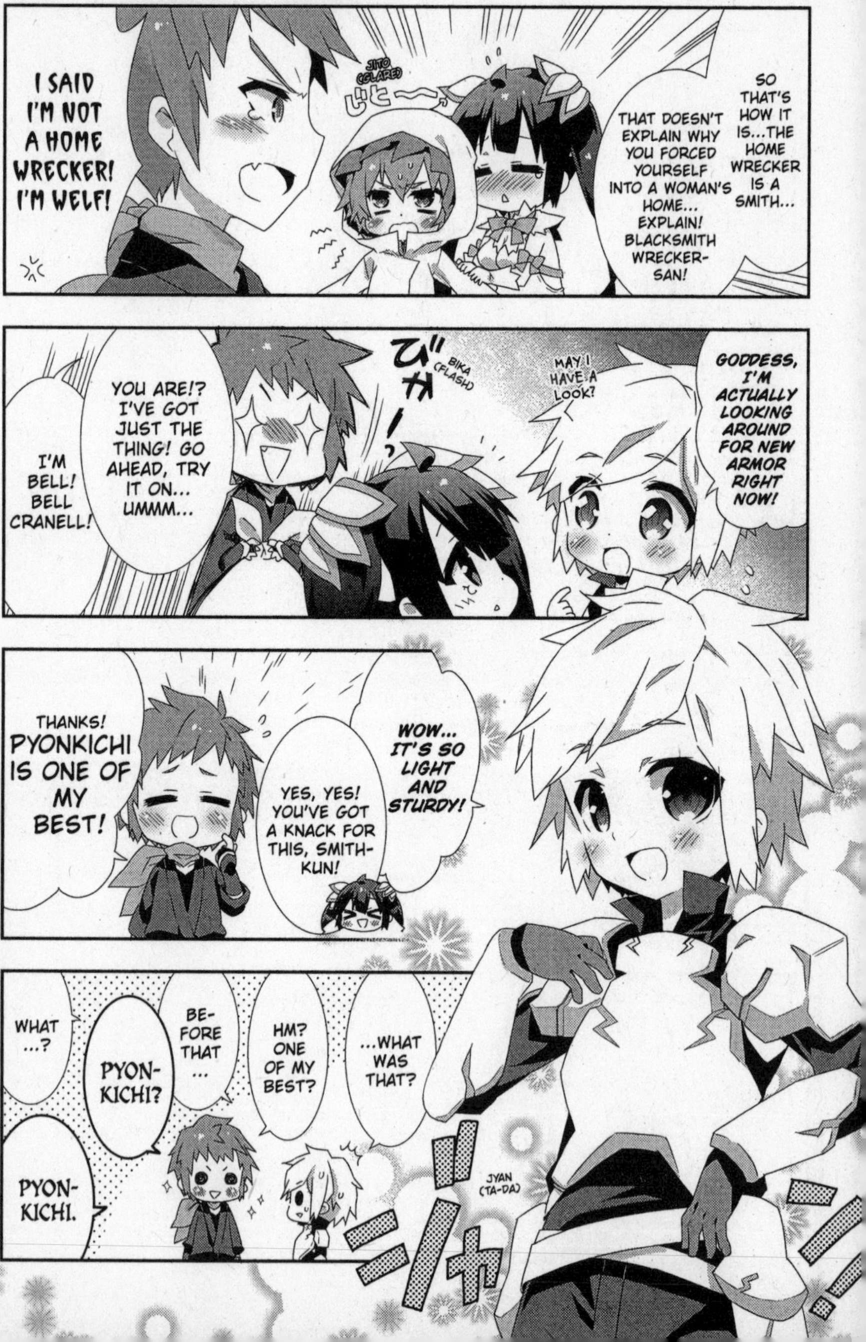
SO THAT'S HOW IT IS...THE HOME WRECKER IS A SMITH...
THAT DOESN'T EXPLAIN WHY YOU FORCED YOURSELF INTO A WOMAN'S HOME... EXPLAIN! BLACKSMITH WRECKER-SAN!
JITO (GLARE)
I SAID I'M NOT A HOME WRECKER! I'M WELF!
GODDESS, I'M ACTUALLY LOOKING AROUND FOR NEW ARMOR RIGHT NOW!
MAY I HAVE A LOOK?
BIKA (FLASH)
YOU ARE!? I'VE GOT JUST THE THING! GO AHEAD, TRY IT ON... UMMM...
I'M BELL! BELL CRANELL!
JYAN (TA-DA)
WOW... IT'S SO LIGHT AND STURDY!
YES, YES! YOU'VE GOT A KNACK FOR THIS, SMITH-KUN!
THANKS! PYONKICHI IS ONE OF MY BEST!
...WHAT WAS THAT?
HM? ONE OF MY BEST?
BE-FORE THAT...
PYON-KICHI?
WHAT...?
PYON-KICHI.

MISHEARD HIM. (HOPEFULLY)

QUITE THE KNACK

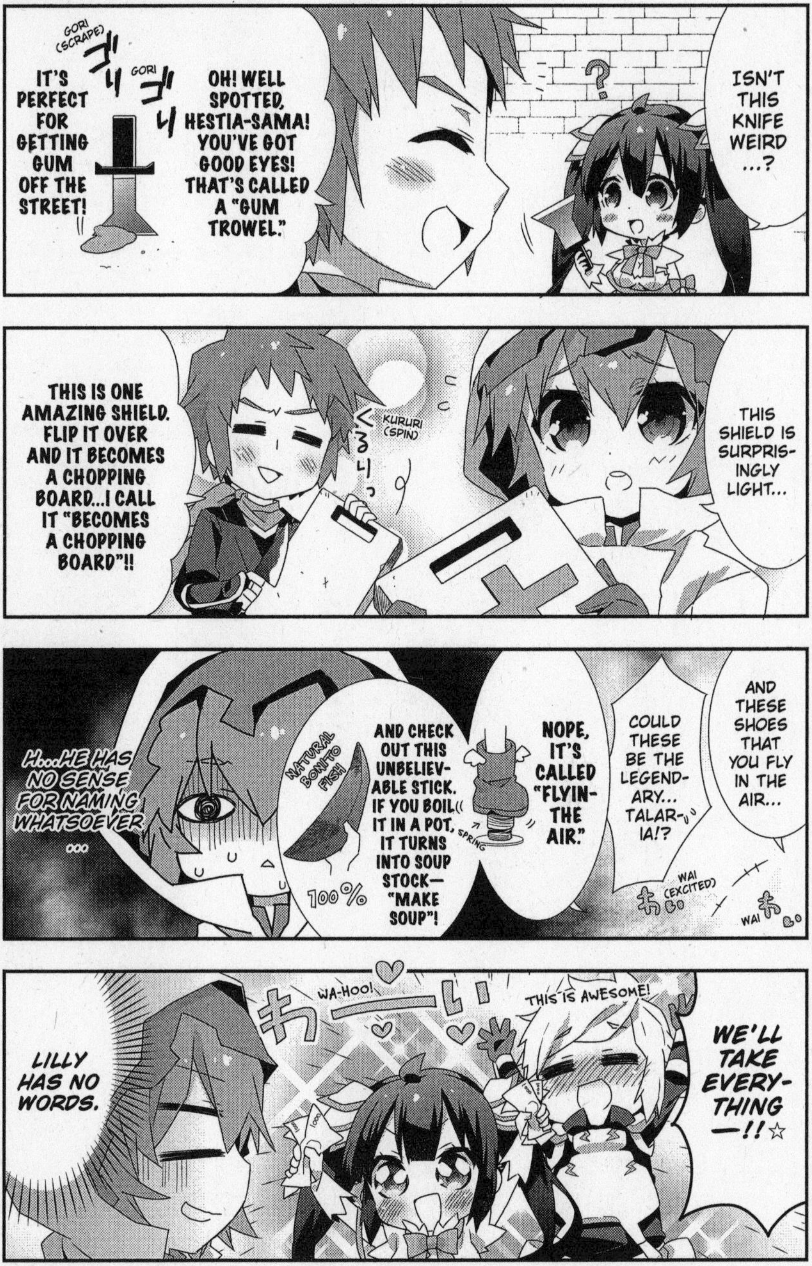
ISN'T THIS KNIFE WEIRD...?
OH! WELL SPOTTED, HESTIA-SAMA! YOU'VE GOT GOOD EYES! THAT'S CALLED A "GUM TROWEL."
ゴリゴリ
GORI (SCRAPE) GORI
IT'S PERFECT FOR GETTING GUM OFF THE STREET!
THIS SHIELD IS SURPRISINGLY LIGHT...
くるりっ
KURURI (SPIN)
THIS IS ONE AMAZING SHIELD. FLIP IT OVER AND IT BECOMES A CHOPPING BOARD...I CALL IT "BECOMES A CHOPPING BOARD"!!
AND THESE SHOES THAT YOU FLY IN THE AIR...
COULD THESE BE THE LEGENDARY... TALARIA!?
わいわい
WAI (EXCITED) WAI
NOPE, IT'S CALLED "FLYIN-THE AIR."
SPRING
AND CHECK OUT THIS UNBELIEVABLE STICK. IF YOU BOIL IT IN A POT, IT TURNS INTO SOUP STOCK—"MAKE SOUP"!
NATURAL BONITO FISH
100%
H...HE HAS NO SENSE FOR NAMING WHATSOEVER...
WE'LL TAKE EVERYTHING—!!☆
THIS IS AWESOME!
わーーい
WA-HOO!
LILLY HAS NO WORDS.

THE REASON THIS FAMILIA IS DIRT-POOR, CONFIRMED.

NEW PARTY MEMBER

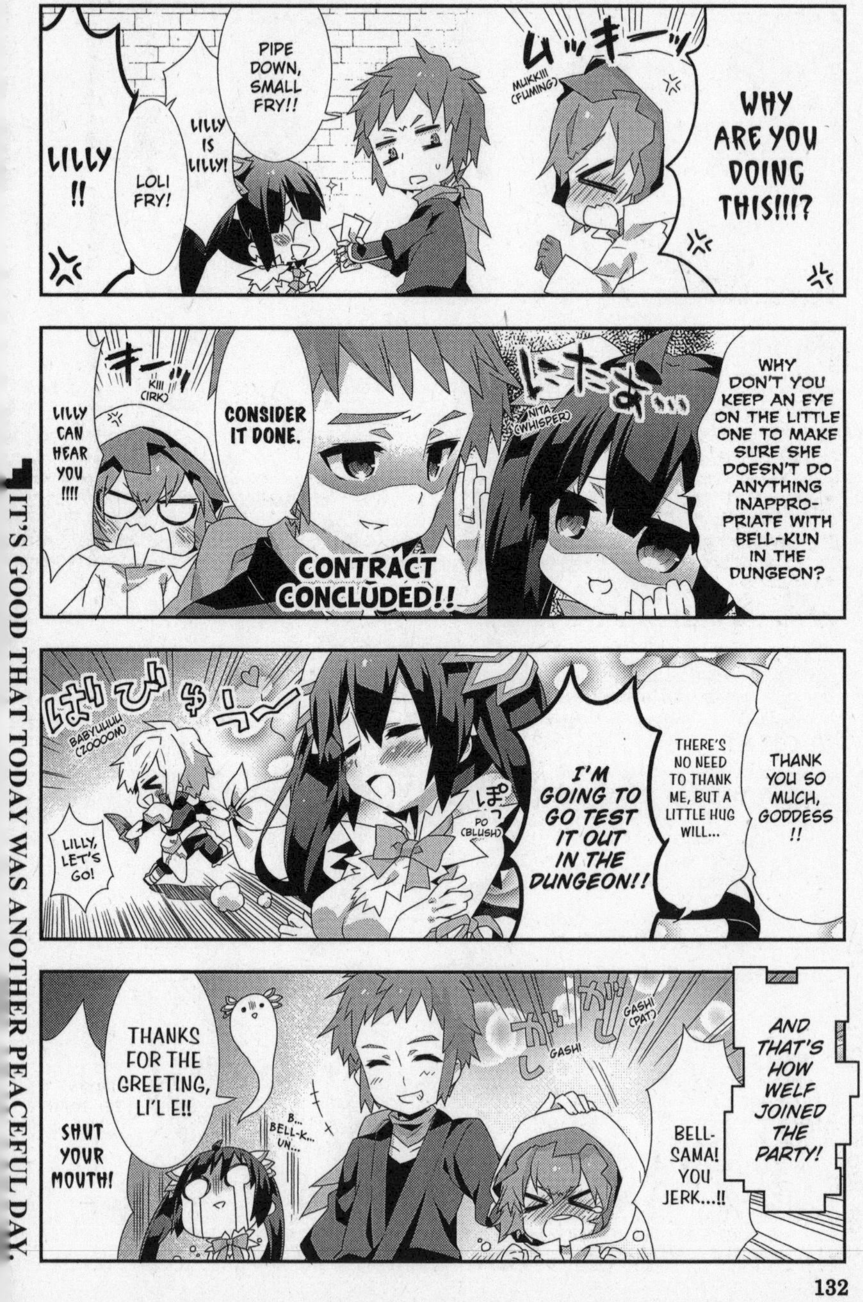
WHY ARE YOU DOING THIS!!!?
ムッキーッ
MUKKIII (FUMING)
PIPE DOWN, SMALL FRY!!
LILLY IS LILLY!
LOLI FRY!
LILLY !!
WHY DON'T YOU KEEP AN EYE ON THE LITTLE ONE TO MAKE SURE SHE DOESN'T DO ANYTHING INAPPRO-PRIATE WITH BELL-KUN IN THE DUNGEON?
にたぁ…
NITA (WHISPER)
CONSIDER IT DONE.
CONTRACT CONCLUDED!!
キーッ
KIII (IRK)
LILLY CAN HEAR YOU !!!!
THANK YOU SO MUCH, GODDESS !!
THERE'S NO NEED TO THANK ME, BUT A LITTLE HUG WILL...
I'M GOING TO GO TEST IT OUT IN THE DUNGEON!!
ぽっ
PO (BLUSH)
ばびゅ〜
BABYUUUN (ZOOOOM)
LILLY, LET'S GO!
AND THAT'S HOW WELF JOINED THE PARTY!
がしっ
GASHI (PAT)
がしっ
GASHI
BELL-SAMA! YOU JERK...!!
B... BELL-K... UN...
THANKS FOR THE GREETING, LI'L E!!
SHUT YOUR MOUTH!

IT'S GOOD THAT TODAY WAS ANOTHER PEACEFUL DAY.

WAITING FOR BELL-KUN ♡

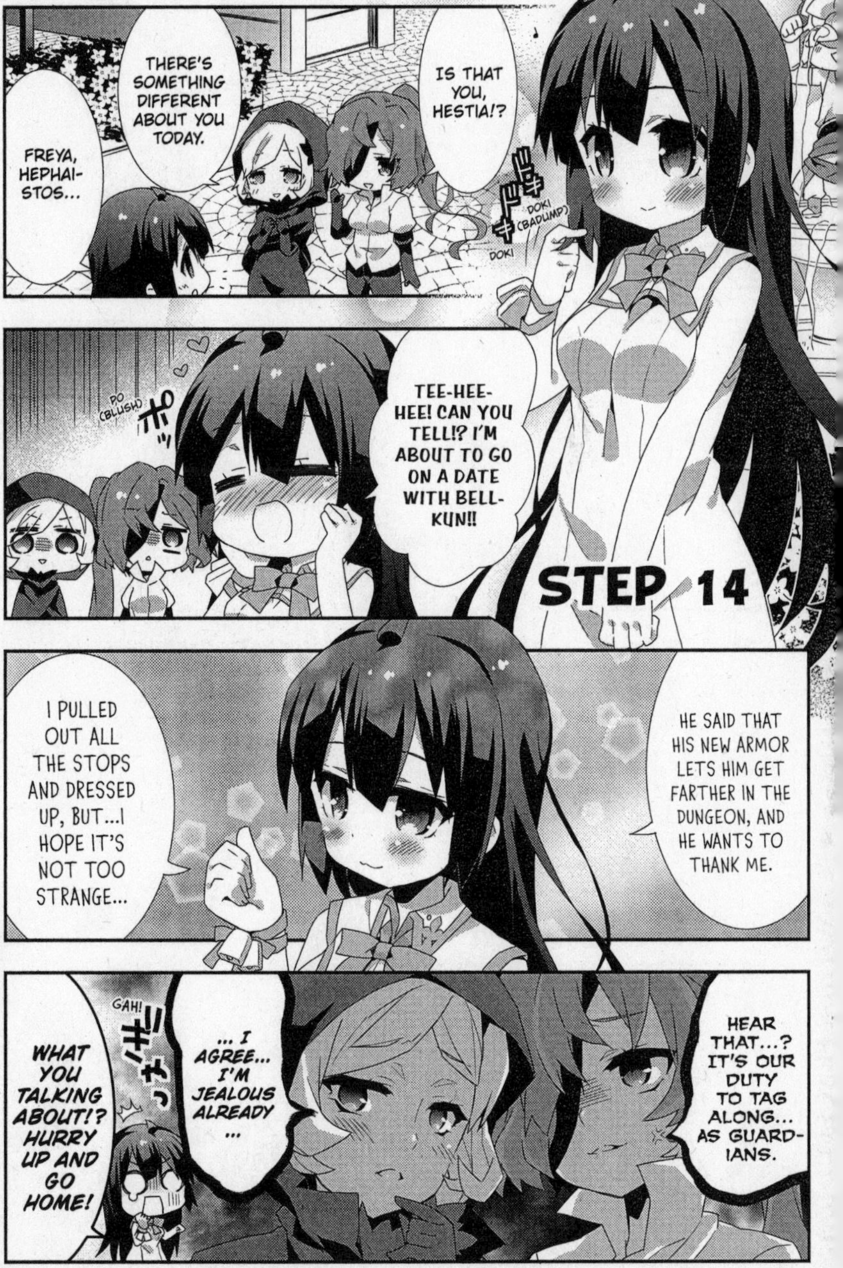
IS THAT YOU, HESTIA!?
DOKI (BADUMP) DOKI
THERE'S SOMETHING DIFFERENT ABOUT YOU TODAY.
FREYA, HEPHAISTOS...
TEE-HEE-HEE! CAN YOU TELL!? I'M ABOUT TO GO ON A DATE WITH BELL-KUN!!
PO (BLUSH)
STEP 14
HE SAID THAT HIS NEW ARMOR LETS HIM GET FARTHER IN THE DUNGEON, AND HE WANTS TO THANK ME.
I PULLED OUT ALL THE STOPS AND DRESSED UP, BUT...I HOPE IT'S NOT TOO STRANGE...
HEAR THAT...? IT'S OUR DUTY TO TAG ALONG... AS GUARDIANS.
... I AGREE... I'M JEALOUS ALREADY ...
GAH!
WHAT YOU TALKING ABOUT!? HURRY UP AND GO HOME!

ENEMIES HAVE APPEARED!

DETERMINED!!

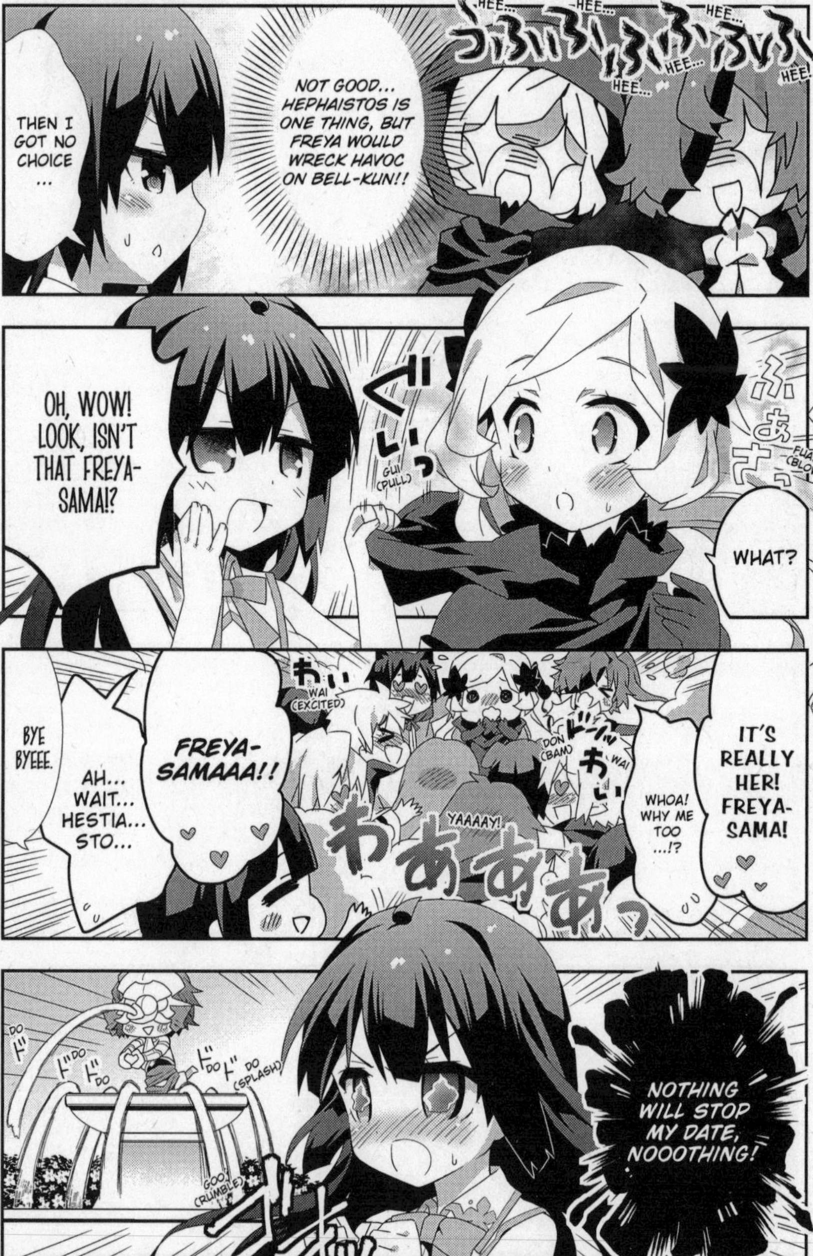
HEE... -HEE... HEE... HEE... HEE... HEE...
NOT GOOD... HEPHAISTOS IS ONE THING, BUT FREYA WOULD WRECK HAVOC ON BELL-KUN!!
THEN I GOT NO CHOICE ...
FUASA (BLOW)
WHAT?
GUI (PULL)
OH, WOW! LOOK, ISN'T THAT FREYA-SAMA!?
IT'S REALLY HER! FREYA-SAMA!
WHOA! WHY ME TOO ...!?
WAI
DON (BAM)
YAAAAY!
WAI (EXCITED)
FREYA-SAMAAA!!
AH... WAIT... HESTIA... STO...
BYE BYEEE.
NOTHING WILL STOP MY DATE, NOOOTHING!
DO (SPLASH)
DO
DO
DO
GOO (RUMBLE)

VICTORY!!

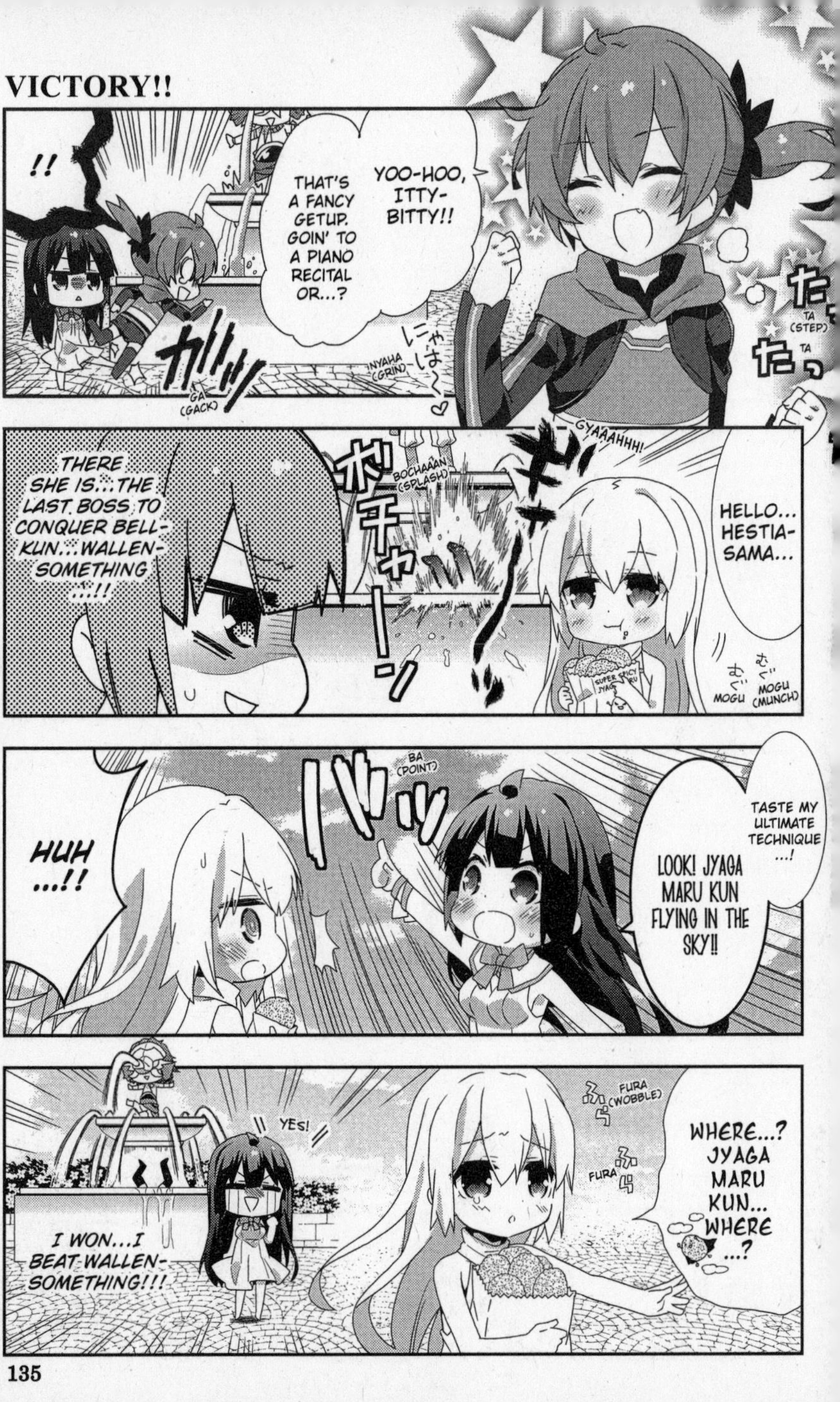

たっ たっ
TA (STEP) TA
YOO-HOO, ITTY-BITTY!!
THAT'S A FANCY GETUP. GOIN' TO A PIANO RECITAL OR...?
にゃはく
NYAHA (GRIN)
ガッ
GA (GACK)
!!
HELLO... HESTIA-SAMA...
むぐ むぐ
MOGU (MUNCH) MOGU
GYAAAHHH!
ボチャーン
BOCHAAAN (SPLASH)
THERE SHE IS...THE LAST BOSS TO CONQUER BELL-KUN...WALLEN-SOMETHING...!!
TASTE MY ULTIMATE TECHNIQUE...!
LOOK! JYAGA MARU KUN FLYING IN THE SKY!!
バッ
BA (POINT)
HUH...!!
WHERE...? JYAGA MARU KUN... WHERE...?
ふら
FURA (WOBBLE)
ふら
FURA
YES!
I WON...I BEAT WALLEN-SOMETHING!!!

A VERY SUBTLY ARTISTIC WATER FOUNTAIN POSE.

THE LAST BOSS!!

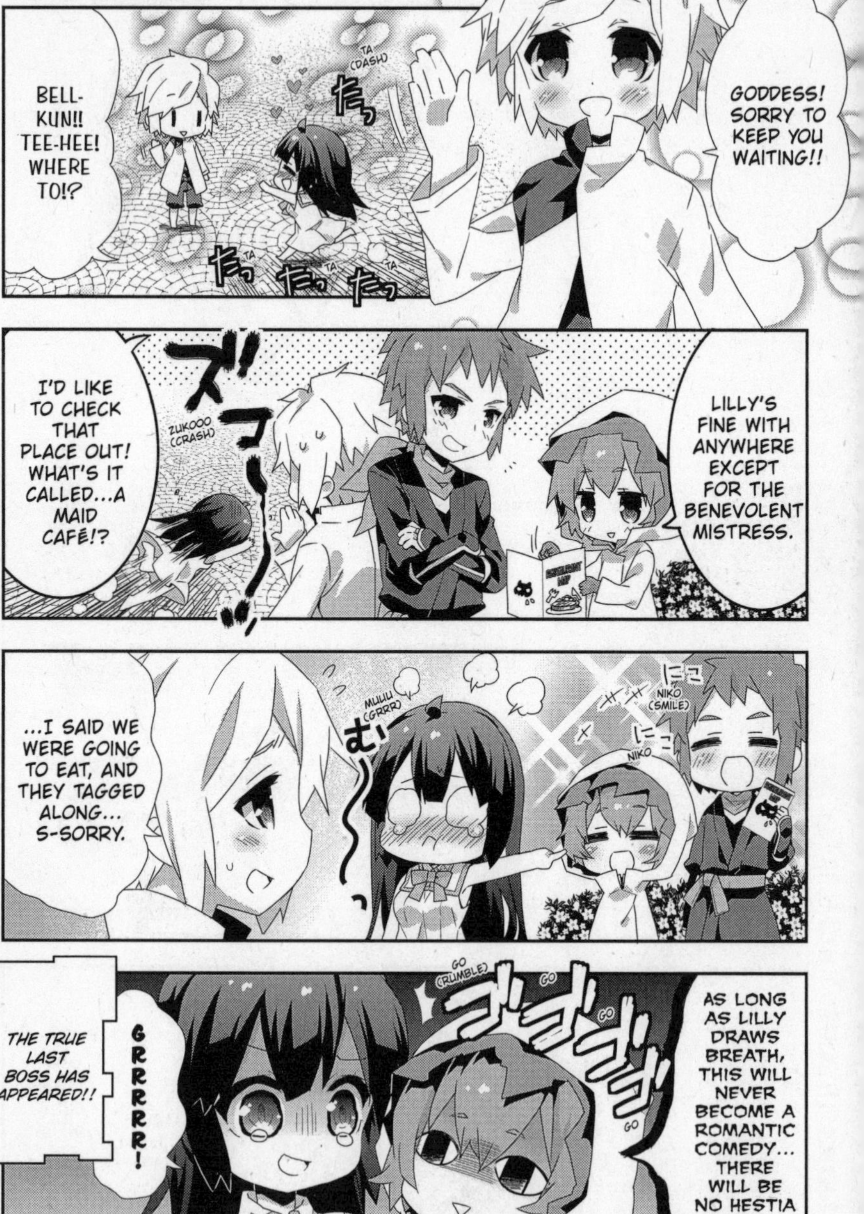
GODDESS! SORRY TO KEEP YOU WAITING!!
TA (DASH)
BELL-KUN!! TEE-HEE! WHERE TO!?
TA
TA
TA
LILLY'S FINE WITH ANYWHERE EXCEPT FOR THE BENEVOLENT MISTRESS.
ZUKOOO (CRASH)
I'D LIKE TO CHECK THAT PLACE OUT! WHAT'S IT CALLED...A MAID CAFÉ!?
NIKO (SMILE)
NIKO
MUUU (GRRR)
...I SAID WE WERE GOING TO EAT, AND THEY TAGGED ALONG... S-SORRY.
AS LONG AS LILLY DRAWS BREATH, THIS WILL NEVER BECOME A ROMANTIC COMEDY... THERE WILL BE NO HESTIA ROUTE... HEH-HEH...
GO (RUMBLE)
GO
GO
GO
GRRRRR!
THE TRUE LAST BOSS HAS APPEARED!!

SHE WON'T SUPPORT HESTIA'S LOVE.

SACRIFICE

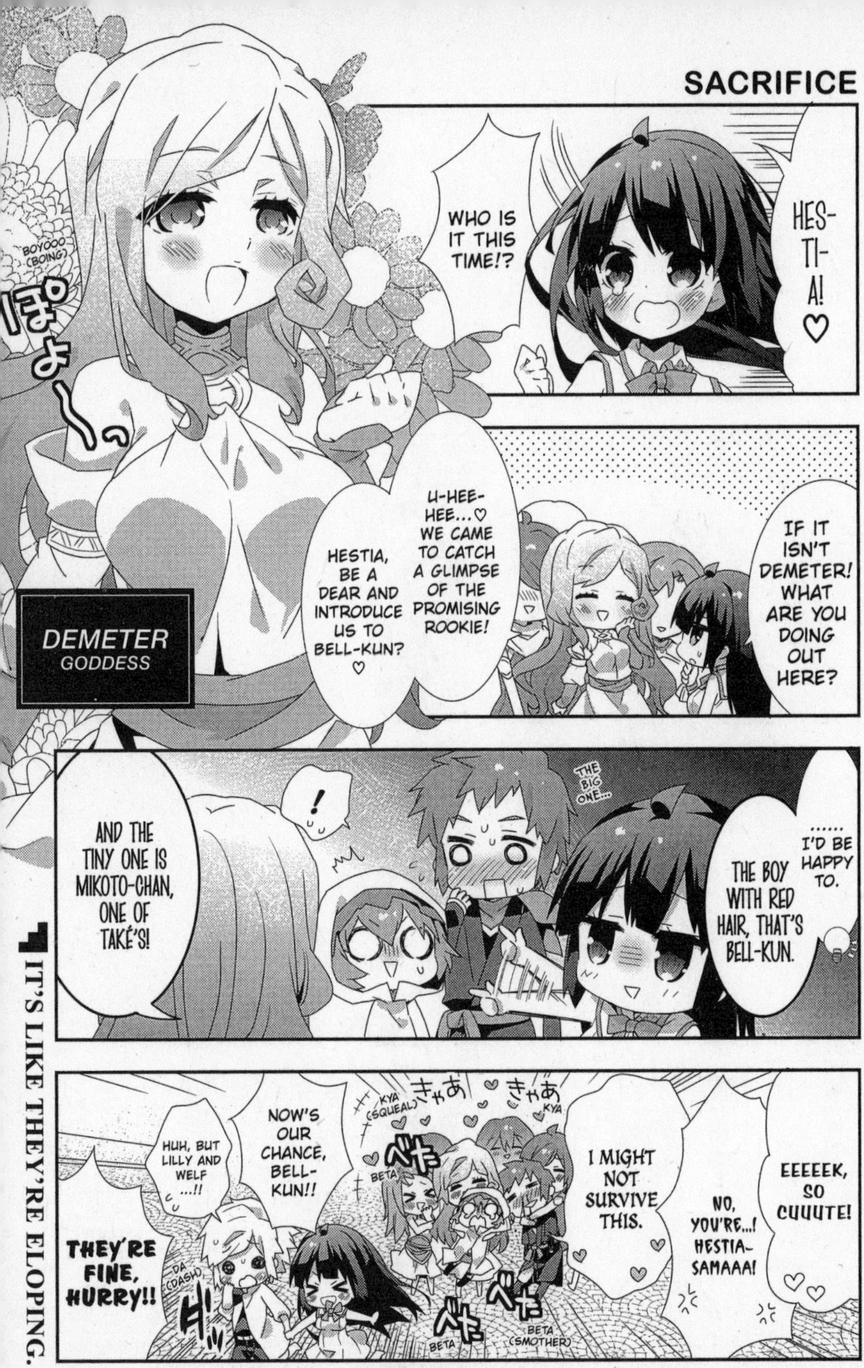
HES-TI-A! ♡
WHO IS IT THIS TIME!?
IF IT ISN'T DEMETER! WHAT ARE YOU DOING OUT HERE?
U-HEE-HEE...♡ WE CAME TO CATCH A GLIMPSE OF THE PROMISING ROOKIE!
HESTIA, BE A DEAR AND INTRODUCE US TO BELL-KUN? ♡
ぽよ〜っ
BOYOOO (BOING)
DEMETER
GODDESS
...... I'D BE HAPPY TO.
THE BOY WITH RED HAIR, THAT'S BELL-KUN.
THE BIG ONE...
!
AND THE TINY ONE IS MIKOTO-CHAN, ONE OF TAKÉ'S!
EEEEEK, SO CUUUTE!
NO, YOU'RE...! HESTIA-SAMAAA!
I MIGHT NOT SURVIVE THIS.
きゃあ
KYA
きゃあ
KYA (SQUEAL)
べた
BETA
NOW'S OUR CHANCE, BELL-KUN!!
HUH, BUT LILLY AND WELF ...!!
THEY'RE FINE, HURRY!!
ダッ
DA (DASH)
べた
BETA (SMOTHER)
べた
BETA

IT'S LIKE THEY'RE ELOPING.

DAYS OF GODDESS

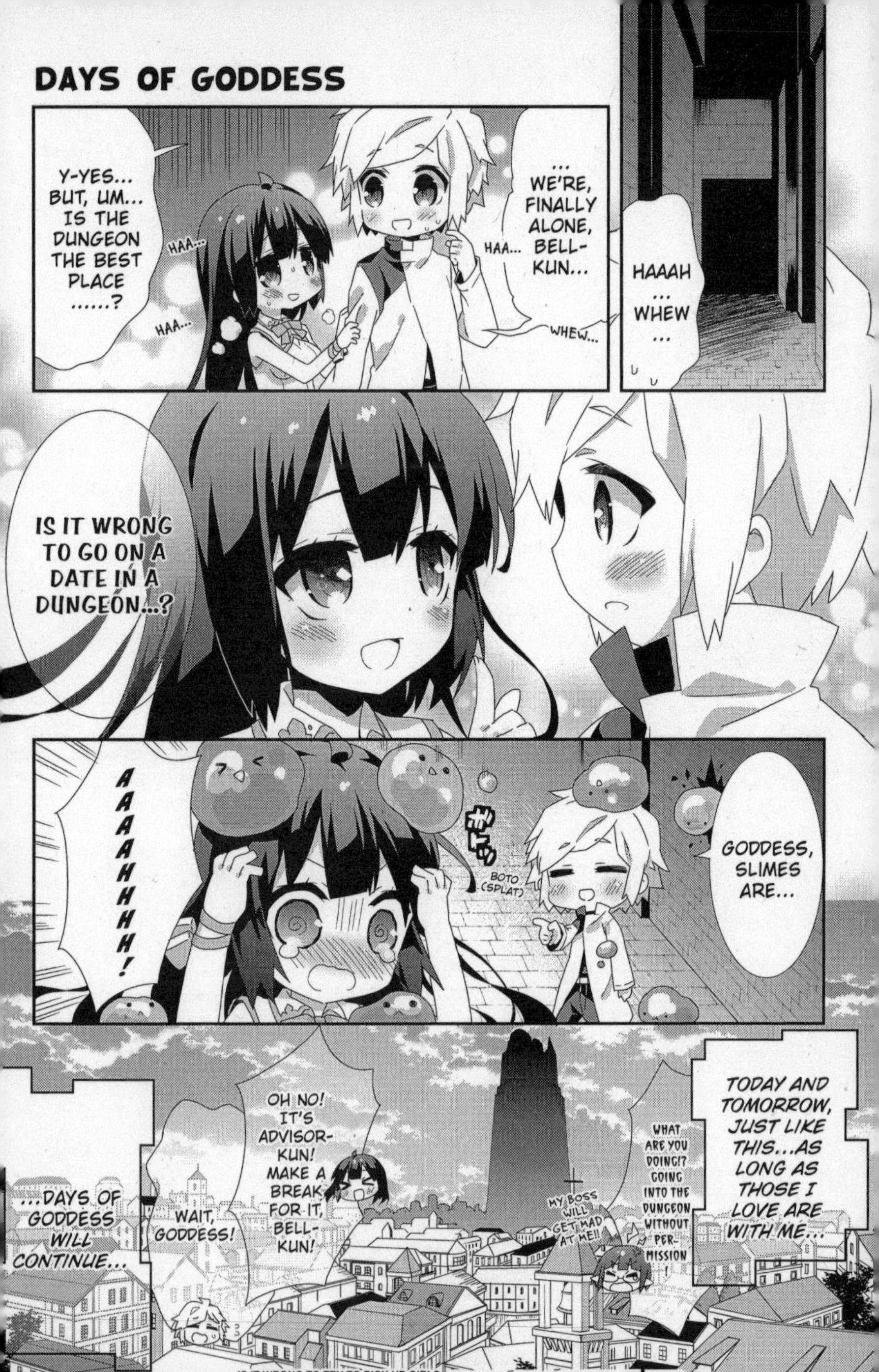
HAAAH ... WHEW ...
... WE'RE, FINALLY ALONE, BELL-KUN...
HAA...
WHEW...
Y-YES... BUT, UM... IS THE DUNGEON THE BEST PLACE ......?
HAA...
HAA...
IS IT WRONG TO GO ON A DATE IN A DUNGEON...?
GODDESS, SLIMES ARE...
BOTO (SPLAT)
AAAAAHHHHH!
TODAY AND TOMORROW, JUST LIKE THIS...AS LONG AS THOSE I LOVE ARE WITH ME...
WHAT ARE YOU DOING!? GOING INTO THE DUNGEON WITHOUT PERMISSION!
MY BOSS WILL GET MAD AT ME!!
OH NO! IT'S ADVISOR-KUN! MAKE A BREAK FOR IT, BELL-KUN!
WAIT, GODDESS!
...DAYS OF GODDESS WILL CONTINUE...

IS IT WRONG TO TRY TO PICK UP GIRLS IN A DUNGEON? FOUR-PANEL COMIC [DAYS OF GODDESS] END

TRANSLATION NOTES

Common Honorifics

no honorific: Indicates familiarity or closeness; if used without permission or reason, addressing someone in this manner would constitute an insult.

-san: The Japanese equivalent of Mr./Mrs./Miss. If a situation calls for politeness, this is the fail-safe honorific.

-shi: Not unlike -san; the equivalent of Mr./Mrs./Miss but conveying a more official or bureaucratic mood

-sama: Conveys great respect; may also indicate that the social status of the speaker is lower than that of the addressee.

-kun: Used most often when referring to boys, this indicates affection or familiarity. Occasionally used by older men among their peers, but it may also be used by anyone referring to a person of lower standing.

-chan: An affectionate honorific indicating familiarity used mostly in reference to girls; also used in reference to cute persons or animals of either gender.

PAGE 3
Jyaga maru kun: Fried potato puffs sold at a popular stall from the *Is It Wrong to Try to Pick Up Girls in a Dungeon* original series.

PAGE 86
Special boxes: The boxes Hestia is filling with food resemble the special packed lunches (*bento*) that people in Japan eat on New Year's Day, called *osechi ryori*.

PAGE 106
Kabe-don: A reference to the pop culture craze that swept Asia, it translates literally to "wall bang" and refers to when a boy slams his hand into a wall, trapping his love interest in order to get her attention.

PAGE 114
Kappa: A creature from folklore whose name combines the words for "river" and "child." It refers to demons who carry a small pool of water on their heads. Said to be based on giant salamanders, they live near water and are roughly humanoid in shape.

Shigeru Mizuki: A manga author and historian known for his work *Gegege no Kitaro*. He also wrote another manga called *Kappa no Sanpei* about a boy who is transported to the realm of the kappa.

I TRIED DRAWING SOME NEVER-BEFORE-SEEN MONSTERS!

NOW YOU KNOW JUST HOW BIG THEY ARE! GODDESS HESTIA ADDED FOR SCALE!!

BONUS STEP 1

BEASTIARY
-Monster Guide-

WHAT DO THE MONSTERS THAT HAVE APPEARED IN THE MAIN STORY BUT HAVE YET TO BE ILLUSTRATED REALLY LOOK LIKE? HAVE A LOOK AT THESE IDEAS DRAWN BY TAKAMURA-SENSEI WITH THEIR OWN DESCRIPTIONS!!

APPEARING IN VOL 4 "QUEST X QUEST!"

BLUE PAPILLON

A BRILLIANTLY BEAUTIFUL BLUE BUTTERFLY. THE SCALES THAT FLAKE OFF ITS WINGS CAN HEAL MONSTERS' WOUNDS TOO. FOR SOME REASON, THIS IS THE ONLY ONE DRAWN PROPERLY. EVEN THE SUPERVISORS WERE CONFUSED.

APPEARING IN VOL 4 "QUEST X QUEST!"

PAPA   MAMA

BLOODSAURUS

A RED CARNIVOROUS DINOSAUR THAT STANDS FIVE MEDERS TALL. SINCE THERE'S A SCENE WHERE BELL AND HIS FRIENDS STEAL ONE OF THEIR EGGS IN THE MAIN STORY, TAKAMURA-SENSEI DREW A MOTHER AND FATHER.

APPEARING IN VOL 5, CHAPTER 1 "MIDDLE LEVELS!"

ゴ゛ー゛
GOO (ROAR)

HELLHOUND

A DOGLIKE MONSTER NICKNAMED BASKERVILLE. ITS MAIN WEAPON IS HIGHLY DESTRUCTIVE FIRE BREATH. TAKAMURA-SENSEI, THIS LOOKS LIKE A CHIHUAHUA... (PERSONAL OPINION)

APPEARING IN VOL 5, CHAPTER 5 "THE OUTLAWS PARTY!"

BUGBEAR

LOVES HONEY CLOUD FRUITS. IT CONSTANTLY SEARCHES FOR THE FRUIT WHILE DROOLING NONSTOP IN THE MAIN STORY. THIS VERSION IS MUCH CUTER THAN WHAT I IMAGINED.

※ OF COURSE, NONE OF THESE HAVE BEEN CONFIRMED BY FUJINO OMORI-SENSEI!!

BONUS STEP 2

THE BEST SCENES FROM *DAYS OF GODDESS* AS CHOSEN BY THE CHARACTERS!!

EMERGENCY PLAN FOR THE INSIDE COVER COMIC!

HAVE YOU READ THE COMIC PRINTED INSIDE THE COVER? WHILE THOSE CHARACTERS DIDN'T APPEAR IN THIS BOOK, THEY GOT TO CHOOSE WHICH SCENES THEY LIKE THE BEST!

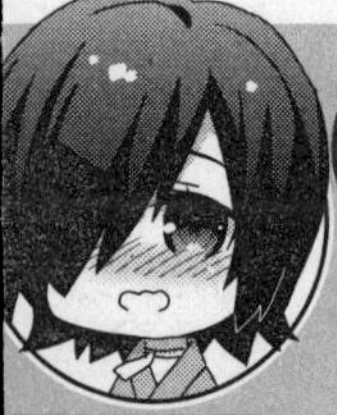

Chigusa's SELECT

APPEARING IN STEP 5 [IT WAS IN A BOOK!!], GODDESS HESTIA'S DOGEZA SCENE.

CHIGUSA

MEMBER OF TAKEMIKAZUCHI FAMILIA. HUMAN ADVENTURER FROM THE FAR EAST.

THE TRUTH BEHIND...ONE OF THE MAIN STORIES' MOST FAMOUS SCENES, THE DOGEZA. IF IT WERE ME...(AT THIS MOMENT) I THINK...BECAUSE IT WAS THE TECHNIQUE OF MY GOD, TAKEMIKAZUCHI-SAMA, IN THE FIRST PLACE, I'D BE BETTER AT IT...MAYBE.

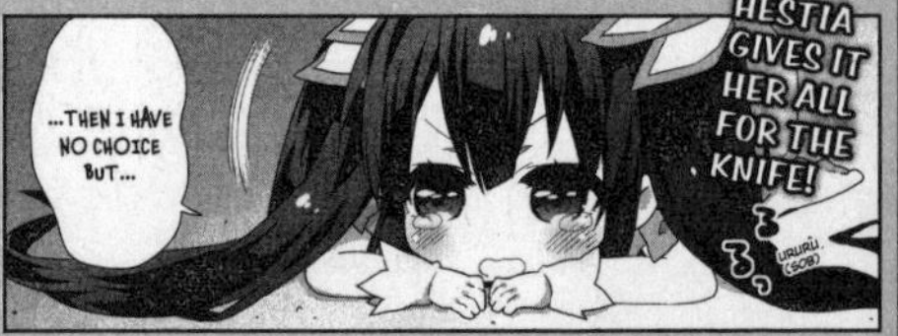
HESTIA GIVES IT HER ALL FOR THE KNIFE!
...THEN I HAVE NO CHOICE BUT...
URURU (SOB)

Mikoto's SELECT

APPEARING IN SPECIAL STEP: LOKI'S DAYS [THE INCREDIBLE KABE-DON!] THE FORBIDDEN LOVE SCENE.

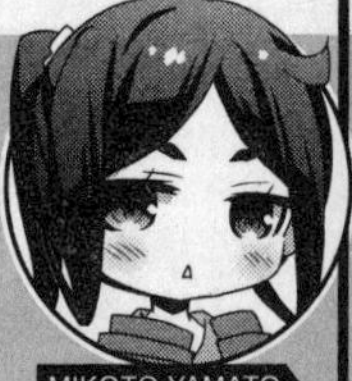

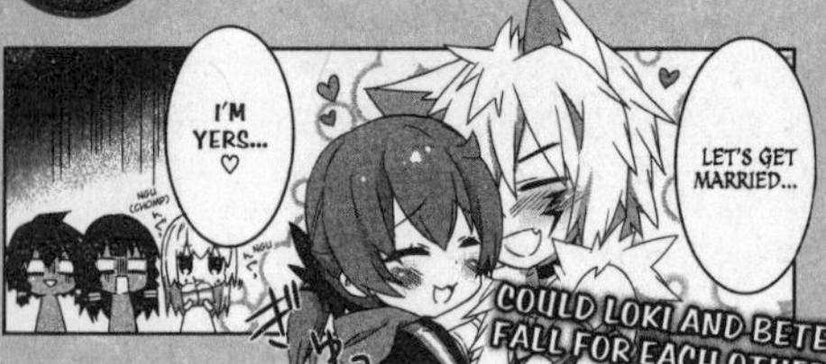
LET'S GET MARRIED...
I'M YERS... ♡
COULD LOKI AND BETE FALL FOR EACH OTHER!?

A MIRACLE SCENE IN WHICH THE DIVIDE BETWEEN US MORTALS AND THE DEITIES OF DEUSDIA WAS CROSSED. IF ONLY I HAD THE COURAGE THAT SIR BETE POSSESSES... ARE YOU ASKING IF TAKEMIKAZUCHI-SAMA EVER APPROACHED ME LIKE THAT...? I CAN'T EVEN IMAGINE IT...!

MIKOTO YAMATO

MEMBER OF TAKEMIKAZUCHI FAMILIA. A LEVEL 2 ADVENTURER WITH THE TITLE ETERNAL SHADOW.

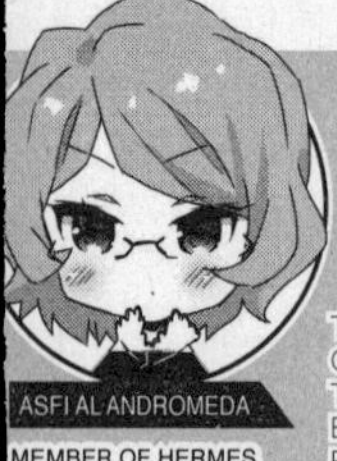

Asfi's SELECT

APPEARING IN STEP 12 [GODDESS' KNIFE!!] WHEN THE KNIFE WAS STOLEN.

ASFI AL ANDROMEDA

MEMBER OF HERMES FAMILIA. AN ERA-DEFINING ITEM MAKER WITH THE RARE ABILITY ENIGMA.

THE MOMENT WHEN BELL CRANELL WAS SURPRISED TO LEARN HIS WEAPON HAS BEEN REPLACED BY A LARGE RADISH. EVEN IF I WERE IN HIS SHOES, I WOULDN'T BE THAT DUMBFOUNDED. HERMES-SAMA HAS GOTTEN ME INTO FAR WORSE SITUATIONS IN THE PAST, SO I'M USED TO IT...

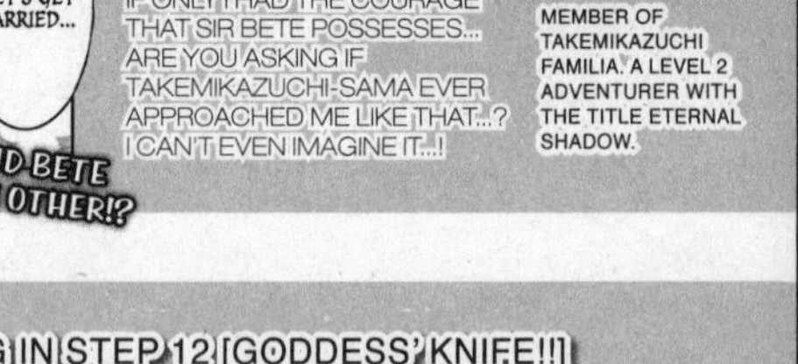
THE HESTIA KNIFE TURNED INTO A RADISH...!?
YEP, THAT'S RIGHT. THIS RADISH HERE IS...
HUH? WHAAAA-AAAAAT!?

BONUS STEP 3

DEITY STATUS + ALPHA [BEHIND THE SCENES☆]

(OF COURSE, UNCONFIRMED BY FUJINO OMORI-SENSEI!)

CONTINUING FROM THE PREVIOUS PAGE, HERE'RE SOME INTRODUCTIONS FOR DEITIES THAT DIDN'T HAVE A PART IN THIS BOOK, ALL AT ONCE. ☆ YOU ONLY GET TO SEE THESE STATUSES HERE—A MUST-SEE. ♡

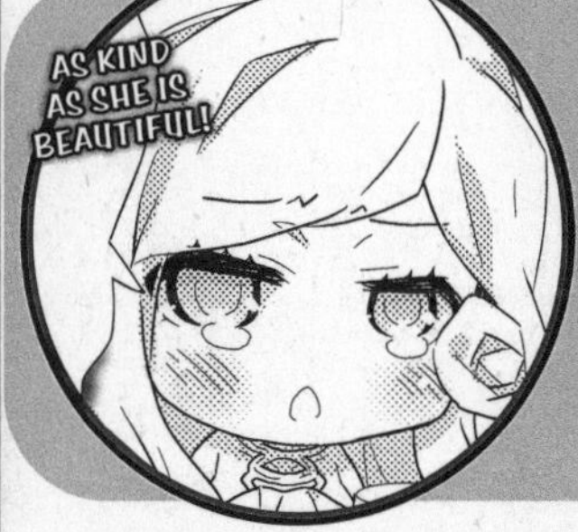
AS KIND AS SHE IS BEAUTIFUL!

DEMETER

GODDESS OF THE HARVEST. HESTIA'S FRIEND. A WELL-MANNERED AND VERY WELL-ENDOWED GODDESS. OF COURSE, THEY JIGGLE WHEN SHE RUNS.

KINDNESS: 130 SUSPICIOUSNESS: 30
FAN GIRL: 240

TAKEMIKAZUCHI

DIRT-POOR DEITY. FRIENDLY WITH HESTIA, AS BOTH HAVE WEAK FAMILIAS. ON A SIDE NOTE, HE'S THE ONE WHO TAUGHT HESTIA HOW TO DO DOGEZA.

TRUST FROM FOLLOWERS: INFINITE
COMPASSION: INFINITE POVERTY: INFINITE

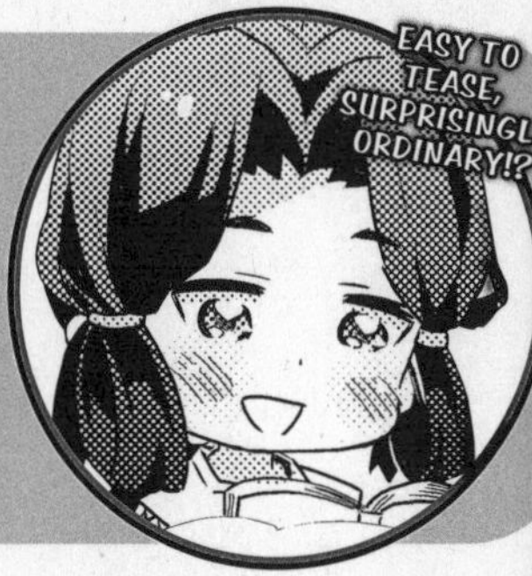
EASY TO TEASE, SURPRISINGLY ORDINARY!?

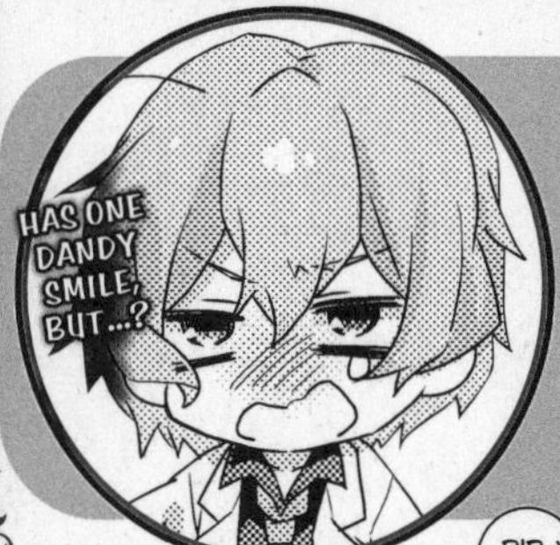
HAS ONE DANDY SMILE, BUT...?

HERMES

A DEITY WHO'S CONSTANTLY ON A JOURNEY. HIS FOLLOWERS AREN'T PROPERLY REGISTERED AT THE GUILD. PAYS A SURPRISING AMOUNT OF ATTENTION TO BELL. SEEMS TO BE HIDING THINGS.

INTELLIGENCE: 180 SUSPICIOUSNESS: 290
ANNOYANCE: ERROR!

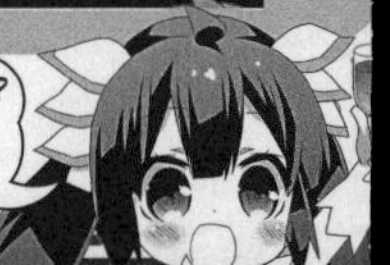
DID YOU GET A KICK OUT OF THE DEITY STATUS? EVERYONE'S GOT THEIR OWN QUIRKS, BUT PLEASE OVERLOOK THEM. ♥

AFTERWORD

NICE TO MEET YOU. THIS IS MASAYA TAKAMURA.

AS THIS COMIC IS BASED ON WHAT HESTIA AND THE OTHER GODDESSES DO WHEN THE ADVENTURERS ARE IN THE DUNGEON, I HAD A GREAT TIME THINKING ABOUT THEIR DAILY LIVES AND WHAT THEIR PART-TIME JOBS WOULD BE LIKE! LOKI WOULD SUDDENLY GET TICKED OFF WHEN I WAS IN THE MIDDLE OF WRITING A NAME AND BECOME THE MAIN CHARACTER, OR GANESHA WOULD SHOUT HIS USUAL "I AM GANESHA!"... SEVERAL COMICS TURNED OUT IN WAYS THAT EVEN I DIDN'T SEE COMING. (HUH!? MIACH IS SHOWING UP QUITE A BIT...? HOW COULD THAT BE...? WELL, FULL DISCLOSURE — HE'S MY FAVORITE DEITY IN THE SERIES.)

AS I'M WRITING THIS, THE ANIME HAS JUST STARTED AIRING! SEEING HESTIA AND EVERYONE MOVE AND TALK EVERY WEEK IS A PROFOUND EXPERIENCE. I CAN'T WAIT TO SEE TAKEMIKAZUCHI, HERMES, AND THEIR FAMILIAS JOIN THE STORY! THEY DIDN'T HAVE MUCH OF A PART IN THESE COMICS, SO I'LL HAVE TO MAKE UP FOR IT WITH MY IMAGINATION!!

LASTLY, I CAN'T EXPRESS HOW GRATEFUL I AM TO THE MAIN AUTHOR, FUJINO OMORI-SENSEI! HE TOOK TIME OUT OF HIS BUSY SCHEDULE TO DO NAME CHECKS FOR MONSTERS AND GIVE HIS OWN ADVICE AND FEEDBACK. THANK YOU SO VERY MUCH!!

THE WORLD IS ONLY CONTINUING TO GROW, AND I'LL BE EXPANDING ON HESTIA, LOKI, AND ALL THE OTHER DEITIES LIVES IN ANOTHER INSTALLMENT OF DAYS OF GODDESS!! I CAN'T WAIT TO SEE THE NEXT STEP IN BELL AND HESTIA'S STORY. THANK YOU SO MUCH FOR READING AND HOPE TO SEE YOU AGAIN!

MASAYA TAKAMURA

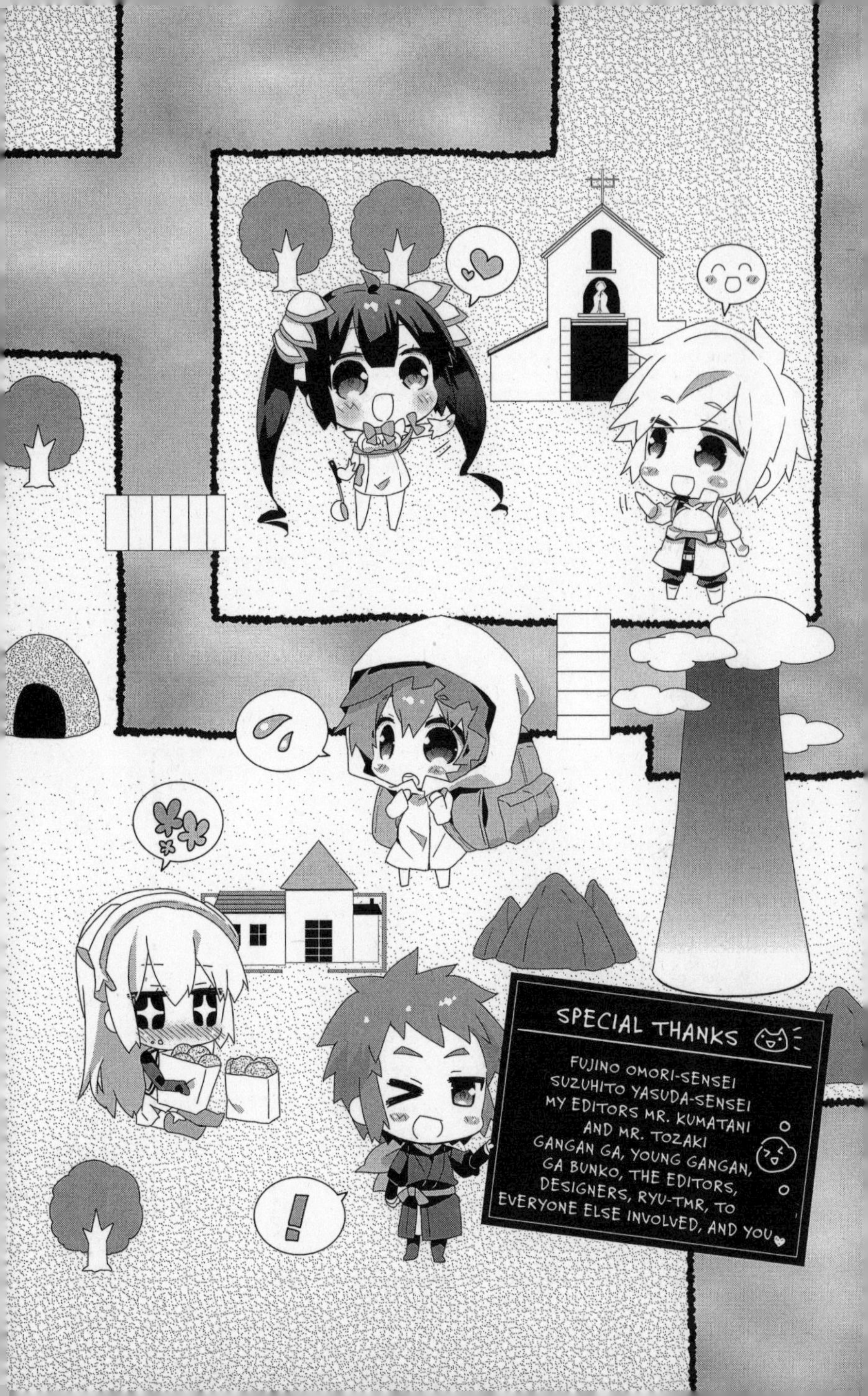
SPECIAL THANKS
FUJINO OMORI-SENSEI
SUZUHITO YASUDA-SENSEI
MY EDITORS MR. KUMATANI
AND MR. TOZAKI
GANGAN GA, YOUNG GANGAN,
GA BUNKO, THE EDITORS,
DESIGNERS, RYU-TMR, TO
EVERYONE ELSE INVOLVED, AND YOU

IS IT WRONG TO TRY TO PICK UP GIRLS IN A DUNGEON? FOUR-PANEL COMIC: DAYS OF GODDESS

Fujino Omori
Masaya Takamura
Yasuda Suzuhito

Translation: Andrew Gaippe • Lettering: D. Kim

DUNGEON NI DEAI WO MOTOMERU NO WA MACHIGATTEIRUDAROUKA YONKOMA
[KAMISAMA NO NICHIJYO]
© Fujino Omori / SB Creative Corp. Character design: Yasuda Suzuhito
© 2015 Masaya Takamura / SQUARE ENIX CO., LTD.
First published in Japan in 2015 by SQUARE ENIX CO., LTD.
English translation rights arranged with SQUARE ENIX CO., LTD. and Yen Press, LLC through Tuttle-Mori Agency, Inc.

English translation © 2018 SQUARE ENIX CO., LTD.

Yen Press
1290 Avenue of the Americas
New York, NY 10104

Visit us at yenpress.com
facebook.com/yenpress
twitter.com/yenpress
yenpress.tumblr.com
instagram.com/yenpress

First Yen Press Edition: February 2018

Yen Press is an imprint of Yen Press, LLC.
The Yen Press name and logo are trademarks of Yen Press, LLC.

The publisher is not responsible for websites (or their content) that are not owned by the publisher.

Library of Congress Control Number: 2017954139

ISBNs: 978-0-316-48013-0 (paperback)
       978-0-316-44816-1 (ebook)

10 9 8 7 6 5 4 3 2 1

BVG

Printed in the United States of America